Modula-3

Samuel P. Harbison

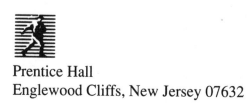

Prentice Hall
Englewood Cliffs, New Jersey 07632

Library of Congress Cataloging-in-Publicataion Data

Harbison, Samuel P.

Modula-3/Samuel P. Harbison
    p. cm.
Includes index
ISBN 0-13-596404-0 (case). -- ISBN 0-13-596396-6 (pbk.)
1. Modula-3 (Computer program language) I. Title. II. Title: Modula three.
QA76.73.M64H37 1992   91-38214
005.13'3--dc20   CIP

Acquisitions editor: Marcia Horton
Production editor: Irwin Zucker
Cover design: Bruce Kenselaar
Prepress buyer: Linda Behrens
Manufacturing buyer: David Dickey
Supplements editor: Alice Dworkin
Editorial assistant: Diana Penha

TRADEMARK INFORMATION

IBM, AIX, and PS/2 are registered trademarks of IBM Corporation. PC-DOS and RISC System/6000 are trademarks of IBM. UNIX is a registered trademark of AT&T Information Systems. DEC, DECstation, VAXstation, and ULTRIX are trademarks of Digital Equipment Corporation. PostScript is a registered trademark of Adobe Systems, Incorporated.

The author and publisher of this book have used their best efforts in preparing this book. These efforts include the development, research, and testing of the theories and programs to determine their effectiveness. The author and publisher make no warranty of any kind, expressed or implied, with regard to these programs or the documentation contained in this book. The author and publisher shall not be liable in any event for incidental or consequential damages in connection with, or arising out of, the furnishing, performance, or use of these programs.

Printed in the United States of America
10 9 8 7 6 5

ISBN 0-13-596404-0 {CASE}

ISBN 0-13-596396-6 {PAPER}

Prentice-Hall International (UK) Limited, *London*
Prentice-Hall of Australia Pty. Limited, *Sydney*
Prentice-Hall Canada Inc., *Toronto*
Prentice-Hall Hispanoamericana. S.A., *Mexico*
Prentice-Hall of India Private Limited, *New Delhi*
Prentice-Hall of Japan, Inc., *Tokyo*
Simon & Schuster Asia Pte. Ltd., *Singapore*
Editora Prentice-Hall do Brasil, Ltda., *Rio de Janeiro*

Contents

Preface

Modula–3 is a new member of the Pascal family of languages. Designed in the late 1980s at Digital Equipment Corporation and Olivetti, Modula–3 corrects many of the deficiencies of Pascal and Modula–2 for practical software engineering. In particular, Modula–3 keeps the simplicity and type safety of the earlier languages while providing new facilities for exception handling, concurrency, object-oriented programming, and automatic garbage collection. Modula–3 is both a practical implementation language for large software projects and an excellent teaching language.

This book is for programmers who want to write clear and efficient programs in Modula–3. The book can be used as a supplementary text in computer science courses, or it can be used for self-study and reference by experienced programmers. A good UNIX™-based implementation of Modula–3 is available free of charge and is described in the book.

For some years I have been involved in developing commercial compilers and programming environments for the C, Modula–2, and Ada languages. When I read the early reports on Modula–3, I was immediately impressed by how it combined elegance and practicality. Here was a programming language as powerful as Ada or C++, but without the complexity of those languages. Although any language can be used effectively by a disciplined programmer, it is consistently easier to write correct and maintainable programs in Modula–3.

Organization

This book describes the complete Modula–3 language. No portions have been omitted or given cursory treatment. I assume you have had some exposure to programming, although novices should have no trouble learning Modula–3. I have organized the book as a compromise between a textbook and a reference manual. In the early chapters I try not to use the advanced features presented later in the book. On the other hand, I've tried to discuss each aspect of the language in only one place. You can follow (or ignore) the inevitable forward references. All the chapters include a set of study and programming exercises that you should attempt in order to get the most out of the book.

Chapters 1 through 6 present the "Pascal subset" of Modula–3, that is, the features that are commonly found in other Pascal family languages. Of course, many of the details of these features are different in Modula–3. Reference types are not discussed in the early chapters since they are often deferred in introductory programming courses.

Chapters 7 through 12 cover more advanced features, including modules, exceptions, object-oriented programming, and concurrency. These chapters are relatively independent and can be used to supplement courses based on languages that lack some or all of these features. Chapter 13 completes the language discussion by covering low-level programming features and the isolation of unsafe code.

Appendix A presents a set of programming conventions that can help you write more consistent and readable Modula–3 programs. Appendix B discusses the SRC Modula–3 compiler and run-time libraries. Appendix C is a summary of the Modula–3 language syntax, and Appendix D contains answers to selected exercises.

Acknowledgments

Modula–3 was designed by Luca Cardelli, Jim Donahue, Mick Jordan, Bill Kalsow, and Greg Nelson as a joint project by the Digital Systems Research Center (SRC) and the Olivetti Research Center. Modula–3 was implemented at SRC by Bill Kalsow and Eric Muller; their implementation is distributed under generous licensing terms by Digital. I made heavy use of SRC Modula–3 while learning and using the language. Mick Jordan, now at SRC, produced the Modula–3 Toolkit from the Olivetti Modula–3 compiler.

Greg Nelson, Bill Kalsow, and the other members of the Modula–3 language committee at SRC provided important feedback on this book and clarified many language details. Bob Taylor and Sam Fuller at Digital were instrumental in supporting Modula–3 in general and my work in particular, making both possible. Several other people spent large amounts of their time reviewing drafts of this book and helping to make it better, including Ken Butler of Tartan, Inc., David Chase of Sun Microsystems, David Emery of MITRE, Stephen Harrison of Digital, Richard Orgass of IBM, and Jeff Perdue of the Software Engineering Institute. I am extremely fortunate to have Marcia Horton as my editor at Prentice Hall, a relationship that so far encompasses two books, four editions, and eight years.

Finally, the many hours devoted to writing this book were too often taken from time I owed to my wife Diana and sons Drew and Michael. Their love continues to support me.

Sam Harbison

1

Introduction

Modula–3 is a modern, general-purpose programming language. It provides excellent support for large, reliable, and maintainable applications. Its clean syntax and semantics, along with its support for object-oriented programming and parallelism, make Modula–3 an excellent teaching and design language. Compared to other languages with a roughly equivalent feature set (e.g., Ada and C++), Modula–3 is easier to learn and safer from runtime misbehavior. Its automatic garbage collection facility greatly simplifies the programming of applications that make use of dynamic memory.

The nature of programming has changed. For many years we were puzzle-solvers, focused on turning algorithms into sets of instructions to be followed by a computer. We enjoyed solving these puzzles, and we often viewed both the complexity of the puzzle and the obscurity of the solution as evidence of our skill. As applications have become more ambitious and programs have grown ever larger, programming has become more of a co-operative effort. We form close-knit teams of programmers. We have code walkthroughs and inspections. We test and maintain other people's programs. Aware of our human limitations, we have come to view complexity and obscurity as faults, not challenges. Now we write programs to be read by people, not computers.

There is a pleasure in creating well-written, understandable programs. There is a satisfaction in finding a program structure that tames the complexity of an application. We enjoy seeing our algorithms expressed clearly and persuasively. We also profit from our clearly written programs, for they are much more likely to be correct and maintainable than obscure ones. You will find that it is easy to write clear programs in Modula–3.

1.1 Modula–3 History

Modula–3 was designed as a joint project of Digital Equipment Corporation's Systems Research Center (SRC) in Palo Alto, California, and the Olivetti Research Center in Menlo Park, California. The designers were Luca Cardelli (SRC), Jim Donahue (ORC), Mick Jordan (ORC), Bill Kalsow (SRC), and Greg Nelson (SRC). The first description of the language was published by Digital and Olivetti in August 1988. A revision based on implementation experience was published in 1989, and a few final adjustments were made in 1990.

Modula–3's immediate ancestor is the language Modula–2+, designed at SRC in the early 1980s as an in-house development language. Modula–2+ is an upward-compatible extension of Niklaus Wirth's Modula–2 language (ca. 1979), which was in turn a successor to Wirth's Pascal (ca. 1970). Wirth himself had designed Oberon in 1987 as a successor to Modula–2, but he still provided helpful suggestions to the Modula–3 designers, who were taking a somewhat different track than Wirth did with Oberon. (See Figure 1–1.) Modula–3 also borrows from Mesa and Cedar systems at the Xerox Palo Alto Research Center. (Mesa's modules influenced Wirth's design of Modula–2.) Other "cousins" of Modula–3 include Object Pascal (Apple Computer) and Euclid (PARC).

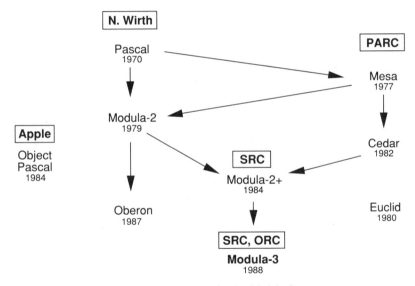

Figure 1–1   Languages related to Modula–3.

1.1.1 Other Relatives

Several popular languages omitted from this family tree deserve some mention. The emerging ISO Modula–2 language extends traditional Modula–2 with a complex type, an exception facility, and several new or different library modules. However, the fundamental character of the language has not changed and its deficiencies remain. From the viewpoint of Modula–3, ISO and traditional Modula–2 are about the same.

Although the Ada language was developed earlier and has approximately the same top-level list of features, Modula–3 is only a cousin once removed. Modula–3 is a simpler language, and it has objects and garbage collection, which Ada implementations lack. You could imagine the Modula–3 designers starting with Ada and coming up with the same language, named "Ada–2"; it just didn't happen that way.

The most aggressive new language is undoubtedly C++, and here there is a sharper philosophical distinction with Modula–3. With the proposed addition of exceptions and templates to C++, both languages will have about the same feature list. Again, Modula–3 is a smaller language. Its object-oriented programming features are much simpler but its module structure is more developed than C++'s. Modula–3 makes other tradeoffs in favor of safety and clarity, whereas C++ opts for power and flexibility. There is sure to be a lively debate on the merits of C++ versus Modula–3, just as there has been between C and Pascal, and C++ and Ada.

1.1.2 Implementations

Both Digital and Olivetti undertook implementations of Modula–3 as the language design progressed. From the outset, both companies hoped for a wide distribution of their compilers, which generated C code for portability. In particular, Digital made SRC's UNIX® implementation publicly available at no charge, for both educational and commercial development of Modula–3 programs. With the closing of ORC in 1990, Digital's implementation became the only one available. (With Olivetti's permission, the ORC software was later modified and included with the SRC release as the "Modula–3 toolkit.") Hundreds of sites all over the world have obtained the SRC software.

1.2 Overview of Modula–3

We'll now do a quick "once-over" of the Modula–3 language to orient you and provide some context for the chapters and examples that follow.

1.2.1 Programs and Execution

Modula–3 programs consist of a sequence of characters that you type into your computer using a text editor of some kind. A Modula–3 *compiler* reads the program and converts it into instructions that the computer can execute. The computer commands that you use to control the compilation and execution of Modula–3 programs are not part of the Modula–3 language, and they will differ from computer to computer.

Example 1–1

Here is a simple Modula–3 program named Hello1 which, when run, types the message "Hello, World!" followed by an end-of-line character (\n) on the display screen:

```
MODULE Hello1 EXPORTS Main;
IMPORT Wr, Stdio;
(* Hello1: Print a greeting on the user's display screen. *)
BEGIN
    Wr.PutText(Stdio.stdout,"Hello, World!\n");
END Hello1.
```

On UNIX systems, you might store the preceding program in a file named Hello1.m3, and you might type the following commands to compile and execute the program. (The > characters are typed by the computer to indicate that it is ready for a command.)

```
> m3 –o hello1 Hello1.m3
> hello1
Hello, World!
>
```

1.2.2 Basic Building Blocks

The Modula–3 compiler checks that each program is correctly written according to the Modula–3 language rules. The checks occur in three steps:

1. The characters making up the program are divided into lexical units called *tokens*.

2. The tokens are grouped into structures according to a *grammar* or *syntax*.

3. The *semantics* (meaning) of the program is analyzed.

By analogy with human languages, tokens are like words, the grammar defines the legal sentences of the language, and the semantics determine which sentences make sense. Each of the three steps is governed by rules that must be met.

Example 1–2

If you were to spell EXPORTS as EXPORT$ in your Modula–3 program, it would cause a lexical error because EXPORT$ is not a legal token in Modula–3.

If you leave out a word in your program, it will probably cause a syntax error, as if you didn't complete a sentence: "Hello, name George" (Does this mean "Hello, my name is George." or "Hello, is your name George?")

Syntactically legal programs, like sentences, can still be nonsensical: "I saw a colorless, blue mistake."

Tokens   There are several kinds of tokens in Modula–3, including identifiers, numbers, string and character literals, and operators. (See Table 1–1.) More details on tokens are provided in Chapter 2 and Appendix C.

Table 1–1   Modula–3 Tokens

Token type	Examples
Reserved word	BEGIN, OBJECT, FROM, TO
Identifier	Book, number, TEN, insideOut, outside_in
Number	0, 1.56, 3.14159d0, 0.1E–10
String literal	"Hello, World!", "Address:\n"
Character literal	'X', '\001', '\t'
Punctuation and operators	:=, {, }, +, <:

Case Sensitivity

Identifiers are case-sensitive in Modula–3, as they are in Modula–2, C, and C++. Identifiers are not case sensitive in Pascal or Ada. Some programmers think it is confusing to use different identifiers whose spelling differs only in letter case, and therefore they believe that case sensitivity is not useful.

The programming conventions listed in Appendix A use letter case to distinguish names for constant entities (e.g., procedures) from names for variables, fields, and methods. It is not considered bad style to use two identifiers that differ only in letter case as long as the identifiers are related in an obvious fashion:

```
VAR
    book: Book;   (* a type, and a variable of that type *)
    from, to: INTEGER;   (* common names; uppercase
                versions happen to be reserved words *)
```

The most common tokens are *identifiers*, which must start with a letter and can contain letters, digits, or underscore characters. Identifiers are used as names for program objects, like modules (Hello1) and procedures (PutText). Identifiers are case sensitive; that is, the identifiers FRED and Fred are different because uppercase letters are considered distinct from lowercase letters. (See "Case Sensitivity," above.)

Certain identifiers have special meanings to the Modula–3 compiler and must not be used by programmers for other purposes; these are called *reserved identifiers*. Reserved identifiers are always spelled with uppercase letters. (Although not all identifiers spelled entirely with uppercase letters are reserved.)

In dividing a program into tokens, the Modula–3 compiler gathers as many characters as can form a single token before trying to find the next token. Therefore, the characters MODULEHello1 would be considered a single identifier rather than the reserved word MODULE followed by the identifier Hello1. If two adjacent tokens could form a single token, they must be separated by one or more *whitespace* characters (spaces, tabs, and carriage returns) to be properly distinguished. Except when needed to separate tokens, whitespace characters have no effect on the meaning of programs.

Example 1–3

The following program is equivalent to the one in Example 1–1 on page 3, but it is harder to read because of its lack of whitespace characters.

```
MODULE Hello1 EXPORTS Main;IMPORT Wr,Stdio;(* Hello1: Print a greeting on the
terminal. *)BEGIN Wr.PutText(Stdio.stdout,"Hello, World!\n");END Hello1.
```

Comments   You can put comments in your program by beginning the comment with (* and ending it with *). Comments can extend over any number of lines and can include any characters (not just legal tokens). If you include (* within a comment, it must be matched by a following *) inside the comment; that is, comments must be properly nested inside one another. Comments are treated like whitespace by the compiler.

Syntax   The Modula–3 grammar specifies how tokens are combined into syntactic "phrases." The major syntactic categories in Modula–3 are modules, interfaces, declarations, statements, types, and expressions. In this book, the grammar is presented in two ways: in a series of "railroad track" diagrams and as a list of BNF-like rules. The BNF rules are presented in Appendix C, whereas the diagrams are spread throughout the book. A sample diagram for a variable declaration (called a VarDecl in the diagram) is shown below. To construct a grammatically correct variable declaration, simply follow the lines,

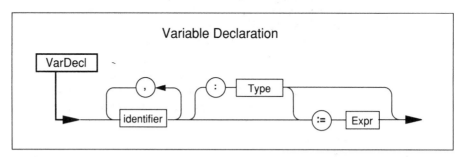

substituting for other syntactic units on the way (e.g., Type and Expr). (There will be other diagrams for those parts of the grammar.) Boxed names beginning with lowercase letters (e.g., identifier) are tokens. Unboxed identifiers and operator symbols enclosed in circles (e.g., :=) must be written exactly as shown.

Semantics   The semantic rules for Modula–3 are more complicated than the grammar. As an example, the semantic rules for a variable declaration include requirements that the same identifier not be declared more than once in the same scope, and that the type of the initialization expression match the declared type (if any). As each part of the language is discussed in the following chapters, the semantic rules are presented.

Conventions   The lexical, syntactic, and semantic rules still leave you with a lot of freedom in writing Modula–3 programs. You can use whitespace to make your program easier to read or harder to read. You can choose names that are clear or obscure. Sometimes it is convenient to introduce conventions, which, when followed, tend to result in more uniform and understandable programs. One set of conventions is presented in Appendix A.

1.2.3 Errors

If you violate the lexical, syntactic, or semantic rules of Modula–3, the compiler will not be able to make sense of your program and will reject it, hopefully with a message that will help you find your error. Mistakes such as these are called *compile-time errors* (or *static errors*) because they are detected when the program is compiled. A *legal* program satisfies all the rules; an *illegal* program does not.

Legal Modula–3 programs can still contain errors. For example, when you execute your program, it might try to perform an impossible or nonsensical operation such as dividing by zero. These kinds of mistakes cannot usually be detected by the compiler. Instead, they are detected as the program executes and are called *checked run-time errors*. They cause your program to print an informative error message and halt, so you can go back and fix the mistake and try again.[1] In some programming languages, nonsensical operations are not detected but simply cause the program to misbehave in some confusing way; these are called *unchecked run-time errors*. Modula–3 programs cannot produce unchecked run-time errors unless you explicitly label part of your program "unsafe" and then write an incorrect piece of code. Programs that cause run-time errors (checked or unchecked) are sometimes called *erroneous*.

Your program might be legal and not have any checked or unchecked run-time errors but still give a wrong answer or behave in a way you didn't expect. This means your program contains a *logic error*. That is, what you wrote in the program (apparently) wasn't what you intended. You will have to study the program to discover your mistake and fix it.

1.2.4 Programs, Modules, and Interfaces

A Modula–3 program consists of a collection of *interfaces* and *modules*. They are compiled individually and then combined to form the executable program. An interface declares procedures, types, variables, etc., that other parts of the program might want to use. For example, the module Hello1 on page 3 *imports* (uses) two interfaces, Wr and Stdio, and thereby gains access to the facilities they provide (the procedure PutText and the variable stdout). Hello1 is called a *client* of Wr and Stdio. When using the form of IMPORT shown in the example, the names declared in the interface must be qualified by the interface name in the client; that is why PutText is referred to as Wr.PutText.

With every interface there must be an associated module that provides the bodies for procedures declared in the interface. The module is said to *export* or *implement* the interface. It is common for a module and the interface it exports to have the same name; if they do not, the module must have an EXPORTS clause to identify the interface, as in the example on page 3. (There is not necessarily a one-to-one correspondence between interfaces and modules, but we'll ignore that possibility for now.) By convention, the module that exports the built-in interface Main is the program's starting point, or "main module."

Some interfaces and modules (like Wr and Stdio) are provided with the Modula–3 compiler, and are automatically available. Of course, you can also write your own interfaces and modules. (See Figure 1–2 on page 8.)

1.2.5 Declarations and Statements

Declarations are used to provide names (identifiers) for the objects your program uses: variables procedures, types, constants, parameters, and exceptions. Figure 1–3 shows

---

[1] Some Modula–3 implementations may raise an exception (Chapter 7) rather than halt the program when a checked run-time error occurs. Consult your compiler's user manual to see what your implementation does.

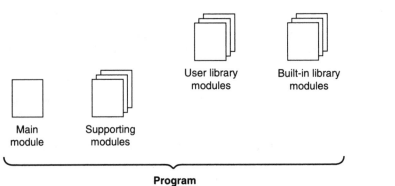

Program

Figure 1–2   A program as a collection of modules.

some typical declarations. *Statements* direct the computer to manipulate the objects in various ways.

```
CONST
    LinesPerInch = 6;
    InchesPerPage = 9;
    LinesPerPage = LinesPerInch * InchesPerPage;
TYPE
    Report = { Monthly, Weekly, Daily };
    Line = [1..LinesPerPage];
VAR
    layout : ARRAY Line OF TEXT;
    thisReport := Report.Weekly;
EXCEPTION
    OutOfRange(INTEGER);
```

Figure 1–3   Declarations.

Example 1–4

Here is another program that prints "Hello, World!":

```
MODULE Hello2 EXPORTS Main;
IMPORT Stdio, Wr;
CONST Greeting = "Hello, World!\n";
PROCEDURE Out(msg: TEXT) =
    BEGIN
        Wr.PutText(Stdio.stdout, msg);
    END Out;
BEGIN
    Out(Greeting);
END Hello2.
```

This program contains a declaration of a constant string named Greeting, and a declaration of procedure Out. It contains two statements: a call on the Wr.PutText procedure (inside the Out procedure) and a call on the Out procedure (inside the module Hello2).

Modula–3 has a typical set of statements, not unlike those found in Pascal or Ada. Table 1–2 is a list of the different statements. Ellipses (…) are used informally to indicate an optional repetition of the preceding part of the statement. Statements are fully described in Chapter 3.

Table 1–2   Modula–3 Statements

Classification	Statement
Assignment statements	Expr := Expr
	INC(var, Expr)
	DEC(var, Expr)
Procedure call and return	Proc(Expr, …)
	EVAL Func(Expr, …)
	RETURN Expr
Blocks of statements	Decls BEGIN Stmts END
	WITH id = Expr,… DO Stmts END
Conditional statements	IF Expr THEN Stmts ELSIF Expr THEN Stmts … ELSE Stmts END
	CASE Expr OF ConstExpr => Stmts | … ELSE Stmts END
	TYPECASE Expr OF Type => Stmts | … ELSE Stmts END
Looping statements	LOOP Stmts END
	WHILE Expr DO Stmts END
	REPEAT Stmts UNTIL Expr END
	FOR var := Expr TO Expr BY Expr DO Stmts END
	EXIT
Exception handling	RAISE Expr
	TRY Stmts EXCEPT Name(var) => Stmts | … ELSE Stmts END
	TRY Stmts FINALLY Stmts END
Thread synchronization	LOCK Mutex DO Stmts END

1.2.6 Procedures

Procedures are often used to encapsulate a group of declarations and statements with a set of parameters that specify information to be passed into the procedure. Procedure declarations include a *signature* giving the number and types of the parameters, and a *body* consisting of a sequence of statements. Signatures can include a list of the exceptions that may be generated by the procedure. (See Figure 1–4 on page 10.) Procedures cannot be overloaded; that is, two procedures with the same name but different signatures cannot be visible at the same time.

```
PROCEDURE Fill (
    VAR dest: ARRAY OF INTEGER;
    value: INTEGER := 0 ) RAISES {OutOfRange} =
BEGIN
    IF NUMBER(dest) = 0 THEN RAISE OutOfRange(0); END;
    FOR i := FIRST(dest) TO LAST(dest) DO
        dest[i] := value;
    END;
END Fill;
```

Figure 1–4   Sample procedure declaration.

1.2.7 Expressions and Types

Expressions specify data to be operated upon in a program. An expression can be as simple as the name of a variable or constant, or it may be composed of many operators, operands, and function calls. The functions can be built-in or user-defined. Table 1–3 lists the operators and built-in functions available in Modula–3.

Table 1–3   Expression Operators (in Precedence Order)

Operator	Description
ABS, ADR[a], ADDRSIZE, BITSIZE, BYTESIZE, CEILING, DISPOSE[a], FIRST, FLOAT, FLOOR, ISTYPE,LAST, LOOPHOLE[a], MAX, MIN, NARROW, NEW, NUMBER, ORD, ROUND, TYPECODE, TRUNC, VAL	Built-in functions
x.a	Field and method selection
f(x), a[i], t{x}	Function calls, subscripts, constructors
^	Pointer dereferencing
+ –	Prefix plus, minus
* / DIV MOD	Multiplicative operators
+ – &	Additive operators; string catenation
= # < <= >= > IN	Relational operators; set inclusion
NOT	Logical negation
AND	Logical conjunction
OR	Logical disjunction

[a] These functions are allowed only in UNSAFE modules.

In a complicated expression, the order in which the operators are applied is important. The operators listed in Table 1–3 are in *precedence* order. That is, the operators listed at the top of the table are applied before the operators listed at the bottom. When operators of the same precedence are combined, they are grouped left-to-right. That is, the operators are *left-associative*. You can also use parentheses to group expressions any way you wish.

Example 1–5

What is the value of the expression 2 + 4 * (5 + 1)?

Solution   The multiplication operator has higher precedence than addition, so this expression is evaluated as 2 + (4 * (5 + 1)), which is 26.

Every expression has a *type*, which determines the values it can take on and the operations that can be performed on those values. Variables, constants, and procedures are given types when they are declared. The types of more complicated operator expressions can be determined by looking at the types of the operands and the rules for the operators. The types available in Modula–3 are listed in Table 1–4.

Table 1–4   Type Expressions

Type	Description
INTEGER	Integers
REAL, LONGREAL, EXTENDED	Floating-point numbers
TEXT, CHAR, BOOLEAN	Strings (any length), characters, booleans
{ identifier,... }	Enumerated types
[low..high], [T.first..T.last]	Subranges (integer and enumerated)
ARRAY index_type... OF element_type	Arrays
RECORD field;... END	Records with default field initializers
BITS n FOR type	Packed types
SET OF base_type	Sets
PROCEDURE signature	Procedure types

parent_type OBJECT field;...
    METHODS method;...
    OVERRIDES override;... END
	Object types

MUTEX	Mutual exclusion semaphore

Example 1–6

Here is a small program fragment:

```
CONST Rate = 5.00;
VAR
    hours: INTEGER;
    salary: REAL;
BEGIN
    salary := FLOAT(hours) * Rate;
END
```

The type of Rate is REAL (determined by the number 5.00), the type of hours is INTEGER, and the type of salary is REAL. The FLOAT built-in function converts an integer value to a REAL value. Therefore the operands to the multiplication both have type REAL, as does the result, which is assigned to the variable salary.

In general, different data types cannot be mixed in expressions. That is, you can't have a REAL and an INTEGER operand to * without inserting an explicit conversion function. Operator precedence follows the C and Fortran tradition, not the Pascal and Modula–2 tradition: relational operators bind more tightly than logical operators. Certain of the built-in functions are permitted only in modules or interfaces that have been labeled UNSAFE.

This book does not contain a chapter on expressions. Instead, the operators applicable to each data type are described in conjunction with the type.

1.3 Input/Output

Modula–3 does not have any built-in facilities for input/output. Instead, you must use procedures from various standard library interfaces to perform I/O. Appendix B discusses the I/O interfaces provided by SRC Modula–3. Since those interfaces are quite general and our needs are usually simple, we'll provide a quick summary here.

Output is always directed towards a *writer*. The interface Wr (page 281) provides basic procedures to output a string or a character to any writer. Interface Stdio (page 283) defines a standard output writer, stdout, which is used for output destined for the user's terminal screen. To write out numbers, you must use the procedures in interface Fmt (page 284) to convert the numbers to strings.

Example 1–7

This program writes out the integers 1 through 10 on separate lines on the user's terminal.

```
MODULE WriteTen EXPORTS Main;
IMPORT Stdio, Wr, Fmt;
BEGIN
    FOR n := 1 TO 10 DO
        Wr.PutText(Stdio.stdout, Fmt.Int(n));
        Wr.PutText(Stdio.stdout,"\n");   (* Write end-of-line *)
    END;
END WriteTen.
```

Input comes from *readers*. Stdio provides a standard reader, stdin, that accepts input from the user's terminal. Input operations are supplied by interface Rd (page 279). Conversions from strings to numbers are provided by procedures in Scan (page 286).

Example 1–8

The following program reads two numbers and prints their sum. (The & operator is used to combine strings.)

```
MODULE WriteSum EXPORTS Main;
IMPORT Wr, Rd, Fmt, Scan, Stdio;

PROCEDURE Read(): INTEGER =
    BEGIN
        RETURN Scan.Int(Rd.GetLine(Stdio.stdin));
    END Read;
```

```
PROCEDURE Write(t: TEXT) =
BEGIN
    Wr.PutText(Stdio.stdout, t);
    END Write;

VAR n1, n2: INTEGER;
BEGIN
    Write("Please type two numbers on separate lines:\n");
    n1 := Read();
    n2 := Read();
    Write("The sum of " & Fmt.Int(n1) & " and " & Fmt.Int(n2) &
        " is " & Fmt.Int(n1 + n2) & ".\n");
END WriteSum.
```

1.4 Exercises

Answers to the exercises marked "[A]" appear in Appendix D.

1. The following English sentences all contain mistakes. Classify the mistakes as lexical, syntactic, or semantic.   [A]

    a. Books listen to reason.

    b. Are? you hospitable.

    c. I like to # at ball games.

    d. I you it don't know where to go.

    e. Snifferblats don't sleep.

2. Explain the difference between importing and exporting an interface. Is a client an importer or an exporter?

3. Where is the end of the comment that begins on the first line of the following example?   [A]

```
(* Ignore the following code:
    (* Swap first and second *)
    temp := first; first := second; second := temp;
*)
```

4. How is the entry point of a Modula–3 program designated?

5. What are the values of the following expressions?   [A]

    a. $1 + 1 + 2 * 5 + 8$

    b. $7 - 1 - 3 * 2$

    c. $7 - (1 - 3) * 2$

6. Write a Modula–3 program that prints the integers from 1 to 10 and their squares in this format:

```
1    1
2    4
3    9
...
```

2

Declarations

In this chapter we'll look at the objects that Modula–3 programs use and manipulate: literal values (e.g., 2, TRUE, "String"), named constants, variables, and types. We'll also look at how declarations are organized, and at their scope and visibility.

2.1 Literals

2.1.1 Integers

Integers are normally written as a sequence of decimal digits (e.g., 0, 24, 15782). A decimal point is not permitted, nor are commas. Negative numbers can be written by preceding an integer with a minus sign, but a negative integer such as −34 is actually considered a constant expression—the negation of the integer literal 34. This distinction doesn't matter in practice. The largest integer you can write without causing an error is given by LAST(INTEGER), which is $2^{31}-1$ (2,147,483,647) on most modern computers. The most negative integer you can use is FIRST(INTEGER), usually -2^{31} (−2,147,483,648). You must write that integer as −2147483647−1, since 2147483648 is too large a (positive) number to write.

You can also write integers using radices (bases) other than 10. Preceding an integer with 8_ signifies that the value is expressed in octal (base 8) notation; 8_12 has the (decimal) value 10. You can also write 10 as 2_1010, 16_A, or 7_13; all bases from 2 through 16 are allowed. For bases 10 and above, the letters A, B, C, D, E, and F (or their lowercase equivalents) stand for the "digits" 10, 11, 12, 13,14, and 15, respectively. Regardless of how you write an integer literal, it always has type INTEGER.

Example 2–1

Legal integers include: 0, −1, 2_10101, 000005, and 16_CAB.

Illegal integers include: 100.,17_GGG, 2_45, and 1,024.

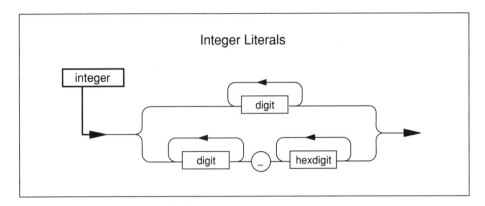

Integer Literals

2.1.2 Floating-Point Numbers

Floating-point numbers are written with an embedded decimal point and possibly an exponent. The numbers 12.34, 1234.0E–2, and 0.1234e2 are all equivalent. You always must have at least one digit before and after the decimal point. Negative floating-point numbers should be preceded by a minus sign. (Again, these are really constant expressions rather than literals.) See "Floating-Point Numbers" below.

There are three types of floating-point numbers: REAL, LONGREAL, and EXTENDED. If a floating-point literal doesn't have an exponent, or if the letters e or E are used for the exponent part, the number will have type REAL. If you want a floating-point number of type LONGREAL, use D or d as the exponent letter; if you want EXTENDED, use X or x.

Example 2–2

Legal floating-point numbers include: 1.0, 3.14D0, –23.45x–5, and 0.1.

Illegal floating-point numbers include: 1., .5, 3e–12, and 8_245.4E8.

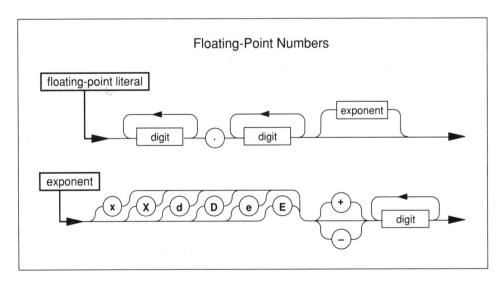

Floating-Point Numbers

2.1.3 Booleans

Boolean (true/false) values are represented by the built-in identifiers TRUE and FALSE. The BOOLEAN type is an enumerated type, and TRUE and FALSE are really abbreviations for the enumerated values BOOLEAN.TRUE and BOOLEAN.FALSE.

2.1.4 Characters

Character values have type CHAR. You can write them in several ways: Printing characters can be enclosed in apostrophes: 'A', '?', '4', '"', ' ' (space), etc. You can write certain special control characters using an "escape" notation by preceding a letter with a backslash \ character. The characters you can write this way include: '\n'(newline, linefeed), '\t' (tab), '\r' (carriage return), '\f' (form feed), '\'' (apostrophe), '\"' (quote), and '\\' (backslash).

You can write other characters (in fact, any character) by specifying their three-digit octal encodings following a backslash (e.g., '\000', '\040', '\277', etc.).

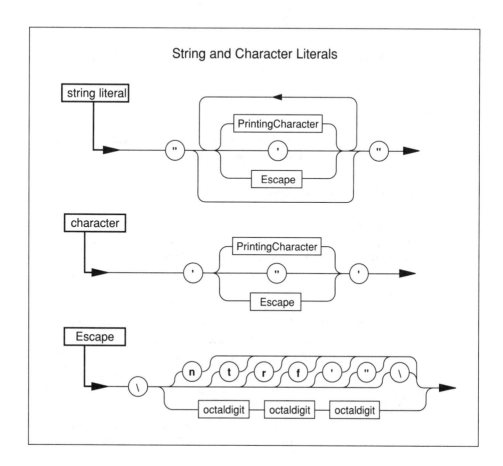

Example 2–3

It is almost always better to refer to characters by name rather than by a numerical escape. Here are some constant declarations for common characters:

```
CONST
    NUL = '\000';
    BS= '\010';
    HT= '\011';
    VT= '\013';
    SP= '\040';
    DEL = '\177';
```

2.1.5 Strings

Strings are sequences of characters, and you write them enclosed in double quotation marks (e.g., "Blue birds"). You can use the same escape notation in strings that was used for characters (e.g., "A string ending in newline\n"). Apostrophes in strings do not have to be escaped, but quotation marks do (e.g., "A string with 's and \"s"). All strings are of type TEXT and may be of any length. The empty string has length 0 and is written "". (See "String and Character Literals" on page 17.)

Your string literals must be contained on one line in the program. If you want a longer string, you have to concatenate it from smaller strings by using the & operator. Strings and type TEXT are described further beginning on page 87.

2.1.6 Constructors

You can also write literal values of record, array, and set types using constructors. These are discussed in Chapter 5, where those types are presented.

2.1.7 Constant Expressions

A *constant expression* is an expression whose value can be determined at compile time. Certain expressions in Modula–3 are required to be constant (for example, the bounds of a subrange and the initialization expression for a variable in an interface).

Constant expressions can include literal values such as numbers, strings, enumerations, and the names of declared procedures. Constant expressions can contain any operators except pointer dereferencing (^) and any built-in functions except ADR, LOOPHOLE, TYPECODE, NARROW, ISTYPE, SUBARRAY, and NEW. The functions from the Word interface can also be used in constant expressions (if their arguments are constant expressions), but no other imported procedures can be used.

Identifiers declared as constants can appear in constant expressions, but a variable can appear in a constant expression only if it is the argument to FIRST, LAST, NUMBER, BITSIZE, BYTESIZE, or ADRSIZE.

Examples of constant expressions include: NUMBER(Subrange) + 1, ORD('A') + 5, 10.6 + FLOAT(2), MAX(BYTESIZE(x), BYTESIZE(y)), and Word.Shift(1, 10).

2.2 Declarations and Identifiers

Programs are made up of many procedures, variables, types, etc. You write declarations to create these things and to associate identifiers with them so that you can refer to them by name. Identifiers must begin with a letter and can be followed by zero or more letters, digits, and underscore characters. Upper- and lowercase letters are distinct; that is, the identifiers BOOK, Book, and book are all different. Also, you cannot declare certain identifiers that are reserved by Modula–3. Table 2–1 lists these identifiers. All reserved identifiers are spelled entirely with uppercase letters.

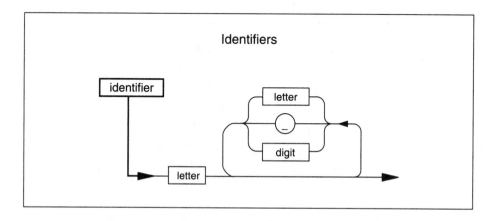

Table 2–1   Reserved Identifiers in Modula–3

ABS	CARDINAL	EXIT	INTEGER	NEW	RECORD	TRY
ADDRESS	CASE	EXPORTS	INTERFACE	NIL	REF	TYPE
ADR	CEILING	EXTENDED	ISTYPE	NOT	REFANY	TYPECASE
ADRSIZE	CHAR	FALSE	LAST	NULL	REPEAT	TYPECODE
AND	CONST	FINALLY	LOCK	NUMBER	RETURN	UNSAFE
ANY	DEC	FIRST	LONGREAL	OBJECT	REVEAL	UNTIL
ARRAY	DISPOSE	FLOAT	LOOP	OF	ROOT	UNTRACED
AS	DIV	FLOOR	LOOPHOLE	OR	ROUND	VAL
BEGIN	DO	FOR	MAX	ORD	SET	VALUE
BITS	ELSE	FROM	METHODS	OVERRIDES	SUBARRAY	VAR
BITSIZE	ELSIF	GENERIC	MIN	PROCEDURE	TEXT	WHILE
BOOLEAN	END	IF	MOD	RAISE	THEN	WITH
BRANDED	EVAL	IMPORT	MODULE	RAISES	TO	
BY	EXCEPT	IN	MUTEX	READONLY	TRUE	
BYTESIZE	EXCEPTION	INC	NARROW	REAL	TRUNC	

Example 2–4

Legal identifiers include: X, Billy, joeBob, brief_encounter, TopMost, Special_, T0089

Illegal identifiers include: 4X, B–grade, _Special, Three thousand, IEF$BR14, Amazin'

With the exception of literals, all program objects are referred to by names that are introduced by declarations. The kinds of objects you declare include variables your program operates on, constant values that you want to refer to by name, procedures, types, and exceptions. Declarations are grouped together in interfaces and modules, inside procedures, and in block statements.

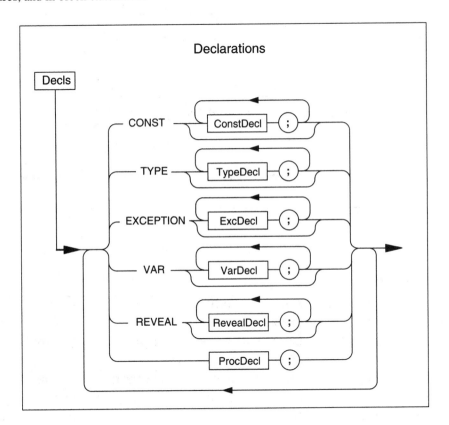

Example 2–5

In the module and interface below, the objects declared include the interface and module themselves; the type Array; the procedure Sort; the parameter array of Sort; and the local variables temp and k. The loop variable i is declared implicitly by the FOR statement.

```
INTERFACE Utilities;
TYPE Array = ARRAY OF INTEGER;
PROCEDURE Sort(VAR array: Array);
END Utilities.
```

```
MODULE Utilities;
PROCEDURE Sort( VAR array: Array)=
   BEGIN
      FOR i := FIRST(array) +1 TO LAST(array) DO
         VAR   (* block *)
            temp := array[i];
            k := i − 1;
         BEGIN
            WHILE k >= FIRST(array) AND array[k] > temp DO
               array[k + 1] := array[k];
               DEC(k);
            END;
            array[k + 1] := temp;
         END;
      END;
   END Sort;
BEGIN
END Utilities.
```

We'll now look at the various kinds of declarations. At the end of the chapter, we'll talk about the visibility and scope of declarations in general.

2.3 Constant Declarations

A constant is a value that does not depend on the execution of the program. A literal such as 23 is a constant. Other constants are *constant expressions*, which are formed by combining constants with expression operators and built-in functions.

Example 2–6

Some examples of constant expressions:

```
-12
TRUNC(15.8) + 34
FLOAT(4) / 5.0
```

A constant declaration is used to give a name to a constant. The name can then be used in other constant expressions or anywhere a value is needed. Named constants can help to make a program more readable in several ways: the name of a constant can suggest the

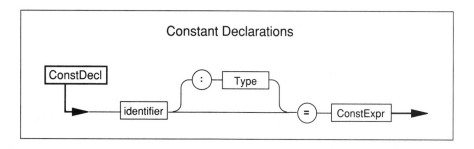

Constant Declarations

constant's use, the name can be used to avoid repeating the same constant expression, and a named constant may be easier than its value to type correctly. By convention in this book (Appendix A), constants are always spelled beginning with an uppercase letter.

Example 2–7

Here are some statements that use constant expressions:

```
area := 3.14159265358979D0 * radius * radius;
sectors := 20 * 256;
least_value := –16_7FFFFFFF-1;
```

See how the statements become more readable when constant declarations are used:

```
CONST
    Pi = 3.14159265358979D0;
    SectorsPerCylinder = 256;
    Cylinders = 20;
    EveryOtherBit = 16_55555555;
...
    area := Pi * radius * radius;
    sectors := SectorsPerCylinder * Cylinders;
    least_value :=  MostNegativeNumber;
```

Named constants have types that are normally determined from the values in the declaration, as in the previous examples. You can see in the accompanying syntax diagram that it is possible to specify the type explicitly, for example,

```
CONST Pi: LONGREAL = 3.14159265358979D0;
```

You need this ability only in a few cases involving reference and object types in which the constant is to have a type that is compatible with, but not the same as, the value. You can also include type if you think it makes your intent more clear.

Example 2–8

In the code below, the types SerialNumber, Size, and INTEGER are all the same, but using Se-rialNumber in the constant declaration tells the reader that None is a kind of "serial number" and not, say, a "size."

```
TYPE
    SerialNumber = INTEGER;
    Size = INTEGER;
CONST
    None: SerialNumber = 0;
```

2.4 Variable Declarations

A variable is an object held in the computer's memory that can contain a number of values as specified by the variable's type. Variables of type INTEGER, for example, hold integers; variables of type CHAR hold characters.

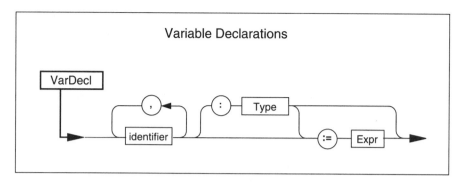

A variable declaration can include an expression used as an initial value for the variable. The initialization expression does not have to be constant, except when the variable declaration appears in an interface. Variables are always spelled beginning with a lowercase letter in this book, which is a convention explained in Appendix A.

Example 2–9

Here are some variable declarations.

```
VAR
    i: INTEGER;
    radius, diameter: REAL := 0.0;
    countOfSamples: [0..100] := ComputeCount();  (* Not legal in an interface *)
    histogram: ARRAY [0..10] OF CARDINAL;
```

It is a good programming practice to use initialization expressions liberally. They remove any doubt in a reader's mind what value the variable begins with. When you do not include an initialization expression in a variable declaration, Modula–3 will initialize the variable to some (unpredictable) value *of its type*. This is an important qualification! Most programming languages allow uninitialized variables to contain arbitrary bit patterns. With Modula–3, using a variable that has never been assigned a value can cause incorrect results, but it cannot cause the program to die horribly.

Example 2–10

In the block below, the variable k is not given a value before being used to index the array vector. Modula–3 guarantees that k will be assigned some value of type Index, but other languages are not as diligent. In those languages, k might start with a value such as 214,123,599, which could cause the program to fail catastrophically by attempting to reference a distant part of memory.

```
TYPE Index = [1..10];
VAR
    k : Index;
    vector: ARRAY Index OF INTEGER;
BEGIN
    vector[k] := 6;
    ...
END
```

Modula–3 encourages using initialization expressions by including a very handy shortcut: if the type of the initialization expression is the same as the desired type of the variable, you can omit the type in the declaration.

Example 2–11

Here are some variable declarations from which the type has been omitted. Comments indicate the type that is assumed. Reference (REF) types are discussed in Chapter 10.

```
TYPE
    Index = [1..10];
    Samples = ARRAY Index OF INTEGER;
    Pointer = REF INTEGER;
CONST First: Index = 1;
VAR
    radius := 0.0D0;              (* type LONGREAL *)
    a, b := 0;                    (* type INTEGER *)
    i := First;                   (* type [1..10] *)
    s := Samples{ 0,.. };         (* type ARRAY [1..10] OF INTEGER *)
    p := NEW(Pointer);            (* type REF INTEGER *)
```

However, you must include the type when the initialization expression doesn't have the correct type. Assuming the same type and constant declarations, here are other variable declarations and the types that would be assumed if they weren't specified:

```
VAR
    i: Index := 1;               (* would be INTEGER *)
    p: REF INTEGER := NIL;       (* would be NULL *)
```

2.5 Type Declarations

A type declaration associates a name with a type; thereafter, using the name is the same as using the original type. Type declarations can be used when the type being named is rather complicated, like an enumeration or record type. However, you should also use your own names for types that are logically different, even if they are really represented in the same way. For example, since integers are used for many purposes in programs, you should define names for INTEGER that suggest their use, and then use them consistently. The syntax

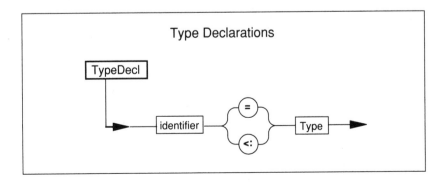

diagram indicates that either = or <: may follow the identifier, but the <: symbol is used only when declaring opaque types, which are not discussed until Chapter 10.

Example 2–12

Suppose you were reading an inventory program that used integers to represent both part numbers and the quantity of parts on hand. This code is confusing; are part numbers or quantities being assigned?

```
VAR p, n: INTEGER;
BEGIN
    ... p := 1; n := 100; ...
END
```

The code becomes clearer with type declarations:

```
TYPE
    PartNumber = INTEGER;
    Quantity = INTEGER;
VAR
    p: PartNumber;
    n: Quantity;
BEGIN
    ... p := 1; n := 100; ...
END
```

However, in neither example would the Modula–3 compiler prevent you from accidentally writing p := n, even though that would probably be a mistake.

2.5.1 Type Equivalence

Type declarations are another area in which Modula–3 differs from other Pascal-family languages. Modula–3 uses *structural equivalence* of types. Roughly speaking, this means that a type isn't different just because you call it by a different name. In contrast to this, some type declarations in other languages treat named types as distinct. The advantage of Modula–3's rules is that they are much easier to describe and to understand. The disadvantage is that two logically different types in Modula–3 may turn out to be the same by coincidence, at which point Modula–3 will allow them to be mixed instead of rejecting such errors. In practice, this does not seem to be a serious problem, and it *is* possible to protect "important" reference types from accidental collisions, as we'll see in Chapter 10. Type compatibility is also discussed further in Chapters 4 and 5.

Example 2–13

After the following declarations, each of the pairs of names A1 and A2, P1 and P2, X1 and X2, E1 and E2, V1 and V2, and R1 and R2 refer to the same type and can be used interchangeably.

```
TYPE
    A1 = INTEGER;
    A2 = A1;
    P1 = REF INTEGER;
    P2 = REF A2;
```

Type Equivalence: By Structure or By Name?

Modula-3's structural equivalence rule is considered by some to be one of the language's weaknesses. These people prefer "name equivalence," in which types that are given different names are treated as distinct and cannot accidentally be mixed just because their structure happens to be the same.

Under the name equivalence rules used by C, Pascal, and Modula-2, new types come into being when special type constructors are used, such as RECORD...END, union{...}, SET OF..., etc. However, a simple "renaming" declaration does not create a new type. Consider these declarations:

```
TYPE
    Apple = RECORD size: REAL END;  (* Pascal, Modula-2*)
    Orange = RECORD size: REAL END;
    Lemon = Orange;
```

In Modula-3, Apple, Lemon, and Orange are all the same type. In Pascal, Modula–2, and C, Apple and Orange would be different types, but you could still mix Lemons and Oranges: they're the same type even though they have different names. Furthermore, you can never create "new" integers or floating-point types. So, name equivalence has its own loopholes.

Ada takes name equivalence further; you can create "new" integer types by writing

```
TYPE InventoryCode = NEW INTEGER;
```

InventoryCode is not the same type as INTEGER. However, since the new type is still an "integers" in some sense, there is a complicated set of rules that allows InventoryCode to inherit many of the INTEGER operations, so that you can assign integer literals to InventoryCode variables, etc.

Structural equivalence is easy to explain and is adequately safe in most cases. It is superior to name equivalence when programming distributed systems, in which separate programs must communicate typed data. There are some important situations in which you want to "disable" structural equivalence to prevent a hidden type from being "guessed"; this is handled in Modula-3 by "branded" types, which are discussed in Chapters 10 and 11.

```
X1 = [0..10];
X2 = [0..10];
E1 = { blue, red, green };
E2 = { blue, red, green };
V1 = ARRAY [0..10] OF P2;
V2 = ARRAY X1 OF REF A2;
R1 = RECORD a, b : INTEGER; END;
R2 = RECORD a: INTEGER; b: INTEGER; END;
```

If these declarations had been written in Modula–2, A1 and A2 would be identical, but P1 and P2 would not, nor would any of the named array, record, or reference types be identical to their anonymous (unnamed) versions. However, nonidentical types can sometimes be mixed in Modula–2; in Modula–3, except for subranges and subtypes, two types are either the same or (completely) different.

2.6 Procedures, Exceptions, and Revelations

The remaining three kinds of declarations—procedure declarations, exception declarations, and type revelations—will be discussed in Chapters 6, 7, and 10, respectively.

2.7 Blocks, Scope, and Visibility

There are a few more important concepts to discuss before leaving declarations.

The location of a declaration in a Modula–3 program determines its *scope*, that is, where in the program the name it defines is *visible* and therefore can be used. All declarations—except those in interfaces—occur in *blocks*, which are sequences of declarations followed by some executable statements:

```
List-of-declarations
BEGIN
    List-of-statements
END
```

Blocks appear inside procedures and in modules. In Modula–3, the scope of a name declared in a block is the entire block, including *all* the other declarations in the block. In contrast to this, the scope of a name in other Pascal-family languages extends only from its declaration to the end of the block—it does not extend to previous declarations. Therefore, in Modula–3 you can organize the declarations in a block in any order that seems appropriate or logical to you; you don't have to declare a name before you use it in another declaration.

Example 2–14

In the following block, the declarations have been arbitrarily arranged in alphabetical order. There are two "forward references" (uses of names before their declarations): Z is used in the declaration of a (for both its value and type), and Q is used in the body of P:

Simultaneous Declarations

Modula–3's "simultaneous declaration" rule simplifies the handling of forward references to procedures and types, but again this is a rule that sets Modula–3 apart from other Pascal-family languages. Languages that require "declaration before use" inevitably have to invent special mechanisms to handle forward references.

In traditional C, for example, you can call a function before it is defined; a new function declaration is implicitly added. Most versions of Pascal have a "forward" declaration to use for mutually recursive procedures:

```
PROCEDURE P(); FORWARD; {Pascal}
PROCEDURE Q(); BEGIN... P(); ... END;
PROCEDURE P(); BEGIN ...Q(); ... END;
```

Types can also be recursive. Modula–2 and C allow limited forward references to types when declaring pointers. Ada provides an incomplete type declaration to introduce a type name before actually defining it. (C has a similar facility for records, and Modula–2 has one for pointers.)

The simultaneous declaration rule makes a little more work for Modula–3 compilers, and it can be abused by programmers who intentionally try to make their programs obscure. However, in general the simplification seems to outweigh any disadvantages.

```
VAR a := Z;
PROCEDURE P(n: INTEGER): INTEGER =
    BEGIN
        IF n > 0 THEN RETURN Q(n – 1); ELSE RETURN 0; END;
    END P;

PROCEDURE Q(n: INTEGER): INTEGER =
    BEGIN
        IF n > 0 THEN RETURN P(n – 1); ELSE RETURN 0; END;
    END Q;

CONST Z = 10.0;
VAR x: INTEGER := 5;
BEGIN
    x := P(x);
END;
```

Although the forward reference to Z could easily be eliminated by placing the declaration of Z before that of A, the functions P and Q call each other and so a forward reference would remain no matter which one was placed first.

The declarations in an interface (Chapter 8) behave in the same manner as declarations in blocks; it's just that there are no executable statements following the declarations in an interface.

2.7.1 **Nested Declarations**

Since blocks can appear as statements, it is possible to place new declarations in a block nested inside the scope of outer declarations. Names declared at outer levels are still visible within the nested scopes unless the nested scope contains declarations of one or more names from the outer scope. In that case, the inner declarations replace the corresponding outer ones throughout the inner scope. At the end of the inner scope, the outer declaration becomes visible again.

Example 2–15

Here is a somewhat contrived example to illustrate how inner declarations can hide outer ones. The inner block extends from the first declaration (the PROCEDURE keyword) through the END (*Inner block*) line. The puzzle is to determine what values the variables i and k have just before exiting the outer block:

```
(* 1 *)    VAR
(* 2 *)       i, k: INTEGER;
(* 3 *)    BEGIN
(* 4 *)       i := 12;
(* 5 *)       PROCEDURE Add_I(n: INTEGER): INTEGER =
(* 6 *)          BEGIN
(* 7 *)             RETURN i + n;
(* 8 *)          END Add_I;
(* 9 *)       VAR i := 3;
(* 10 *)      BEGIN
(* 11 *)         k := Add_I(4);
(* 12 *)      END (*Inner block*);
(* 13 *)   (* What are the values of i and k here? *)
(* 14 *)   END;
```

Solution   k has the value 7, not 16, and i has the value 12. The use of i within procedure Add_I refers to the innermost declaration of i, which appears after the procedure on line 9 but whose scope covers the entire inner block, lines 5–12. Therefore, Add_I adds 3 to its argument. The outer variable i (declared on line 2) is not affected and thus keeps the value of 12 that it was given at the beginning of the outer block.

You shouldn't redeclare names in nested blocks just to be confusing, as in this example. However, it is a good idea to declare names close to where they are needed, giving them the *smallest* scope possible. In large programs it is not unusual to accidentally choose a name in a procedure that just happens to have been declared somewhere in the outer scopes. This usually does no harm: since you weren't aware of the outer name, you obviously don't need it inside the procedure. It would be very tedious to have to check an entire program before you declared each new variable in a procedure.

Example 2–16

Suppose we wanted to exchange the values of variables a and b, which have the same type. To do this, we need to use a third variable temporarily, and it's convenient to create a block that limits the scope of this temporary variable:

```
VAR temp := a;
BEGIN
  a := b;
  b := temp;
END;
```

This way, we don't care if temp had been declared in an outer scope. (By the way, see how we also avoid having to know the type of a and b!)

Visibility always extends inward, never outward from blocks. The declarations at the top level of a module are never visible outside that module (i.e., in any other module or interface). Declarations in an interface (Chapter 8) *are* visible in the module that implements that interface. By using IMPORT statements, other modules or interfaces can see declarations inside an interface.

2.7.2 Lifetimes

The *lifetime* of a variable determines when during program execution the variable is usable; that is, the time during which it actually occupies a location in memory).

Declarations in an interface or in the topmost block of a module are called *top-level declarations*, and variables declared there exist throughout program execution. The declared names always refer to the same variables, and these variables are initialized once, when the program is first started. (See Chapter 8.)

All other blocks occur inside procedures or inside the top-level block of a module. Declarations in those blocks are called *local declarations*, and variables declared there exist only while the enclosing procedure is being executed. Each time the procedure is called, new copies of the variables are created and initialized. Each time the procedure returns, the variables are destroyed.

There are also variables with a *dynamic lifetime*, but these variables are not declared. They are discussed in Chapter 10.

2.7.3 Variable Initialization Order

There is one exception to the "declarations can occur in any order" statement: variable initializations can be affected by the order of declarations. All initializations take place in the order the variables are declared, as if they were assignments at the beginning of the statements of the block. This can result in a variable getting a different value than might be apparent.

Example 2–17

The following three variable declarations are legal, and it might appear (to a programmer thinking "order of declarations doesn't matter") that each variable will be initialized to 10:

```
VAR
  a: INTEGER := b;
  b: INTEGER := c;
  c: INTEGER := 10;
```

In fact, however, the initializations occur in order, as if this code had been written:

```
VAR
    a, b, c: INTEGER;
BEGIN
    a := b;
    b := c;
    c := 10;
    ...
END;
```

This rewriting makes clear what is happening. In accordance with Modula–3's rules for default (missing) initializations, a, b, and c are first initialized to arbitrary values of their types (INTEGER). Only then are the assignments performed. The result is that a and b are assigned arbitrary values. Only c gets the expected value of 10.

Example 2–18

This example is similar to the last one, except it *does* work as expected:

```
VAR
    a: INTEGER := C;
    b: INTEGER := C;
CONST
    C = 10;
```

Again, the effect can be seen clearly by rewriting:

```
VAR a, b: INTEGER;
CONST C = 10;
BEGIN
    a := C;
    b := C;
    ...
END;
```

In an interface (Chapter 8), the order of variable initializations is not a problem since all initialization expressions must be constant.

2.7.4 Recursive Declarations

A *recursive declaration* is one in which the name being declared is used (directly or indirectly) in its own declaration, as in these examples:

```
TYPE List = REF RECORD item: INTEGER; next: List; END;         (* OK *)
VAR ptr: REF ARRAY [0..BYTESIZE(ptr)] OF INTEGER;              (* OK *)
CONST N = N + 1;                                              (* Illegal! *)
PROCEDURE Fib(n: CARDINAL): CARDINAL =                        (* OK *)
    BEGIN
        IF n = 0 THEN RETURN 1; ELSE RETURN n * Fib(n – 1); END;
    END Fib;
```

Modula–3 permits recursive declarations as long as the recursive use of the name is enclosed in a REF, OBJECT, or PROCEDURE type, or in a procedure body. This places a level of pointer indirection around the name. By this rule, the declarations of List, ptr, and Fib above are legal recursive declarations, but the declaration of N is illegal.

In a variable declaration of the form V := E, where the type is omitted, the declaration is considered recursive only if V is used in the definition of the type of E. Therefore the declaration

```
VAR n := BITSIZE(n);   (* Legal, if silly *)
```

is not considered to be recursive because the result type of BITSIZE (page 258) is always CARDINAL. On the other hand, the following recursive declaration of v is illegal:

```
VAR v := P();   (* Illegal! *)
PROCEDURE P(): ARRAY [0..LAST(v)] OF T;
```

2.8 Exercises

Answers to the exercises marked "[A]" appear in Appendix D.

1. Which of the following statements about Modula–3 are true?   [A]
   a. All integer literals have type INTEGER.
   b. The literal '\xFF' is the character encoded by the value 16_FF (i.e., 255).
   c. Declarations can appear only at the top level of interfaces, modules, procedures, and blocks.
   d. The type of a named constant is the type of the expression appearing in the constant declaration.
   e. Identifiers written with all uppercase letters are reserved.
   f. Two types with different names might or might not be the same.
   g. The order of declarations doesn't affect their scope.

2. Given the following declarations, which of the types A, B, C, and D are the same?

```
TYPE
    A = INTEGER;
    B = RECORD f: INTEGER; END;
    C = RECORD f: A; END;
    D = REAL;
    E = A;
```

3. Which of the following literals are legal? For those that are legal, what are their types?   [A]
   a. 1.0
   b. –2_0010
   c. 0xFF
   d. 1.0X4
   e. '' (two consecutive apostrophes)
   f. "" (two consecutive quotation marks)
   g. '\0'

4. Given the following declarations, what is the type of the declared identifier in each of the variable declarations?

```
TYPE
    Number = INTEGER;
    Sub = [1..10];
    CONST Five: Sub = 5;
```

a. VAR x := 0;
b. VAR x: INTEGER;
c. VAR x: Number := 0;
d. VAR x: Sub;
e. VAR x: Sub := 0;
f.   VAR x := Five;
g. VAR x: Number := Five;

5. What can you say about the values of the variables a, b, and c just after the BEGIN below?   [A]

```
VAR
    a := k;
    b := c;
    c := b;
    CONST k = 10;
BEGIN
    ...
END;
```

6. What value is assigned to variable x in the following code fragment?

```
VAR
    k := 10;
    x: INTEGER;
BEGIN
    PROCEDURE P(): INTEGER =
        BEGIN RETURN k; END P;
    VAR k := 5;
    BEGIN
        x := P();
    END;
END;
```

7. Are the following recursive declarations legal or illegal?
    a.   CONST N = BYTESIZE(ARRAY [0..N] OF REAL);
    b.   CONST N = BYTESIZE(REF ARRAY [0..N] OF REAL);
    c.   TYPE T = RECORD one: INTEGER; two: T; END;
    d.   TYPE T = OBJECT x: T; END;
    e.   TYPE T = T OBJECT x: INTEGER; END;

3

Statements

There are fifteen different kinds of statements in the Modula–3 language, as shown in the syntax diagram below. The exception-related statements (RaiseStmt, TryFinStmt, and TryXptStmt) are covered in Chapter 7 (Exceptions). The TYPECASE statement (TCase-Stmt) is discussed in Chapter 10 (Dynamic Programming). The thread-related statement (LockStmt) is covered in Chapter 12. All the other statements are described in this chapter.

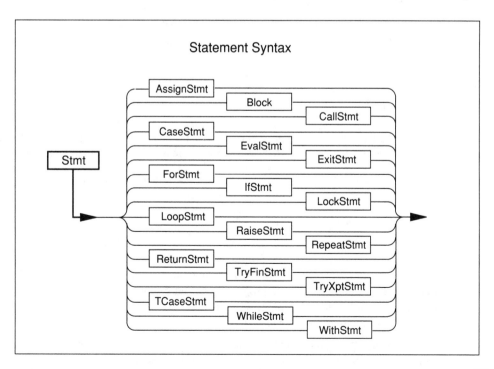

Statement Syntax

3.1 Statements and Statement Sequences

Statements can appear in the block at the top level of a module and inside procedures. *Compound* statements can contain statements inside them. Because Modula–3's compound statements always include a keyword (e.g., END) at the end of any enclosed statements, you can put a sequence of statements separated by semicolons wherever a single statement would be allowed. In the syntax diagrams, the word Stmts refers to a sequence of statements.

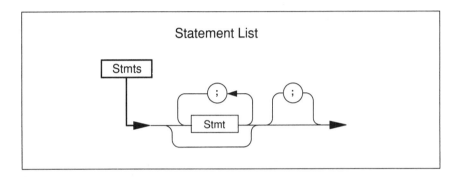

Statement List

Example 3–1

An IF statement is a compound statement. Here is an example which contains two statements inside it:

```
IF a > b THEN
    larger := a;
    Wr.PutText(Stdio.stdout, "a is bigger\n");
END
```

If you are a Pascal (or C) programmer, notice that you don't need extra BEGIN-END (or {-}) brackets in Modula–3 (or Modula–2 or Ada). Here is the Pascal version of the statement:

```
IF a >  b THEN                        { PASCAL: note the extra BEGIN }
    BEGIN
        larger := a;
        writeln("a is bigger");
    END
```

As you can see from the syntax, you can include a semicolon after the last statement in a sequence if you wish. Some programmers find it more natural to think of the semicolon as terminating each statement, whereas others think of the semicolon as a separator. You can have it either way in Modula–3.

A statement sequence can be empty (or consist of a single semicolon). If you use an empty sequence, you should probably include a comment explaining why you did so.

3.2 Assignment Statement

Assignment statements are the most common statements in Modula–3 programs. They simply compute the value of an expression and store the value in a variable. Assignments can involve constant values or lengthy calculations. In Modula–3, you can assign values of any type, including procedures, records, and arrays.

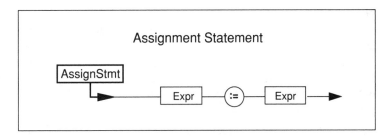

Example 3–2

Below are some sample assignment statements that assume these declarations:

```
VAR
    i, j : INTEGER;
    r1, r2: RECORD ... END;
    a, b: ARRAY [1..10000] OF REAL;
    p, q: REF INTEGER;
    proc1, proc2: PROCEDURE (x: REAL): REAL;
...
    i := 0;                      (* Assign to an integer variable *)
    a[j] := a[j+i] * b[j];       (* Assign an array element *)
    p := q;                      (* Assign pointers *)
    p^ := q^;                    (* Assign variables designated by pointers *)
    a := b;                      (* Assign arrays *)
    r1 := r2;                    (* Assign records *)
    proc1 := proc2;              (* Assign procedures *)
```

In judging whether an assignment statement is allowable, Modula–3 applies three criteria:

1. The expression on the left-hand side (LHS) of the assignment must denote a variable that can be modified. (It must be a *writable designator*.)

2. The type of the right-hand-side (RHS) expression must be assignable to the type of the LHS variable in the assignment.

3. The value of the RHS expression must be a member of the LHS variable's type.

The first two criteria can be checked when the program is compiled; the third criterion may have to be checked at run time. We'll look at each of these criteria in more detail in the next three sections.

3.2.1 Writable Designators

The LHS expression of an assignment statement must designate a writable variable, i.e., a variable whose value you can change. If the LHS is a simple identifier, for example, that identifier must be declared as a variable—not an exception, or a type, or a procedure, or a constant. The designated variable also must not be *read-only*. For example, you can assign to an identifier declared as a procedure parameter as long as the parameter's mode is not READONLY.

A few Modula–3 statements introduce variable identifiers and you might want to know if you can assign to them. You can assign to the local identifiers declared in TYPE-CASE (page 185) and TRY-EXCEPT (page 135) statements, but *not* to the identifier declared in a FOR statement (page 49)—it's read-only. You can assign to an identifier bound in a WITH statement (page 54) if the expression to which it was bound is assignable; otherwise, the bound identifier is read-only.

If the LHS expression is not a simple identifier, it must be an expression in one of the following forms (after removing any outer parentheses). These are the only expressions that can be writable designators:

p^   p can be any pointer expression

a[i]   a must be a writable array designator. If a is a pointer to an array, a[i] is always a writable designator.

r.f   r must be a writable designator for a record, and f must be one of its fields. If r is a pointer to a record, r.f is always a writable designator.

o.f   o must be an object and f must be one of its fields

I.x   x must be a variable declared in interface I

SUBARRAY(a,pos, len)
         a must be a writable array designator (see page 104)

LOOPHOLE(v, T)
         v must be a writable designator and this expression can appear only in an UNSAFE module (see page 262)

Example 3–3

What return type(s), if any, for function F would make the following assignments legal? (a) F() := x; (b) F()^ := x; (c) F()[i] := x;

Solution   (a) The return value from a function is never a designator itself, so the statement F() := x can never be legal. (b) If the return type of F is any pointer type, the statement F()^ := x is legal (assuming that the type of x matches the pointer referent type). (c) The expression F()[i] can be a designator only if F() is; therefore, F must return a reference to an array and not an array itself. (This depends on the expression F()[i] being equivalent to F()^[i] when F returns a reference to an array.)

By the way, be careful if either the LHS or RHS of the assignment involves function calls that might produce side effects. Modula–3 does not specify whether the LHS or RHS is evaluated first.

Example 3–4

The AddOne function increments the variable k by one and returns its new value. What is the effect of the assignment statement, array[k] := AddOne()?

```
VAR
    array: ARRAY [1..10] OF INTEGER;
    k := 1;
PROCEDURE AddOne(): INTEGER =
    BEGIN k := k + 1; RETURN k; END AddOne;
BEGIN
    array[k] := AddOne();
END;
```

Solution   There are two possible outcomes of the assignment, and you cannot tell which will be chosen. If the LHS of the assignment is evaluated first, the effect is the same as array[1] := 2. If the RHS of the assignment is evaluated first, the effect is the same as array[2] := 2.

3.2.2 Type Assignability

Once you are sure that the LHS of the assignment is a writable designator, the next question is: Are the types of the LHS and RHS compatible? That is, is the RHS type assignable to the LHS type? Assignability is a relationship between types (page 60) and is discussed with the individual types in later chapters. However, here are some common situations that result in assignability:

1. The types are the same. (Recall that type declarations simply introduce synonyms for types, not different types.)

2. Both types are INTEGER, or integer subranges ([n..m]), sharing at least one value.

3. Both types are CHAR, or CHAR subranges (['x'..'y']), sharing at least one value.

4. Both types are some enumeration type T, or subranges of T ([T.A..T.B]), sharing at least one value.

5. The LHS is an open array and the RHS is a fixed array of the same dimension and element type (see page 103).

If you have been programming in a less strict language, keep in mind these common illegal assignments: you can't assign an integer value to a floating-point variable, or vice versa, and you can't assign a value of one floating-point type (e.g., REAL) to a variable of a different floating-point type (e.g., LONGREAL). In these cases you must convert the value of the RHS to the type of the LHS variable using one of the built-in conversion functions such as FLOAT or ROUND.

Example 3–5

In the following assignment statements, some of the types are compatible and some are not:

```
TYPE Color= { red, blue, green };
VAR
    lf: LONGREAL;  ef: EXTENDED;
    i: INTEGER;  sub_1: [1..10];  sub_2: [11..20];
    c1: { red, blue, green };  c2: [Color.blue..Color.green];
    int_p: REF INTEGER;  char_p: REF CHAR;

    i := sub_1;                    (* OK *)
    sub_1 := sub_2;                (* illegal; types share no values *)
    ef := lf;                      (* illegal; mixing floating-point types *)
    lf := sub_1;                   (* illegal; mixing integer and flt-pt. *)
    c1 := c2;                      (* OK; c1's type Color are assignable *)
    int_p := char_p;               (* illegal; types are different *)
```

Some other assignments involving reference, object, procedure, and array types are permitted although they don't appear in the "compatible" list above. The additional rules are discussed when the corresponding types are described in later chapters.

3.2.3 Value Assignability

After determining that the LHS and RHS types in an assignment are compatible, there remains a final test: Is the RHS value assignable to the LHS variable? The first two assignment tests can be performed by the Modula–3 compiler, but this test may require a run-time check. There are, roughly speaking, three cases that give rise to run-time checks:

1. The LHS is a subrange, and the RHS type includes values outside that subrange. A check is needed to be sure the value lies within the subrange.

2. The LHS is a reference or object and a subtype of the RHS type (page 188 and page 212). A check is needed to be sure the RHS value has the appropriate type.

3. The LHS and RHS are procedure variables. A check is needed to be sure the RHS is a top-level procedure (page 126).

If the run-time checks fail, the Modula–3 program will halt with a suitable diagnostic message. (Implementations may instead raise an exception, but none do so at present.)

Example 3–6

Some the following assignment statements will require run-time checks. (Variables of type REFANY can hold values of any reference type; see page 183.)

```
VAR
    sub: [1..10];  i: INTEGER;
    any_p: REFANY;  int_p: REF INTEGER;
    ...
    i := sub;                      (* OK, no check required *)
    sub := i;                      (* run-time check required *)
    int_p := any_p;                (* run-time check required *)
    any_p := int_p;                (* OK, no check required *)
```

3.3 INC and DEC Statements

The INC and DEC statements are kinds of assignment statements, used to increment and decrement variables by some amount. Syntactically, they appear to be procedure calls, but they are built into the Modula–3 language. The first argument to INC and DEC must be an expression that would be allowed as the LHS of an assignment statement. The second must be an integer.

If v is a writable designator for an integer variable, and n is an integer expression, then the effect of executing the statement INC(v, n) is to add the value of n to the current value of v. Likewise, the effect of DEC(v, n) is to subtract the value of n from v. If the addition or subtraction causes the value of v to exceed its range, it is a checked run-time error. This includes, if v is an INTEGER variable, computing a value greater than LAST(INTEGER) or less than FIRST(INTEGER). (Some other languages ignore those errors.)

INC and DEC can be applied to variables of integer, enumeration, and CHAR types, and to subranges of those types. (That is why INC and DEC have to be built in to the language.) In all cases, n must be an integer expression. When the variable v is not an integer, the effect of INC is to change the value of v to the n'th following enumeration value or character, and the effect of DEC is to change the value to the n'th preceding value.

If you omit the second argument to INC and DEC it is taken to be 1.

Example 3–7

INC and DEC are very useful when v is a complicated expression. Consider the problem of decrementing by k the value of a[F(x)], an element of an integer array indexed by the function call F(x). The best solution is to write

    DEC(a[F(x)], k);

The naive way to write this without DEC is

    a[F(x)] := a[F(x)] – k;

However, this will cause F to be called twice—once when the RHS is evaluated and once when the LHS is evaluated. DEC only evaluates its argument once, so to simulate it you have to write the more complicated statement

    WITH v = a[F(x)] DO v := v – k; END;

(The WITH statement is discussed on page 54.) If a were a CHAR array, the DEC statement would look the same, but the rewritten form would be even more complicated:

    WITH v = a[F(x)] DO v := VAL(ORD(v) – k, CHAR); END;

(The VAL and ORD functions for type CHAR are described beginning on page 77.)

3.4 Procedure Calls and EVAL

Procedure calls are other common statements in virtually all Modula–3 programs. They are used to execute the statements of a procedure, after providing values for the procedure's parameters. When the called procedure completes, execution continues after the procedure call. Procedures are discussed in more detail in Chapter 6.

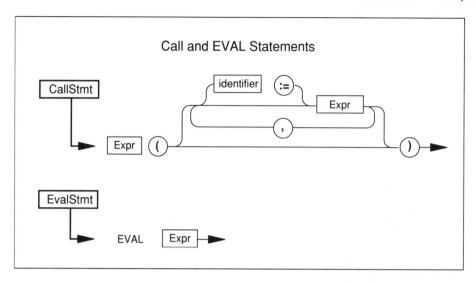

A procedure call statement must name a "proper" procedure—one that returns no value. Calls of value-returning procedures, called functions, appear in expressions—not in statements. However, if you want to call a function as a statement, ignoring the returned value, simply precede the call with the keyword EVAL.

Example 3–8

Here is a proper procedure that writes out its single integer argument:

```
PROCEDURE PutInt(x: INTEGER) =
  BEGIN
      Wr.PutText(Stdio.stdout, Fmt.Int(x));
  END PutInt;
```

You can call this procedure by writing, say,

```
PutInt(i + 7);
```

When PutInt is executed, formal parameter x will have the value of the expression i + 7. Similarly, here is a function WriteSum that uses PutInt to write out the sum of two integers. WriteSum also returns the sum as its value:

```
PROCEDURE WriteSum(x, y: INTEGER): INTEGER =
  BEGIN
      Wr.PutText(Stdio.stdout, "The sum is ");
      PutInt(x + y);
      Wr.PutText(Stdio.stdout, ".\n");
      RETURN x + y;
  END WriteSum;
```

To write out the sum of two integers and ignore the computed result, you could write

```
EVAL WriteSum(3, 5);              (* Returned value discarded *)
```

Variations on Procedure Calls

In Modula–3, like C, a procedure call can always be identified by a paren-
thesized list following the procedure name. Even if there are no arguments,
an empty set of parentheses must be present. In Pascal, Modula–2, and
Ada empty argument lists are omitted entirely from proper procedure calls.
In Pascal and Ada empty argument lists are also omitted from function calls,
so the expression x + P could involve a call of two function procedures, x
and P. By requiring empty argument lists in Modula–3 you are always
reminded that you are calling a procedure.

    The languages also differ in how they let you ignore function return
values. Modula–3 provides the EVAL statement for this purpose. C just si-
lently ignores the return value of a function call standing alone as a statement. In Ada, Pascal, and Modula–2, you cannot ignore function values; you
have to put them somewhere even if you never use them. Many programmers think this is cumbersome.

3.4.1 Argument Compatibility

When calling a procedure, you must be careful that the arguments in the call are compatible with the corresponding formal parameters. Unless the parameter has mode VAR, the
rule is the same as for assignment—the argument value must be assignable to the formal
parameter, as if the formal parameter were the LHS of an assignment statement and the argument were the RHS.

    If the formal parameter does have mode VAR, the rule is more strict: The type of the
actual must be the same as the type of the formal, and the actual must be a writable designator (i.e., it must be allowable as the LHS of an assignment statement).

Example 3–9

Here is an Inc procedure, which increments its integer argument exactly as the built-in INC
does:

```
PROCEDURE Inc(VAR v: INTEGER; n: INTEGER) =
  BEGIN
    v := v + n;
  END Inc;
```

Here are some legal and illegal calls of Inc:

```
CONST Five = 5;   VAR i: INTEGER;    s: [1..10] := Five;
...
Inc(i, 1);                           (* OK; increments i by 1 *)
Inc(i, s);                           (* OK, because s is assignable to N *)
Inc(s, 1);                           (* Illegal: the types of s and v are different *)
Inc(i, Five);                        (* OK *)
Inc(Five, i);                        (* Illegal; the constant Five is not writable *)
```

Modula–3 also allows procedure calls to name their arguments and to omit arguments for which the procedure has specified default values. These additional features are discussed in Chapter 6.

3.5 RETURN Statement

The RETURN statement terminates the innermost procedure, returning control to the caller. In a function procedure, the RETURN statement must provide a result value that is assignable to the result type of the function. In a proper procedure, the RETURN statement must not supply a value.

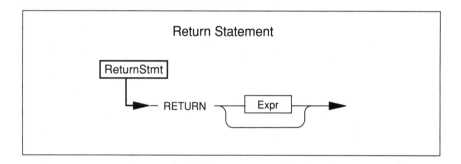

If the last statement in the body of a proper procedure completes and it is not a RETURN statement, then the effect is as if the last statement were immediately followed by RETURN statement. It is a checked run-time error if this situation arises in a function procedure, because no return value can be supplied.

Example 3–10

Consider the following function:

```
PROCEDURE ReturnIt(n: INTEGER): [1..10] =
   BEGIN
      IF n > 0 THEN RETURN n; END;
   END ReturnIt;
```

If ReturnIt is passed an argument whose value is in the range 1..10, then the function will return without error. If ReturnIt is passed a value greater than 10, then a run-time error will occur because the function will attempt to return a value that is outside the range of the return type. If ReturnIt is passed a value less than 1, then a (different) run-time error will occur because function body will complete without encountering a RETURN statement.

3.6 Block Statement

The block statement is a sequence of statements, usually preceded by some declarations. Blocks support locality by giving you the opportunity to declare variables, types, con-

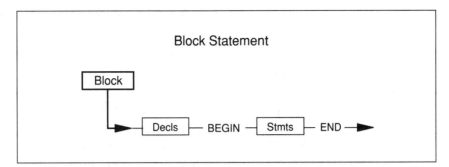

stants, etc., that are visible within only a small section of a procedure or module. The syntax of the block statement is shown above.

The block statement is quite general, but you may be able to accomplish the same purpose with a more specialized statement. The FOR statement (page 49) and WITH statement (page 54) both introduce local variables, as do the TRY-EXCEPT statement (page 135) and the TYPECASE statement (page 185).

Example 3–11

Suppose you want to read an integer value and, if the value is greater than 10, write it out. You will need a variable to hold the input value while you test it. A block statement lets you declare the variable, isolated from the surrounding program:

```
VAR k: INTEGER;
BEGIN
    k := Scan.Int(Rd.GetLine(Stdio.stdin));
    IF k > 10 THEN Wr.PutText(Stdio.stdout, Fmt.Int(k) & "\n"); END;
END;
```

If k were declared further away—at the top of the procedure, say—a reader might wonder if k were used for something other than the short input/output sequence. The only way to be sure would be to scan the entire procedure. A slightly more compact form of the above example is

```
VAR k := Scan.Int(Rd.GetLine(Stdio.stdin));
BEGIN
    IF k > 10 THEN Wr.PutText(Stdio.stdout, Fmt.Int(k) & "\n"); END;
END;
```

Since the value of k does not change, this could also be written using a WITH statement.

3.7 IF Statement

The IF statement is used to execute one or another sequence of statements, depending on the value of one or more Boolean expressions. It may be helpful to think of there being three idioms involving IF, which can be selected depending on how a problem is worded:

1. "If <some condition>, then <take some action>." This is the simplest, IF-THEN form.

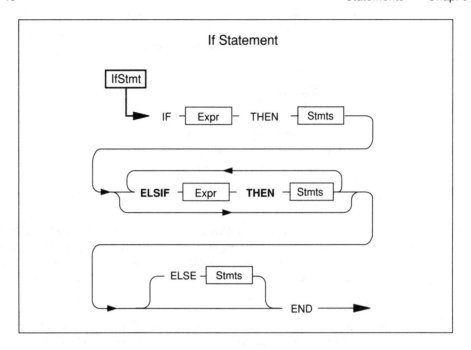

2. "If <some condition>, then <take some action>; otherwise <take some other action>." This is the IF-THEN-ELSE form.

3. "If <some condition>, then <take some action>, or if <some other condition>, then <take some other action>, or if…; otherwise, <take this default action>." This is the most general IF-ELSIF form.

Each of these forms is illustrated in the following example problems.

Example 3–12

If INTEGER variable divisor is not zero, print the quotient and remainder from dividing dividend by divisor. (The expression a # b means that a is not equal to b.)

Solution

```
IF divisor # 0 THEN
    Wr.PutText(Stdio.stdout, Fmt.Int(dividend DIV divisor) & "\n");
    Wr.PutText(Stdio.stdout, Fmt.Int(dividend MOD divisor) & "\n");
END
```

Example 3–13

If divisor is not zero, then compute quotient and remainder from dividing dividend by divisor; otherwise, set quotient and remainder to 0.

Solution

```
IF divisor # 0 THEN
    quotient := dividend DIV divisor;
    remainder := dividend MOD divisor;
ELSE
    quotient := 0;
    remainder := 0;
END
```

Example 3–14

If x is greater than HighTemp, then set temp to 1. If x is less than LowTemp, then set temp to -1. Otherwise, set temp to 0.

Solution

```
IF x > HighTemp THEN
    temp := 1;
ELSIF x < LowTemp THEN
    temp := -1;
ELSE
    temp := 0;
END;
```

3.8 Looping Statements

Modula–3 has four looping statements that can be used to execute a sequence of statements repeatedly: WHILE, REPEAT, LOOP, and FOR. The EXIT statement is provided as a way to terminate loops.

3.8.1 WHILE and REPEAT

The WHILE and REPEAT loops contain Boolean expressions that control termination of the loop. In the case of WHILE, the test is at the top of the loop and the loop continues while the test expression is true. In the case of REPEAT, the test is at the bottom of the loop and the

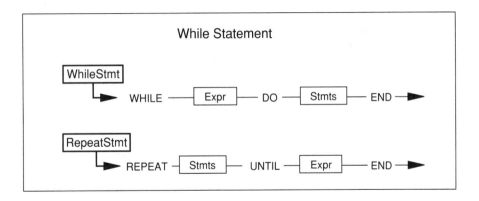

loop continues while the test expression is false. Which statement you use depends on how the termination condition is expressed in the algorithm. Loops you could express saying, "As long as X, do Y" probably fit WHILE; loops you could describe as "Do Y until X" probably fit REPEAT.

Example 3–15

Euclid's algorithm for computing the greatest common divisor (GCD) of x and y can be stated as follows: "As long as y is not 0, replace y by x MOD y and replace x by the value of y (before alteration). When y becomes 0, x will be the greatest common divisor of the original x and y." This algorithm can be expressed in the following Modula–3 function (the name CARDINAL is a built-in abbreviation for the integer subrange [0..LAST(INTEGER)]):

```
PROCEDURE GCD(x, y: CARDINAL): CARDINAL=
(* Return the greatest common divisor of x and y using Euclid's algorithm. *)
  BEGIN
      WHILE y # 0 DO
        VAR
          temp: CARDINAL := y;
        BEGIN
          y := x MOD y;
          x := temp;
        END;
      END;
      RETURN x;
  END GCD;
```

Example 3–16

The following procedure reads and discards characters from the input stream until a specified character is read.

```
PROCEDURE SkipTo(lastChar: CHAR) =
    VAR ch: CHAR;
    BEGIN
      REPEAT
          ch := Rd.GetChar(Stdio.stdin);
      UNTIL ch = lastChar;
    END SkipTo;
```

This can be shortened to:

```
PROCEDURE SkipTo(lastChar: CHAR) =
    BEGIN
      REPEAT (* nothing *) UNTIL Rd.GetChar(Stdio.stdin) = lastChar;
    END SkipTo;
```

3.8.2 LOOP and EXIT

The LOOP statement has no termination condition, so the repetition continues until some other statement causes it to stop. One such statement is EXIT, which causes the innermost loop to terminate, passing control to the first statement following the loop. (The other statements that could terminate the loop are RETURN and RAISE.) We saw how the WHILE

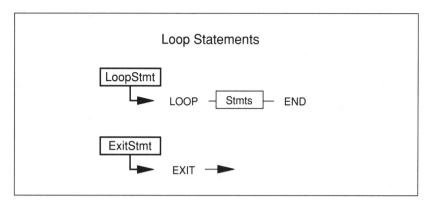

statement was useful when the termination condition was at the top of the loop, and how REPEAT was useful when the condition was at the bottom. The LOOP statement is frequently used when the termination condition is conveniently tested in the middle of the statement sequence.

Example 3–17

Read integers from the input stream until one with a specified value is read. Return the sum of all the integers read up to, but not including, the ending value.

Solution

```
PROCEDURE Sum(endingValue: INTEGER): INTEGER =
    VAR sum := 0;
    BEGIN
        LOOP
            WITH n = Scan.Int(Rd.GetLine(Stdio.stdin)) DO
                IF n = endingValue THEN EXIT; END;
                INC(sum, n);
            END;
        END;
        RETURN sum;
    END Sum;
```

Although often used with LOOP, the EXIT statement also works with the other loop statements, WHILE, REPEAT, and FOR.

3.8.3 FOR Statement

The FOR statement repeats the execution of its enclosed statements while stepping a loop variable from a starting value to an ending value. A typical FOR statement looks like this:

```
FOR v := A TO B DO  (* Stmts *)  END;
```

The expressions A and B must both be integers, or they must both be values of the same enumeration type (which could be CHAR). The expressions A and B are evaluated once, before the loop begins. The identifier v is declared as a read-only variable by the FOR

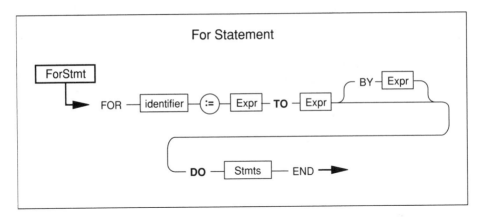

statement; its scope is the body of the loop and its type is either INTEGER or the common enumeration type of A and B.

Each time the body of the FOR statement is executed, V takes on the successive values A, A+1, A+2, etc. The loop stops as soon as the next value of V would be greater than B. The execution of this FOR statement is quite similar to the following code fragment. The only differences are that, in the FOR loop, the variable V is read-only and there is no explicit variable temp:

```
VAR
    v := A;
    temp := B;
BEGIN
    WHILE v <= temp DO
        (* Stmts *)
        INC(v);
    END;
END;
```

Example 3–18

The FOR statement provides an easy way to execute a series of statements a fixed number of times. Here is a loop that prints out Hello 10 times:

```
FOR i := 1 TO 10 DO
    Wr.PutText(Stdio.stdout, "Hello\n");
END;
```

The loop variable, i, is not used in this loop body, but in most cases it is used. Here's a procedure that returns the sum of the first n positive integers:

```
PROCEDURE SumOfIntegers(n: CARDINAL): CARDINAL =
    VAR sum: CARDINAL := 0;
    BEGIN
        FOR i := 1 TO n DO INC(sum, i); END;
        RETURN sum;
    END SumOfIntegers;
```

The FOR loop can be made slightly more general. If you add a BY C clause to the FOR statement, you can cause v to increase by a value different than 1 on each iteration. That is, after the body completes, v is increased as if by the statement INC(v, C). The value C must be a constant expression, but it may be negative, in which case the value of v is decremented on each iteration as if by DEC(v, –C), and the loop terminates when v < B.

Example 3–19

Procedure SumOfIntegers in Example 3–18 summed n integers with the loop

```
FOR i := 1 TO N DO INC(sum, i); END;
```

However, by the associative and commutative laws of addition, the loop could equally well have been written

```
FOR i := N TO 1 BY –1 DO INC(sum, i); END;
```

If you were to leave out the BY –1, the effect would be different. The loop

```
FOR i := N TO 1 DO INC(sum, i); END;
```

will execute 0 times if n > 1, leaving sum = 0 for all values of n except n = 1.

FOR statements are also commonly used in conjunction with arrays. The loop variable is often used as an index into the array.

Example 3–20

The loop below reads 10 characters from the input stream and places them in the character array buffer[1..10]. However, if a newline character is read, the loop stops after storing the newline character.

```
FOR i := 1 TO 10 DO
    buffer[i] := Rd.GetChar(Stdio.stdin);
    IF buffer[i] = '\n' THEN EXIT; END;
END
```

In general, loops tend to be easier to understand when they have only one exit point. Since the REPEAT, WHILE, and FOR statements already have an exit point, EXIT should be used sparingly with those statements. In particular, if the EXIT appears at the top or bottom of the loop, consider whether it can be replaced by adding another condition to the Boolean expression controlling a WHILE or REPEAT statement.

Example 3–21

The loop in Example 3–20 is rewritten below without using the EXIT statement. Which version seems more readable?

```
VAR  i := 0;
BEGIN
    REPEAT
        INC(i);
        buffer[i] := Rd.GetChar(Stdio.stdin);
    UNTIL (buffer[i] = '\n' OR i >= 10);
END
```

This version has the advantage of a single loop exit, but it is longer and the values taken on by i are much less obvious. In this case, the FOR statement with EXIT should be kept. However, if you need the value of i (the number of characters read) after the loop, the second version might be preferable.

3.9 CASE Statement

The CASE statement is used to select one of a number of statement sequences ("arms") based on the value of an ordinal (integer or enumeration) expression. Each statement sequence is preceded by a list of values that the sequence is to be used for; these values can be combinations of constant expressions and ranges of the form low..high. The values of the expressions in the case arms must be members of the type of the ordinal expression. An ELSE clause can be included to catch any values that are not listed in a previous case. No value may be listed in more than one case arm.

When the CASE statement is executed, each of the cases is examined in turn to see if it matches the value of the ordinal expression. When one does match, the associated statement sequence is executed and that completes the CASE statement. If no value matches, the ELSE sequence is executed, if any. It is a checked run-time error if no case matches the ordinal expression and no ELSE clause is included.

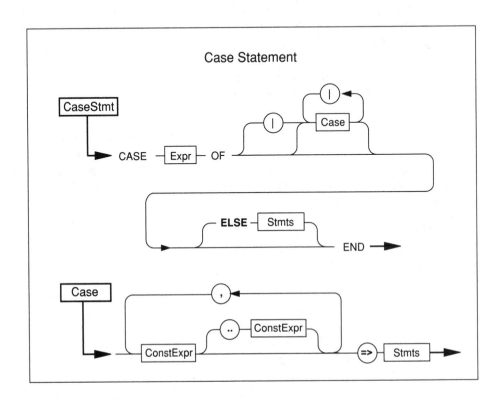

Case Statement

Example 3–22

A lexical analyzer reads characters making up some structured text (like a Modula–3 program) and groups the characters into units called tokens. The function NextToken below examines the next character to be read (held in variable nextChar) and dispatches to a specialized function to read a particular kind of token.

```
PROCEDURE NextToken(): Token =
  VAR token: Token;
  BEGIN
    CASE nextChar OF
    | 'a'..'z', 'A'..'Z' =>
        token := ReadIdentifier();
    | '0'..'9' =>
        token := ReadInteger();
    ELSE
        token := ReadPunctuation();
    END;
    RETURN token;
  END NextToken;
```

A CASE statement with only one arm and an ELSE clause might be better written using an IF statement. CASE statements that return constant values for many values of the control expression might be better replaced by a table of values. Tables (arrays) are discussed beginning on page 98.

Example 3–23

The function DayString below translates an enumeration value to a string:

```
TYPE Day =
  {Sunday, Monday, Tuesday, Wednesday, Thursday, Friday, Saturday};
PROCEDURE DayString(day: Day): TEXT =
  BEGIN
    CASE day OF
    | Day.Sunday => RETURN "Sunday";
    | Day.Monday => RETURN "Monday";
    | Day.Tuesday => RETURN "Tuesday";
    | Day.Wednesday => RETURN "Wednesday";
    | Day.Thursday => RETURN "Thursday";
    | Day.Friday => RETURN "Friday";
    | Day.Saturday => RETURN "Saturday";
    END;
  END DayString;
```

However, this function can be replaced by a table:

```
CONST DayStrings = ARRAY Day OF TEXT{
  "Sunday", "Monday", "Tuesday", "Wednesday",
  "Thursday", "Friday", "Saturday" };
```

It is more efficient to convert Day.Wednesday to a string by writing DayStrings[Day.Wednesday] rather than writing DayString(Day.Wednesday).

The first arm of the CASE statement does not have to start with a | character, although we always do so. This is a convenience akin to the extra semicolon that can appear at the end of a statement sequence. Placing | before each case arm makes them more symmetric and makes it is easier to reorder them or add a new case arm on the front.

3.10 WITH Statement

The Modula–3 WITH statement is used to *bind* names to variables or values. Like the block statement, the WITH statement supports locality by allowing you to introduce identifiers that are visible only within a limited part of a module or procedure. In the statement

```
WITH V = E DO  (* Stmts *)  END;
```

the name v is *bound* to an expression E. Binding V to E is different than declaring V as a variable and initializing it to the value E. The exact effect depends on whether or not E is a writable designator (i.e., a variable that could appear on the LHS of an assignment statement). If the expression E is not a writable designator, the binding makes v a read-only name for the expression's value. This is like declaring v as a new variable, initializing it to E, and then prohibiting assignment to v. This use of WITH is very common in well-structured Modula–3 programs.

Example 3–24

Example 3–11 on page 45 used a block statement to declare a temporary variable to hold an input value. Since the variable's value never changed, a WITH statement could be used instead:

```
WITH k = Scan.Int(Rd.GetLine(Stdio.stdin)) DO
    IF k > 10 THEN Wr.PutText(Stdio.stdout, Fmt.Int(k)); END;
END;
```

The advantage of this version is that it clearly indicates that k is unchanging over its lifetime. In larger programs this information can be very helpful.

3.10.1 Using WITH to Introduce Aliases

If E is a writable designator, then within the statement

```
WITH v = E DO  (* Stmts *)  END;
```

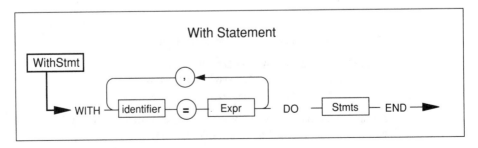

the name v becomes an *alias* for E. That is, any operations or assignments to v actually reference E. As a trivial example, if j is an integer variable, then the statement

```
WITH k = j DO INC(k); END;
```

has the effect of incrementing the value of j. A more realistic use of the WITH statement is to introduce a new name as an abbreviation for a more complicated variable expression.

Example 3–25

The following code is from a larger sorting procedure; this code swaps the values in two array elements (v[i,j1] and v[i+k,j2]) if the first is larger than the second. A temporary variable t is used to perform the swap:

```
IF v[i, j1] > v[i+k, j2] THEN
    VAR
        t := v[i+k, j2];
    BEGIN
        v[i+k, j2] := v[i, j1];
        v[i, j1] := t;
    END;
END;
```

It's hard to have confidence in this code because the many array subscripts make it difficult to read. We can use WITH to introduce abbreviations for the two array elements, making the swapping code more compact and easier to understand:

```
WITH
    a = v[i, j1],
    b = v[i+k, j2]
DO
    IF a > b THEN
        VAR t := b; BEGIN b := a; a := t; END;
    END;
END;
```

The WITH statement can be like a sharp knife: it doesn't require much effort to cut yourself with it. Be especially careful when replacing blocks by WITH statements; you may get an alias when you don't want one.

Example 3–26

What is the effect of changing the statement

```
VAR t := b; BEGIN b := a; a := t; END;
```

to

```
WITH t = b BEGIN b := a; a := t; END; ?
```

Solution   The block statement swaps the values of the variables a and b. The WITH statement, on the other hand, sets both a and b to a's initial value. Because t is aliased to b, the WITH statement is equivalent to writing

```
b := a;  a := b;
```

WITH in Pascal and Modula–2

Pascal and Modula–2 provide a WITH statement that is quite different from Modula–3's. In those languages, the WITH statement is

```
WITH expression DO    (* Modula–2 *)
    statements
END
```

The expression must be a designator for a record variable. (Records are described beginning on page 107.) The effect is to make the component names of the designated record directly visible inside the WITH statement. That is, if r is a record variable with INTEGER components a and b, then you can set r.a to x and r.b to y by writing

```
WITH r DO    (* Modula–2 *)
    a := x;
    b := y
END
```

Unfortunately, to determine the names made visible by WITH you must locate the record type definition, which may be far away. Adding a new component to the record type can change the meaning of WITH statements unexpectedly. Suppose a field x were added to the type of record r. The WITH statement above would then have the effect of

```
r.a := r.x;
r.b := y;
```

The Modula–3 WITH is more general and the new names are explicit. Getting the precise effect of the Pascal WITH in Modula–3 would be cumbersome. It is better to bind a short name to the common record designator and not bother to introduce bindings for the field names.

A WITH statement can bind several expressions at the same time:

```
WITH a = x, b = y, c = z DO  (* Stmts *)  END;
```

Unlike a sequence of declarations in a block, the names and bindings in WITH are introduced sequentially, as if the statement above were written

```
WITH a = x DO
    WITH b = y DO
        WITH c = z DO
            (* Stmts *)
        END;
    END;
END;
```

This means that later bindings can refer to earlier bindings in the same WITH statement:

WITH a = v[k], b = a.field, c = b[k] DO ... END;

3.11 Exercises

Answers to the exercises marked "[A]" appear in Appendix D.

1. Which of the following statements about Modula–3 are true?   [A]
    a. A semicolon is optional after the last statement in a statement sequence.
    b. Integers and pointers can be assigned but arrays and records cannot.
    c. If x is a field of record r, r.x is always a writable designator.
    d. SUBARRAY is a designator, but it is not writable.
    e. A function call cannot stand alone as the left side of an assignment statement.
    f. If INC(v, n) is legal, then DEC(v, n) is legal.
    g. In the expression v := F;, F might be a function that is called as part of the statement.
    h. The operator <> means "not equal to."
    i. The control variable in a FOR loop is declared automatically.
    j. In the statement WITH v = e DO...END, whether v is an alias for e depends only on e.

2. On page 41, the following statement was presented as an example of how you should *not* decrement a variable, for reasons of both efficiency and correctness:

    A[F(x)] := A[F(x)] – k;

    Rewrite this statement using a WITH statement, but not using INC or DEC, so that the problems of efficiency and correctness are eliminated.

3. Given these declarations, which assignments are legal? Of those that are legal, which will require a run-time check? Note: The type of all integer literals, and the type of integer expressions like x+y, is INTEGER.   [A]

    ```
    VAR
        a: INTEGER;
        b: [1..10];
        c: [11..20];
    ```

    a. a := b;
    b. b := a;
    c. b := c;
    d. c := 5;
    e. b := a + c;

4. Rewrite the procedure Sum in Example 3–17 on page 49 twice: once using a WHILE statement instead of LOOP and EXIT, and once using REPEAT. Which of the three versions is more readable?

5. Rewrite the generalized FOR statement: FOR v := A TO B BY C DO Stmts END; using other statements. Take into account the possibility that C is be negative and that A and B could be enumeration values.

6. Look at the rewriting of the FOR statement on page 50. What will happen if both A and B are LAST(INTEGER)? (In fact, the FOR statement is defined precisely as this kind of rewriting.)

7. Write the following Modula–2 statement in Modula–3. Assume that a and b are components of the record variable recs[j, k] but x and y are not.   [A]

```
WITH recs[j, k] DO   (* Modula–2 *)
    a := x;
    b := y;
END
```

4

Basic Types

The description and use of data types is central to traditional programming languages, including Modula–3. You might think of declarations, expressions, procedures, and statements as merely the tools you use to create and manipulate abstract data types. In this book, for example, expressions and operators are discussed with the data types to which they apply. We don't have a separate chapter just on "expressions," for instance.

After a general discussion of types, this chapter describes the simple, nonstructured type abstractions provided by Modula–3: integers, enumerations, Booleans, characters, and floating-point numbers. Chapter 5 continues by discussing most of the structured types: sets, strings, arrays, and records. Procedure types are described in Chapter 6. Chapters 10 and 11 complete the discussion by describing reference types and object types.

Modula–3's built-in types will be familiar to most programmers, but its underlying model of types has some interesting differences. Chief among these are the use of structural equivalence and the introduction of the subtype relation.

4.1 Basic Concepts of Types

4.1.1 Types of Variables, Values, and Expressions

Every variable in Modula–3 has a *type* which determines the values the variable can hold and how those values are represented in the computer's memory. If a particular type includes a certain value, we say that the value is a *member* of the type and that the type *contains* the value. In general, a value can be a member of many types. For example, the value 6 is a member of both the type INTEGER and the subrange type [0..10], which consists of the integers 0, 1, …, 10. Likewise, the types REAL, LONGREAL, and EXTENDED each contain the value 3.14.

Expressions like a + b also have types, which are determined statically in Modula–3 by examining the operators and operands in the expression. A variable name like a, for example, has the type of the variable. Literal values are assigned types; for example, the value 3.14 has type REAL. The specification of each expression operator includes the type of the resulting expression. The addition operator +, for example, produces an INTEGER result when applied to integer arguments.

The type assigned to an expression always contains all the values the expression can produce, but often those values can be members of other types. Thus, if you say that "a + b has type INTEGER," you are referring to the expression's statically determined type. If you say that "a + b is a member of [0..1]," you are asserting that the value produced by a + b is additionally a member of the type [0..1].

4.1.2 Type Expressions, Equivalence, and Subtypes

You specify a type by writing a type expression. The expression can be a predefined type identifier like INTEGER or REAL, a more complicated expression such as SET OF [0..19], or a *type name* you have assigned to a type expression in a type declaration (Section 2.5 on page 24). Type expressions are used in variable declarations (Section 2.4 on page 22) and in other declarations and statements. "Type Syntax" below lists the various kinds of type expressions, which are individually described in this and later chapters.

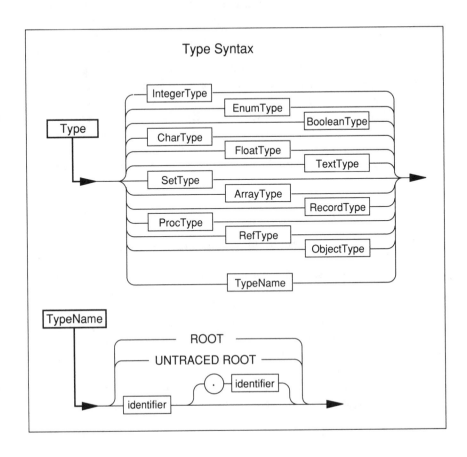

There are several important relationships among types. First, two types (i.e., type expressions) are the *same* if their definitions are the same after expansion. Expanding a type definition means replacing all the included type names with their definitions and replacing all constant expressions with their values. (In some recursive type expressions, this expansion is theoretically infinite, but it's still easy to tell if the two types are the same.) Modula–3 determines if two types are the same based only on their structure, not their names. When two types are the same, we sometimes say they are *equivalent*.

Example 4–1

Consider the following type declarations.

```
CONST
    Ten = 5 + 5;
TYPE
    A = [0..Ten];
    B = [1..10];
    C = SET OF B;
    D = C;
    E = SET OF [1..Ten];
    F = SET OF A;
```

The types C, D, and E are the same because each of them expands to SET OF [1..10]. Type declarations do not of themselves create new types. However, C, D, and E are different from F, which expands to SET OF [0..10].

The second relationship between types is called the *subtype* relation. If type S is a subtype of type T (written S <: T), then expressions of type S can appear many places where expressions of type T are permitted, and vice versa. Whether two types are related by the subtype relation depends on specific rules for each kind of type. That is, there is a rule for integer types, one for arrays, one for records, etc. If S <: T, then all members (values) of S are also members of T. (But, that is not a sufficient condition to establish the subtype relation.) If S and T are the same, then S <: T and T <: S.

Example 4–2

If low and high are constant integer expressions, then the declaration

```
TYPE Sub = [Low .. High];
```

declares Sub to be an integer subrange type. Sub is a subtype of INTEGER that contains values from Low to High, inclusive. Expressions of type Sub can generally be used anywhere INTEGER expressions are allowed. For example, the built-in function ABS takes an argument of type INTEGER, computes its absolute value, and returns a value of type INTEGER. You can use a variable of type Sub as an argument to ABS because Sub <: INTEGER. However, using an argument of type Sub does not change the return type of the ABS function; it is still INTEGER.

Finally, two types can be *assignable*. (The term *compatible* is also used; they mean the same thing in Modula–3.) For example, the assignment statement v := e is legal only if the type of e is assignable to the type of v. Assignability also determines if an expression can appear as the argument to a procedure or function. The assignability relation is similar to the subtype relation, but they are different. Type assignability was discussed on page 39, and it is discussed in more detail with the individual types.

4.1.3 Classification of Types

The remainder of this chapter describes the "basic types" in Modula–3: the ordinal types and the floating-point types. Chapter 5 continues with some of the structured types: strings, sets, arrays, and records. Procedure types are discussed in Chapter 6, and the non-object reference types in Chapter 10. Object types are discussed in Chapter 11.

The ordinal types are divided into several classes, shown in Figure 4–1. The major division is between the integer types and the enumeration types, but there are also subranges of both enumerations and integers. The *base type* of an integer subrange is the type INTEGER; the base type of an enumeration subrange is the enumeration type from which it is taken.

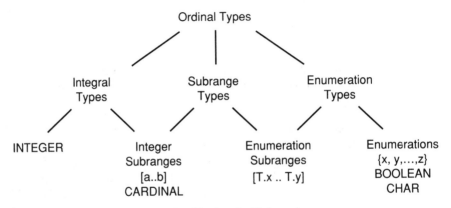

Figure 4–1   Classification of ordinal types.

4.2 Integer Types

Modula–3's integer types consist of INTEGER and integer subranges of the form [n..m], where n and m are constant integer expressions. An integer subrange is a subtype of INTEGER; it is also a subtype of any other subrange that completely contains it. The name CARDINAL is predefined as the subrange of all non-negative integers, [0..LAST(INTEGER)]. The type Word.T, defined in interface Word, is the same as INTEGER but is used in conjunction with the unsigned arithmetic functions in that interface. (See page 69.)

A variable of an integer type can take on any value in that type. If variable choice has type [1..10], for example, then choice can hold the value 5 but not the value 12. Modula–3 ensures that this rule is not violated when values are assigned to variables. (Recall the discussion of assignment on page 37.) Within expressions, however, all integer values can be freely mixed, as long as you don't attempt to compute a value outside the range of type

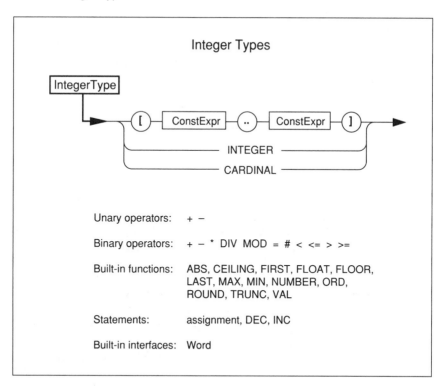

INTEGER. The careful use of integer subrange types can make your programs more readable and safer.

Most computers represent integers using a 32-bit, two's complement representation. (See "Two's Complement Integer Representation" on page 65.)

Example 4–3

Consider the following code fragment. Will either of the assignment statements result in an error?

```
VAR
    a, b: [1..10] := 7;
    c: INTEGER := 2000000;
    i: INTEGER;
...
    i := a + b;
    i := c * c;
```

Solution   The first assignment is OK. Although the value of a+b is 14, which is outside the range of the type [1..10], all integral expressions have type INTEGER, and 14 is certainly representable in that type. The expression c*c, however, will result in a checked run-time error whenever the product (4,000,000,000,000) is larger than LAST(INTEGER).

4.2.1 Arithmetic Operators

The usual arithmetic operators can be used in integer expressions. For binary operations, both operands must be integers and the result has type INTEGER. The two unary operations are:

     –   (unary minus) inverts the sign of its operand
     +   (unary plus) returns the operand unchanged

The five binary arithmetic operators are:

     +   (addition) computes the sum of its operands
     –   (subtraction) computes the difference of its operands
     *   (multiplication) computes the product of its operands
   DIV   (integer division) computes the integer quotient of its operands
   MOD   (modulus) computes the integer remainder after dividing its operands

The DIV operator is always used for integer division; the / operator is not permitted with integers. DIV computes the integer quotient of its operands; if the quotient is not an exact integer, the result is the next-lower integer. That is, DIV truncates towards minus infinity. (In this way Modula–3 differs from Modula–2 and many other languages which truncate integer quotients towards zero.)

The MOD operator is defined with DIV: x MOD y is defined to be $(x - y * (x$ DIV $y))$. This means:

if $y \geq 0$, then $0 \leq (x$ MOD $y) \leq y - 1$
if $y < 0$, then $y + 1 \leq (x$ MOD $y) \leq 0$

It is a checked run-time error for the right operand of DIV or MOD to be 0.

Example 4–4

Here are some integer expressions and their values:

```
5 DIV 3 = 1
–8 DIV 3 = –3
5 MOD 3 = 2
–8 MOD 3 = 1
–8 DIV –3 = 2
–8 MOD –3 = –2
```

Example 4–5

The MOD operator may be used to determine if an integer is even or odd. An even number is exactly divisible by 2; therefore, the value of x MOD 2 will be 0 for even numbers and 1 for odd numbers.

4.2.2 Relational Operators

There are six comparison (relational) operators defined for integers. Each operator yields a BOOLEAN (true or false) value depending on the numerical relationship of its operands:

a = b   true if a equals b

a # b   true if a does not equal b

a < b   true if a is less than b

a > b   true if a is greater than b

a <= b   true if a is less than or equal to b

a >= b   true if a is greater than or equal to b

4.2.3 Arithmetic Functions

Modula–3 also includes some built-in arithmetic functions that can be used with integer arguments a and b:

ABS(a)   returns −a if a < 0; otherwise, returns a

MAX(a, b)   returns the greater of a and b

MIN(a, b)   returns the lesser of a and b

Two's Complement Integer Representation

The range of values representable by type INTEGER depends both on the number of bits used to hold values of the type and on the encoding technique. The most common encoding is *two's complement notation*, in which a signed integer represented in n bits will have a range from -2^{n-1} through $2^{n-1}-1$. (On modern computers, n is typically 32.) Here is how the integers are represented:

The high-order (leftmost) bit of the word is the sign bit. If the sign bit is 1, the number is negative; otherwise, the number is positive. Positive numbers follow the normal binary sequence:

$$0 = 000...0000_2$$
$$1 = 000...0001_2$$
$$2 = 000...0010_2$$
$$3 = 000...0011_2$$
$$...$$

To negate an integer, complement all the bits in the word and then add 1 to the result. Thus, to form the integer −1, start with 1 ($000...0001_2$); complement the bits (yielding $111...1110_2$); and add 1, producing $111...1111_2$. Other arithmetic can be performed in base 2 just as you would normally do it by hand in base 10.

Notice that the maximum negative value—FIRST(INTEGER) or $100...0000_2$ or -2^{n-1}—has no positive equivalent. Negating this value produces the same, negative value (and a checked run-time error).

Example 4–6

> MAX and MIN take only two arguments, but they can be combined to operate on more arguments. To compute the maximum value among the three integers, a, b, and c, write MAX(a, MAX(b, c)).

4.2.4 Conversion Functions

There are several predefined functions for converting values of type INTEGER to other types, and vice versa. There are four functions for converting floating-point values to integers: FLOOR, CEILING, ROUND, and TRUNC, which are described on page 80 in conjunction with the floating-point types. The FLOAT function converts an integer value to the corresponding value in one of the floating-point types:

> FLOAT(x, T)   returns the floating-point number of type T that is closest in value to the integer x. T must be REAL, LONGREAL, or EXTENDED. If T is omitted, REAL is assumed.

FLOAT is also used to convert between floating-point types; see Section 4.6.2 on page 80.

The conversion functions ORD and VAL are designed primarily for use with enumeration types and are described later along with those types. They can be applied to integers, but they are not very interesting:

> ORD(n) = VAL(n, T) = n, for any integer n and integer type T

4.2.5 Inquiry Functions

The FIRST, LAST, and NUMBER functions can be used to inquire about the range of integers in a type. They take an integer type as their argument:

> FIRST(T)   returns the smallest integer in type T
>
> LAST(T)   returns the largest integer in type T
>
> NUMBER(T)   returns the number of integers in type T: LAST(T) − FIRST(T) + 1

It is a checked run-time error if the value of NUMBER(T) is too large to represent as a value of type INTEGER, as in the case of NUMBER(INTEGER) or NUMBER(CARDINAL).

Example 4–7

> Suppose that T is an integer type. Write a function Next that takes an argument x of integral type T and returns x + 1 if x + 1 is a member of T and otherwise returns the smallest value of T.

Solution

```
PROCEDURE Next(x: T): T =
BEGIN
    IF x # LAST(T) THEN
        RETURN x + 1;
    ELSE
        RETURN FIRST(T);
    END;
END Next;
```

Example 4–8

The volume control on a newly designed digital stereo system can take on values (levels) from 0 through 10. In a computer simulation of the design, the current volume is represented by variable Volume. Write a top-level declaration for Volume and a procedure ChangeVolume which changes Volume by N units (N is an INTEGER parameter). N may have any value, but do not allow Volume to go outside its limits. By the way, the designers think the range 0..10 might be changed later; try to make it easy to change this range in your code.

Solution   We will develop the problem solution in three stages. Here is the most obvious first attempt:

```
VAR volume : [0..10];
PROCEDURE ChangeVolume(n: INTEGER) =
    BEGIN
        INC(volume, n);
    END ChangeVolume;
```

Unfortunately, this is wrong. The declaration of volume is fine, but the INC statement will cause a run-time error if volume + n is less than 0 or greater than 10. To protect against this, the second solution tests for out-of-range values:

```
VAR volume: [0..10];
PROCEDURE ChangeVolume(n: INTEGER) =
    BEGIN
        IF volume + n >= 10 THEN volume := 10;
        ELSIF volume + n <= 0 THEN volume := 0;
        ELSE volume := volume + n;
        END;
    END ChangeVolume;
```

This solution works and is easy to understand, but it has some characteristics that adversely affect maintainability. The range constants 0 and 10 appear several places in the code, which means there are several places that have to be altered if the range changes. The expression volume + n is also repeated needlessly. By naming the subrange type, using FIRST and LAST, and introducing a WITH statement, we get larger but more efficient and maintainable code:

From A to B: Subranges

Pascal, Modula–2, and Modula–3 all provide constant integer (or enumeration) subrange types, although the syntax varies slightly:

```
TYPE ModulaSubrange = [1..10];   (* Modula–2 or Modula–3 *)
TYPE PascalSubrange = 1..10;   { Pascal }
SUBTYPE AdaSubrange IS INTEGER RANGE 1..10;   — Ada
```

Ada also allows nonconstant subranges, plus subranges on floating-point types. Nonconstant subranges impose a small run-time penalty, and seem to be overkill to many programmers. The C and C++ languages do not provide built-in subranges. Subrange information can be recorded as comments for documentation purposes, but cannot be enforced by the compiler:

```
typedef int CSubrange;   /* can have values from 1 to 10 */
```

```
TYPE VolumeLevel = [0..10];
VAR volume: VolumeLevel;
PROCEDURE ChangeVolume(n: INTEGER) =
    BEGIN
        WITH NewVolume = volume + n DO
            IF NewVolume >= LAST(VolumeLevel) THEN
                volume := LAST(VolumeLevel);
            ELSIF NewVolume <= FIRST(VolumeLevel) THEN
                volume := FIRST(VolumeLevel);
            ELSE
                volume := NewVolume;
            END;
        END;
    END ChangeVolume;
```

Now, changing the volume range only involves changing the definition of VolumeLevel; the rest of the code will work without modification.

4.2.6 Statements and Assignability

The assignment statement can be used to set an integer variable to an integer value. In the assignment statement $v := n$, n must be an integer value that is a member of the type of v. This means, for instance, that you cannot write an assignment of a floating-point value to an integer. The statement INC(v, n) is permitted if $v := v + n$ is; DEC(v, n) is permitted if $v := v - n$ is.

4.2.7 The Word Interface for Unsigned Arithmetic

The predefined type CARDINAL represents the subrange [0..LAST(INTEGER)], which is the set of nonnegative integers. This type is quite useful, for you often want to prohibit integer variables from taking on negative values. As with all integer subranges, CARDINAL and INTEGER can be freely mixed in expressions and assignments.

If you are familiar with the Modula–2 language, notice that the definitions of CARDINAL in Modula–2 and Modula–3 are quite different. In Modula–2, CARDINAL is designed to permit *unsigned arithmetic* on integers. (See "CARDINAL and Unsigned Types" below.)

CARDINAL and Unsigned Types

Computers typically have a single primary integer type—a word—but two sets of integer instructions: one that treats the word as a signed integer and one that treats the word as an unsigned integer. The same bit pattern in a 32-bit word could be interpreted as the signed integer −1 or as the largest unsigned integer, 4,294,967,296. Unsigned arithmetic lets the programmer use a larger set of positive integers, and is also convenient for manipulating addresses. Language designers have struggled over how to give system programmers access to unsigned arithmetic and comparisons.

A typical solution, adopted in C, C++, and Modula–2, is to provide both signed and unsigned integer types. This works fine as long as the signed and unsigned types are not mixed, but in practice mixing is hard to avoid. Is the literal 5 signed or unsigned? Is the subrange [1..10] a subrange of the signed or unsigned integers? Doesn't it make sense to allow s := s + u, where s is a signed integer and u is an unsigned integer?

C and C++ allow the types to be freely mixed and provide rules that specify when signed and unsigned operators will be used. There is no checking, and the programmer is responsible for ensuring that what happens is what he or she intended.

Modula–2 tries to keep the types distinct. It limits how the programmer can mix the signed and unsigned (CARDINAL) types. The result can be confusing. For example, if s has type INTEGER and u has type CARDINAL, Modula–2 permits s:=u but not s<u.

Pascal and Ada simply don't support unsigned arithmetic at all.

In a clean departure from Modula–2, Modula–3 threw out the rules for CARDINAL and reused the same name as a simple subrange of INTEGER. However, recognizing the need for unsigned and bit-level operations on integers, the Word interface was defined as part of the language. Since Word.T is the same as INTEGER, Modula–3 in effect allows the mixing of signed and unsigned operations. However, since a completely different notation must be used for unsigned operations, the chance of mixing signed and unsigned operations inadvertently is reduced.

In Modula–3, unsigned arithmetic is performed by the required interface Word, which is shown in Listing 4–1 below. If you wish to use unsigned integers, declare them as type Word.T rather than INTEGER, and use the operations in Word. Although these operations appear to be procedure calls, you should expect good Modula–3 compilers to implement them as in-line code, so you will not suffer any performance penalty.

```
NTERFACE Word;
(* A Word.T w represents a sequence of Word.Size bits
w(0), ..., w(Size–1). It also represents the unsigned number
sum of 2^i * w(i) for i in 0, ..., Size-1. *)
TYPE
     T = INTEGER;                    (* implementation-dependent; e.g., 2's compl.. *)
CONST
     Size = 32;                      (*implementation-dependent*)
PROCEDURE Plus (x, y: T): T;                      (* (x + y) MOD 2^Size *)
PROCEDURE Times (x, y: T): T;                     (* (x * y) MOD 2^Size *)
PROCEDURE Minus (x, y: T): T;                     (* (x – y) MOD 2^Size *)
PROCEDURE Divide (x, y: T): T;                           (* x DIV y *)
PROCEDURE Mod (x, y: T): T;                              (* x MOD y *)
PROCEDURE LT (x, y: T): BOOLEAN;                  (* unsigned x < y *)
PROCEDURE LE (x, y: T): BOOLEAN;                  (* unsigned x <= y *)
PROCEDURE GT (x, y: T): BOOLEAN;                  (* unsigned x > y *)
PROCEDURE GE (x, y: T): BOOLEAN;                  (* unsigned x >= y *)
PROCEDURE And (x, y: T): T;                  (* bitwise AND of x and y *)
PROCEDURE Or (x, y: T): T;                    (* bitwise OR of x and y *)
PROCEDURE Xor (x, y: T): T;                   (* bitwise XOR of x and y *)
PROCEDURE Not (x: T): T;                  (* bitwise complement of x *)

PROCEDURE Shift (x: T; n: INTEGER): T;
     (* For all i such that both i and i - n are in the range [0 .. Word.Size–1],
     bit i of the result equals bit i–n of x. The other bits of the result are 0. *)

PROCEDURE LeftShift (x: T; n: [0..Size-1]): T;             (* = Shift (x, n) *)
PROCEDURE RightShift (x: T; n: [0..Size-1]): T;            (* = Shift (x, -n) *)
PROCEDURE Rotate (x: T; n: INTEGER): T;
     (* Bit i of the result equals bit (i – n) MOD Word.Size of x. *)
PROCEDURE LeftRotate (x: T; n: [0..Size–1]): T;           (* = Rotate (x, n) *)
PROCEDURE RightRotate (x: T; n: [0..Size–1]): T;          (* = Rotate (x, –n) *)

PROCEDURE Extract (x: T; i, n: CARDINAL): T;
     (* Take n bits from x, with bit i as the least significant bit, and return
     them as the least significant n bits of a word whose other bits are 0.  *)
PROCEDURE Insert (x, y: T; i, n: CARDINAL): T;
     (* Return x with n bits replaced, with bit i as the least significant bit, by
     the least significant n bits of y. The other bits of x are unchanged. *)
END .
```

Listing 4–1   The Word interface for unsigned arithmetic.

Example 4–9

The value of the expression (–1 < 0) is TRUE, but the value of Word.LT(–1, 0) is FALSE. This is because the bit pattern for the signed integer –1 is interpreted as a large positive number using the unsigned arithmetic rules.

Example 4–10

The Next procedure of Example 4–7 on page 66 can be rewritten for type INTEGER and take advantage of the Word interface. Unlike the + operator on integers, Word.Add does not check for overflow, so it naturally "wraps around" when the computer uses a two's complement representation for integers.

```
PROCEDURE Next(x: INTEGER): INTEGER=
  BEGIN
    RETURN Word.Add(x, 1);
  END Next;
```

4.3 Enumerations

Some of the real-world objects and qualities we want to model in computer programs are not naturally represented by numbers. The position of a light switch, for instance, is not 0 or 1, but "off" or "on."

An enumeration type consists of a set of values that are named with identifiers. For example, an object's color might best be represented by a value from an enumeration type Color:

```
TYPE Color = {Red, Blue, Green, White, Black};
VAR color: Color;
```

The values of the enumeration type are prefixed with their type name when they are used in expressions. That is, for example, to assign the color Blue to the newly declared variable color, you write

```
color := Color.Blue;
```

This naming convention, which is not used by most other programming languages that have enumerations, has several advantages. First, you don't have to worry that an enumeration value (e.g., Blue) might conflict with a variable or type declaration, or with a value in some other enumeration type. Second, the enumeration values automatically "follow" the type name in a program, much like record field names.

Example 4–11

Declare an enumeration type, Gear, that represents the positions of a car's gear-shift lever. (Pick suitable values from your own experience.) Declare a variable, ShiftPosition, of this type and initialize it to the "neutral" gear.

Solution   My car has an automatic transmission, so I would declare the following type. If your car has a manual transmission, your definition might be different. The type of the variable shiftPostion (i.e., Gear) is determined by the type of the initialization value:

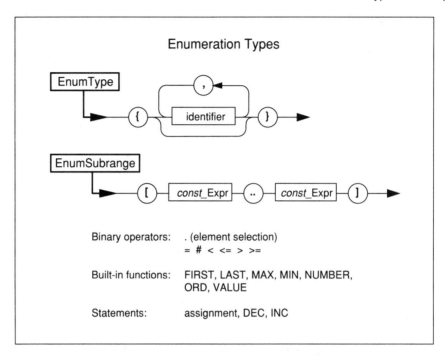

```
TYPE Gear = {Park, Reverse, Neutral, Overdrive, Drive, Low };
VAR shiftPosition := Gear.Neutral;
```

An enumeration subrange is a subset of some enumeration type T, called the *base type* of the subrange. The subrange is specified by giving two enumeration values as lower and upper bounds; it is written [T.A..T.B]. A variable with an enumeration subrange type is restricted to having values within the specified range. Otherwise, an enumeration type and subranges of that type can be freely mixed in expressions and assignments.

4.3.1 Relational Operators

Enumeration types, like integer types, are ordinal types. That is, the types have discrete values with an ordering relation imposed on them. For integers, the ordering is by numeric values. For enumerations, the order is implied by the order in which the values are listed in the enumeration type declaration. For instance, in the enumeration type T={A, B, C}, the value T.B is greater than the value T.A but less than the value T.C.

The same six binary relational operators defined for integers are also defined for enumeration types: =, #, <, <=, >=, and >. The operand expressions must both be values from the same enumeration type, and the result is a BOOLEAN value.

The MAX and MIN functions are also defined on enumeration types, using the same ordering relationship. They return values from the same base type that the operands have.

How the Shepherd Becomes a Shepherd_Dog

All members of the Pascal family of languages provide enumerations. C and C++ have an enumeration facility, but enumeration constants in those languages are simply integers; there is no type checking.

Consider the problem of defining and using an enumeration of dog breeds in Modula–3:

```
TYPE Dog = { Shepherd, Collie, Mutt };    (* Modula-3 *)
VAR dog: Dog;
IF dog = Dog.Shepherd THEN …
```

A good Ada programmer might write:

```
TYPE Dog_Type IS ( Shepherd_Dog, Collie_Dog, Mutt_Dog );    -- Ada
dog: Dog_Type;
IF dog = Shepherd_Dog THEN …
```

Why do Dog and Shepherd in Modula–3 become Dog_Type and Shepherd_Dog in Ada? Ada is not a case-sensitive language, so the identifiers Dog and dog are the same. Thus there is a tendency to use type names such as Dog_Type, Dog_Kind, Dogs, etc, so that dog can be used as a variable name. In Modula-3, the capitalization convention (page 269) permits the same basic name to be used for types and variables.

Also, in Ada (as in Pascal, Modula-2, and C), enumeration constant names are declared in the same scope as the type itself. They do not have to be qualified by the type name, as in Modula–3, but it is easy to choose names that conflict with other enumerations or with a type or variable name. To avoid accidental conflicts, many programmers spell enumeration names with a common prefix or suffix (e.g., Shepherd_Dog) that is unlikely to be duplicated elsewhere in the program. This has the added benefit of increasing readability by connecting the constant to the type. By requiring enumeration names to be qualified, Modula–3 reduces the chances of conflict, increases readability, and imposes no more verbosity than a good programmer would probably have to use in the other languages.

Direct visibility of enumeration constants in Ada and Modula–2 also leads to complications when importing interfaces. Should enumeration constant names be imported explicitly, or do they "come along" with the type name? If they come along with type names, what are the rules for collisions with other names? Modula–3 neatly avoids the collision problem by requiring qualification with the type name.

4.3.2 Conversion Functions

Using the ORD function, you can convert an enumeration value to an integer that represents the "position" of the value in its enumeration type. The VAL function converts an integer position back to an enumeration value. The position of the first value in an enumeration type is 0, the position of the second one is 1, etc. If an enumeration type has n values, the position of the last one is $n-1$. If e is an enumeration value with position p in enumeration type T, then ORD(e) is p and VAL(p, T) is e. Notice that VAL's second argument is a type name. It is a checked run-time error if VAL is given an integer argument that is out of the range of T.

Example 4–12

If type Evaluation is {Poor, Fair, Good}, what are the values of ORD(Evaluation.Fair), ORD(Evaluation.Good), VAL(0,Evaluation), and VAL(3,Evaluation)?

Solution The ORD function computes positions, so the value of ORD(Evaluation.Fair) is 1 and the value of ORD(Evaluation.Good) is 2. VAL is the opposite mapping, so the value of VAL(0,Evaluation) is Evaluation.Poor. Attempting to compute the value of VAL(3,Evaluation) causes a run-time error because there is no value with position 3 in type Evaluation.

The ORD and VAL functions do not behave differently for subranges. The position associated with an enumeration value of a subrange is the position in the base type.

Example 4–13

After the declarations shown below, what are the values of ORD(day) and VAL(0, Weekday)?

```
TYPE
    DaysOfWeek = {Sun, Mon, Tue, Wed, Thu, Fri, Sat};
    Weekday = [DaysOfWeek.Mon..DaysOfWeek.Fri];
VAR day: Weekday := DaysOfWeek.Fri;
```

Solution The value of ORD(day) is 5, the same as ORD(DaysOfWeek.Fri). The value of VAL(0, Weekday) would be DaysOfWeek.Sun (the same as VAL(0, DaysOfWeek)), but that value is not a member of Weekday, so a checked run-time error occurs.

4.3.3 Inquiry Functions

The FIRST, LAST, and NUMBER functions can be used to inquire about the range of enumeration types. If T is an enumeration type, then

FIRST(T)	returns the first enumeration value
LAST(T)	returns the last enumeration value
NUMBER(T)	returns the number of elements in the enumeration type

The type of FIRST and LAST is the base type of T. The type of NUMBER is CARDINAL. For example, if S is the enumeration subrange type [T.A..T.B], then:

FIRST(S)	returns T.A and has type T
LAST(S)	returns T.B and has type T
NUMBER(S)	returns the number of elements in S, i.e., ORD(T.B)–ORD(T.A)+1

4.3.4 **Statements and Assignability**

The assignment statement is used to set the value of an enumeration variable to an enumeration value. In the assignment statement v := e, if the designator v has enumeration type T, then the type of the expression e must be T or a subrange of T.

The INC and DEC statements can also be used with enumeration variables. Since addition and subtraction are not defined for enumeration types, INC and DEC are defined in terms of ORD and VAL. If v is a variable of type T, the effect of the statement INC(v, n) is to set v to the value VAL(ORD(v)+n, T). It is a checked run-time error if INC or DEC causes a variable to assume a value outside its range.

Example 4–14

Rewrite procedure ChangeVolume in Example 4–8 on page 67 assuming VolumeLevel is defined as the enumeration type {Off, Soft, Medium, Loud, Ear_splitting}.

Solution   You cannot compute the tentative value of NewVolume as VAL(ORD(volume)+n, VolumeLevel) without getting a checked run-time error if n is too large or too small. This makes the procedure somewhat more cumbersome. Here is one possibility, in which the range testing is hidden in the functions MIN and MAX:

```
PROCEDURE ChangeVolume(n: INTEGER) =
  BEGIN
    WITH
      biggest = ORD(LAST(VolumeLevel)),
      smallest = ORD(FIRST(VolumeLevel)),
      proposed = ORD(volume) + n
    DO
      volume := VAL(MAX(MIN(biggest, proposed), smallest), VolumeLevel);
    END;
  END ChangeVolume;
```

Now suppose that v has the subrange type [T.A..T.B]. For the assignment v := e to be legal, the type of e must either be T or else it must be a subrange of T that includes at least one value in T.A..T.B. That is, the types of v and e must share at least one value. Even if the assignment is legal, it is a checked run-time error if the actual value of e is not in T.A..T.B.

Example 4–15

In the code fragment below, which assignment statements are legal, and which will cause runtime errors?

```
TYPE T = {A, B, C, D, E, F};
VAR
    bc: [T.B .. T.C];
    df: [T.D .. T.F];
    af: T;
BEGIN
    bc := T.C;
    af := df;
    bc := df;
END
```

Solution   The type of the expression T.C is T. The assignment bc := T.C is legal because the two types share the values T.B..T.C, and no run-time error will occur since T.C is one of the shared values. The assignment af := df is also legal and cannot result in a run-time error because all the values of df are also values of af. The assignment bc := df is illegal at compile time because the types of bc and df do not share any values.

4.4 BOOLEAN

The predefined type BOOLEAN represents the Boolean values true and false. The type is predefined in Modula–3 as an enumeration:

    TYPE BOOLEAN = {FALSE, TRUE};

The predefined identifiers FALSE and TRUE are synonyms for BOOLEAN.FALSE and BOOLEAN.TRUE.

Although all the predefined operations on enumerations are available for type BOOLEAN (e.g., relational operators, LAST, ORD, etc.), they are seldom used. BOOLEAN values are usually computed by using relational operators on other data types or by combining them with the logical operators NOT, AND, and OR. If expressions p and q have type BOOLEAN, then:

NOT p   is true if p is false, and false if p is true

p AND q   is true if p and q are true, and otherwise is false

p OR q   is true if p or q is true, and otherwise is false

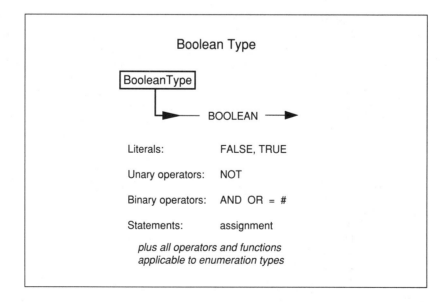

Boolean Type

BooleanType

BOOLEAN

Literals: FALSE, TRUE

Unary operators: NOT

Binary operators: AND OR = #

Statements: assignment

plus all operators and functions
applicable to enumeration types

The NOT operator has a lower precedence than the relational and arithmetic operators, AND is lower than NOT, and the OR operator has the lowest precedence. (This precedence is different from Pascal and Modula–2, and the same as in C and Ada.)

Example 4–16

What is the value of the Boolean expression

–3 < 8 AND TRUE > FALSE OR NOT 6 < 10 ?

Solution   The expression's value is TRUE. Here is the expression written with parentheses showing the order of evaluation and the sequence of evaluations that are made:

((–3 < 8) AND (TRUE > FALSE)) OR (NOT (6 < 10))
((TRUE) AND (TRUE)) OR (NOT (TRUE))
(TRUE) OR (FALSE)
TRUE

The logical operators in Modula–3 are known as *short-circuit operators*, because they do not necessarily evaluate their operands. In particular, if the left operand of AND is false, then the result of the expression is false and the right operand is not evaluated. (Its value could not affect the outcome of the expression.) Similarly, if the left operand of the OR operator is true, then the result of the expression is true and the right operand is not evaluated. The short-circuiting of AND and OR may be important if the operands include function calls with side effects.

Example 4–17

Attempting to divide by zero will cause a run-time error. Will either of the following two expressions cause run-time errors?

6 < 2 AND 6 DIV 0 > 10
6 < 2 OR 6 DIV 0 > 10

Solution   The first expression (involving AND) will not cause an error: since 6 < 2 is false, the right operand of AND will not be evaluated and the division by zero will not be attempted. On the other hand, the second expression (involving OR) will cause a run-time error: since 6 < 2 is false, the right operand will have to be evaluated.

4.5 CHAR

The CHAR type is another predefined enumeration type, this time representing characters (A, b, $, ?, etc.). In Modula–3, the CHAR type has at least 256 elements, representing the characters of the ISO-Latin-1 alphabet (an extension of the ASCII alphabet). The order of characters in the type CHAR is significant, because ORD(c) must correspond to the ISO-Latin-1 encoding for character c. Character literals were discussed in Section 2.1.4 on page 17.

Since the ordering relationship on type CHAR corresponds to the ISO-Latin-1 alphabet, you should be careful when using the relational operators to sort English characters (or those for some other language). In type CHAR, the uppercase letters are correctly sorted ('A' < 'B' < ... < 'Z'), the lowercase letters are sorted ('a' < 'b' < ... < 'z'), and the digits are

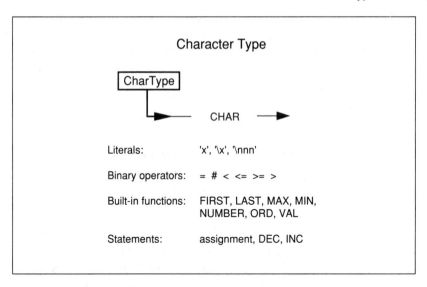

Character Type

CharType

→ CHAR →

Literals: 'x', '\x', '\nnn'

Binary operators: = # < <= >= >

Built-in functions: FIRST, LAST, MAX, MIN,
                      NUMBER, ORD, VAL

Statements: assignment, DEC, INC

sorted ('0' < '1' < '2' < ... '9'). However, depending on your expectations, other relationships between characters may not appear "natural." For example, all lowercase letters follow all uppercase letters, and the following relationships also hold:

'#' < '4'
'4' < 'P'
'P' < '_'
'_' < 'a'
'a' < '|'

The ORD function maps between characters and their position (encoding) in type CHAR. Therefore, ORD('A') is the encoding of 'A'. VAL(ORD(C), CHAR) is equal to C, for any CHAR value C.

Example 4–18

Write a procedure LetterNumber that accepts a CHAR parameter and returns an INTEGER value which is the index of the letter argument in the English alphabet. That is, the function should return 1 for 'A' or 'a', 2 for 'B' or 'b', and so forth. If the argument is not a letter, return 0.

Solution   The solution below depends on the knowledge that the upper- and lowercase letters are each encoded contiguously and in ascending order.

```
PROCEDURE LetterNumber(c: CHAR): [0..26] =
    VAR number: [0..26];
    BEGIN
        CASE c OF
        | 'A' .. 'Z' => number := ORD(c) – ORD('A') + 1;
        | 'a' .. 'z' => number := ORD(c) – ORD('a') + 1;
        ELSE number := 0;
        END;
        RETURN number;
    END LetterNumber;
```

4.6 Floating-Point Types

Modula–3 provides the built-in types REAL, LONGREAL, and EXTENDED to provide approximations to the "real" numbers of mathematics. These types are referred to as *floating-point types* and their values as *floating-point numbers*. Any number with a fractional part (i.e., not just an integer) must be represented with one of the floating-point types.

How do you choose among the three floating-point types? It depends on what you need. It is always safe to use EXTENDED whenever you need a floating-point type, although this choice may not be the most efficient one for your application. Generally speaking, variables of type REAL occupy the least storage (usually about as much as an integer), and variables of type EXTENDED occupy the most storage (perhaps three times as much). However, EXTENDED can represent larger numbers and numbers with more digits of precision than type REAL. Type LONGREAL represents an intermediate choice between REAL and EXTENDED. An implementation is free to choose appropriate representations for the three types, and can use the same representation for two or even all three types.

Different floating-point types cannot be mixed in expressions or assignment statements, although there are built-in functions that can be used to convert between them. Therefore, you have to make a choice between the three types when designing or coding your programs.

4.6.1 Arithmetic Operations

The operations provided for the floating-point types take operands of type REAL, LONGREAL, or EXTENDED. However, when two operands are required, they must both be the

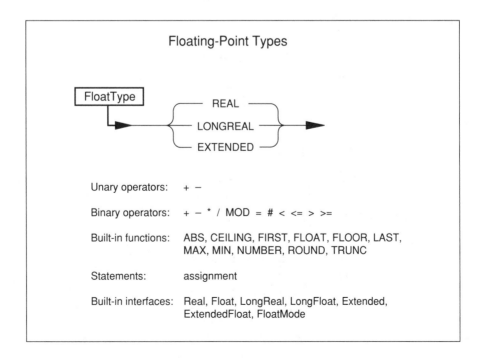

same type; they cannot be mixed. Except for the conversion operations, the result is always of the same type as the operands.

The two unary arithmetic operations are − (unary minus) and + (unary plus). The five binary operators are + (addition), − (subtraction), * (multiplication), / (division), and MOD (remainder). The remainder operation x MOD y is defined to be

    x − y * FLOOR(x / y)

Notice that the / operator must be used for floating-point division, whereas DIV must be used for integer division.

The six relational operators (=, #, <, <=, >=, and >) are defined on the floating-point types. Each yields a BOOLEAN value depending on the numerical values of its operands.

There are three built-in arithmetic functions:

ABS(x)	returns −x if x < 0 and otherwise returns x
MAX(x, y)	returns the greater of x and y
MIN(x, y)	returns the lesser of x and y

Example 4–19

Write a procedure Third that takes three REAL arguments and returns one third the magnitude of the difference between the largest and smallest arguments.

Solution   This problem has two parts: finding the largest and smallest arguments, and then computing the result. It's possible to write this procedure using several IF statements to determine which of the six possible pairs of arguments are largest and smallest, but it is clearer to use MAX and MIN, even though it may be slightly less efficient:

```
PROCEDURE Third(a, b, c: REAL): REAL =
  BEGIN
    WITH
        largest = MAX(MAX(a, b), c), smallest= MIN(MIN(a, b), c)
    DO
        RETURN (largest − smallest) /3.0;
    END
  END Third;
```

4.6.2 Conversion Functions

There are several predefined functions for converting values of type REAL, LONGREAL, and EXTENDED to other types, and vice versa. There are four functions for converting floating-point values to integers; their single argument can be of any floating-point type:

FLOOR(x)	returns the greatest integer not exceeding x
CEILING(x)	returns the least integer not less than x
ROUND(x)	returns the nearest integer to x; ties are broken according to the constant RoundDefault in the FloatMode interface (page 83)
TRUNC(x)	returns the nearest integer to x in the direction of 0.0

If $x \geq 0$, TRUNC(x) = FLOOR(x). If $x < 0$, TRUNC(x) = CEILING(x).

Example 4–20

What are the values of FLOOR(x), CEILING(x), ROUND(x), and TRUNC(x) for x = –2.5 and for x = 3.8?

Solution

FLOOR(–2.5) = –3   FLOOR(3.8) = 3
CEILING(–2.5) = –2   CEILING(3.8) = 4
ROUND(–2.5) = –3 or –2   ROUND(3.8) = 4
TRUNC(–2.5) = –2   TRUNC(3.8) = 3

The FLOAT function can be used to convert between floating-point types; it takes a floating-point value x (of any type) and the name of one of the floating-point types, T:

FLOAT(x, T)   returns the value of type T closest to x

If you omit the type T, it is assumed to be REAL. This function is also used to convert an integer argument to one of the floating-point types.

4.6.3 Statements and Assignability

The assignment statement is used to set the value of a floating-point variable to a floating-point value. In the assignment statement V := R, the designator V and the expression R must have the same floating-point type.

Example 4–21

If r is a variable of type REAL, what is wrong with the assignment statement r := 3.0d0, and how can it be corrected?

Solution   The type of 3.0d0 is LONGREAL and therefore it can't be assigned to a variable of type REAL. You can correct the problem either by writing 3.0d0 as 3.0 (or 3.0e0), or by using the FLOAT function: r := FLOAT(3.0d0).

4.6.4 Standard Interfaces for Floating Point

Modula–3 includes several built-in interfaces for programmers doing floating-point calculations.

The interfaces Real, LongReal, and Extended each define a type T that is the corresponding built-in floating-point type. (Real.T is REAL, and so forth.) Each interface also defines five constants that characterize the floating-point numbers of that type:

Base   the integer radix of the floating-point representation for T
Precision   the number of digits of precision (in the given base) for T
MaxFinite   the maximum finite value in T
MinPos   the minimum positive value in T
MinPosNormal   the minimum positive "normal" value in T

For non-IEEE implementations, MaxFinite is the same as LAST(T). MinPosNormal differs from MinPos only for implementations with denormalized numbers. The values of some IEEE constants are shown in Table 4–1.

Table 4–1 Constants from Real and LongReal Interfaces for IEEE Implementations

Constant	Real	LongReal
Base	2	2
Precision	24	53
MaxFinite	3.40282347E+38	1.7976931348623157D+308
MinPos	1.40239846E–45	4.9406564584124654D–324
MinPosNormal	1.17549435E–38	2.2250738585072014D–308

The interface FloatMode (Listing 4-2) characterizes the behavior of rounding operations and describes how numerical conditions (e.g., overflow) are handled. On some implementations the interface also allows you to change this floating-point behavior, on a per-thread basis. This interface was designed to cover IEEE floating-point capabilities, but may be used with other floating-point representations. There are two major sections in interface FloatMode: rounding behavior, and handling of conditions. In all cases, if an operation in this interface is requested but cannot be satisfied, the exception FloatMode.Failure is raised. (Exceptions are described in Chapter 7.)

Rounding   The interface defines an enumeration type RoundingMode and procedures for testing and setting the mode. RoundingMode includes the following values:

MinusInfinity	rounding is towards minus infinity
PlusInfinity	rounding is towards plus infinity
Zero	rounding is towards zero
Nearest	rounding is to the nearest integer
Vax	DEC VAX-style rounding
IBM370	IBM 370-style rounding
Other	another rounding convention

The first four rounding options are part of the IEEE standard. The constant RoundDefault defined in FloatMode is the default mode for rounding arithmetic operations, which is used by a newly forked thread. This constant also specifies how rounding occurs in half-way cases.

Conditions   Associated with each thread is a set of boolean status flags recording whether the condition represented by the flag has occurred in the thread since the flag has last been reset. The flags are defined in an enumeration type, Flag, which includes:

Invalid	An invalid argument was passed to an operation.
Inexact	An operation produced an inexact result

```
INTERFACE FloatMode;
CONST IEEE: BOOLEAN = ...;              (* TRUE for full IEEE implementations. *)
EXCEPTION Failure;

TYPE RoundingMode =
    {MinusInfinity, PlusInfinity, Zero, Nearest, Vax, IBM370, Other};
CONST RoundDefault: RoundingMode = ...;
PROCEDURE SetRounding(md: RoundingMode) RAISES {Failure};
PROCEDURE GetRounding(): RoundingMode;

TYPE Flag =
    {Invalid, Inexact, Overflow, Underflow, DivByZero, IntOverflow, IntDivByZero};
CONST NoFlags = SET OF Flags {};
PROCEDURE GetFlags(): SET OF Flag;   (* Return the flags for this thread *)
PROCEDURE SetFlags(s: SET OF Flag): SET OF Flag;
PROCEDURE ClearFlag(f: Flag);
EXCEPTION Trap(Flag);

TYPE Behavior = {Trap, SetFlag, Ignore};
PROCEDURE SetBehavior(f: Flag; b: Behavior) RAISES {Failure};
PROCEDURE GetBehavior(f: Flag): Behavior;
END FloatMode.
```

Listing 4–2   Interface FloatMode.

Overflow	A floating-point operation produced a result whose absolute value is too large to be represented.
Underflow	A floating-point operation produced a result whose absolute value is too small to be represented.
DivByZero	Floating-point division by zero occurred.
IntOverflow	An integer operation produced a result whose absolute value is too large to be represented.
IntDivByZero	An integer DIV or MOD by zero occurred.

The meaning of the first five flags is defined precisely in the IEEE floating-point standard. The other two are provided for the convenience of programmers. The behavior of an operation that causes one of the flag conditions is specified by one of the elements of the enumeration Behavior:

Ignore	Return some result and do nothing.
SetFlag	Return some result and set the condition flag. For IEEE implementations, the result will be what the standard requires.
Trap	Possibly set the condition flag; in any case raise the Trap exception with the appropriate flag as the argument.

The generic Float interface (Listing 4–3), and its instantiations RealFloat, Long-RealFloat, and ExtendedFloat, provide access to specific IEEE floating-point functions. Computers not using IEEE floating point may have different versions of these interfaces. Generic interfaces are discussed in Chapter 9. In this case, the Float interface is used to define three nongeneric interfaces: RealFloat, LongFloat, and ExtendedFloat, which differ only in the type used for T.

```
NTERFACE RealFloat = Float(Real) END RealFloat.
INTERFACE LongFloat = Float(LongReal) END LongFloat.
INTERFACE ExtendedFloat = Float(Extended) END ExtendedFloat.

GENERIC INTERFACE Float(Real);
TYPE T = Real.T;
PROCEDURE Scalb(x: T; n: INTEGER): T;                    (* Return x * (2ⁿ). *)
PROCEDURE Logb(x: T): T;                          (* Return the exponent of x. *)
PROCEDURE ILogb(x: T): INTEGER;
    (* Like Logb, but returns an integer, never raises an exception, and always returns
    the n such that ABS(x) / Baseᴺ is in [1..Base–1] even for denormalized numbers. *)
PROCEDURE NextAfter(x, y: T): T;
    (* Return the next neighbor of x in the direction towards y. If x = y, return x. *)
PROCEDURE CopySign(x, y: T): T;                     (* Return x with the sign of y. *)
PROCEDURE Finite(x: T): BOOLEAN;
    (* Return TRUE if x is strictly between -infinity and +infinity. *)
PROCEDURE IsNaN(x: T): BOOLEAN;
    (* Return FALSE if x represents a numerical (possibly infinite) value, and TRUE if x
    does not represent a numerical value.  *)
PROCEDURE Sign(x: T): [0..1];                        (* Return the sign bit x. *)
PROCEDURE Differs(x, y: T): BOOLEAN;             (* RETURN (x < y OR y < x). *)
PROCEDURE Unordered(x, y: T): BOOLEAN; (* Return NOT (x <= y OR y <= x). *)
PROCEDURE Sqrt(x: T): T;                          (* Return the square root of T. *)
TYPE IEEEClass = {SignalingNaN, QuietNaN, Infinity, Normal, Denormal, Zero};
PROCEDURE Class(x: T): IEEEClass;
    (* Return the IEEE number class containing x. *)
END Float.
```

Listing 4–3 Float generic interface for IEEE floating point.

4.7 Exercises

Answers to the exercises marked "[A]" appear in Appendix D.

1. Which of the following statements about Modula–3 are true?   [A]
   a. The two predefined integer types are INTEGER and LONGINTEGER.
   b. BOOLEAN is the only built-in enumeration type.
   c. The largest integer can be written as MAX(INTEGER).
   d. There are four separate built-in functions that convert floating-point values to integers.
   e. The base type of a subrange must be INTEGER or an enumeration type.
   f. An subrange that includes all the elements of its base type is the same as the base type under the structural equivalence rules.
   g. If the computer uses the value 55 to represent the character '7', then ORD('7') will be 55 on that computer.
   h. CARDINAL is an unsigned integer type.

2. Write type declarations for the following types. If you can't declare a type that contains exactly the indicated values, declare a type that contains the values plus as few other values as possible.
   a. Positive contains the positive integers.
   b. Odd contains the odd integers, including 0.
   c. Negative contains the negative integers.
   d. Languages contains the values C, Ada, Pascal, Modula3, and FORTRAN.
   e. PascalLangauges is the Languages subrange that omits C and FORTRAN.
   f. Letters contains the 26 lowercase letters.
   g. Alphanumerics contains the values of Letters plus the digit characters '0' through '9'.
   h. Temperature contains floating-point values from –100.0 through +100.0.
   i. Tautology contains only the value TRUE.
   j. Empty contains no values.

3. Given the following declarations, what are the types and values of the listed expressions?   [A]

   ```
   TYPE
       PizzaToppings = {Pepperoni, Sausage, Mushrooms, GreenPeppers, Onions };
       VeggieToppings = [PizzaToppings.Mushrooms..PizzaToppings.Onions];
       PizzasOrdered = [1..10];
   VAR
       topping := PizzaToppings.Sausage;
       veggie: VeggieToppings := PizzaToppings.GreenPeppers;
       howMany: PizzasOrdered := 3;
   ```

   a. ORD(veggie)
   b. ORD(howMany)
   c. NUMBER(PizzasOrdered)
   d. FIRST(VeggieToppings)
   e. VAL(howMany, VeggieToppings)

4. Write a procedure ToUpper that accepts a CHAR parameter and returns a CHAR value. If the argument character is a lowercase letter, the corresponding uppercase letter is returned. If the argument is any other character, it should be returned unchanged. You can assume that the lower- and uppercase letters are each encoded with contiguous integers (i.e., ORD('a')=k, ORD('b')=k+1, ... ORD('z')=k+25 and similarly for 'A' through 'Z').

5. When do FIRST(T) and VAL(0, T) return the same value?   [A]

6. On a computer that uses 16-bit words to represent type INTEGER, what would be the values of FIRST(INTEGER) and LAST(INTEGER), assuming a two's complement representation? What are the smallest and largest unsigned integers, and what would their representations be as signed integers?

7. What are the values of the following expressions? Assume a two's complement representation for signed integers.   [A]

   a. Word.Add(−1, 4)

   b. Word.Add(LAST(INTEGER), 1)

   c. Word.Shift(4, 2)

   d. Word.Shift(4, −2)

   e. Word.GE(−1, 10)

   f. Word.And(5, 3)

   g. Word.Or(6, 5)

   h. Word.Not(0)

5

Structured Types

This chapter continues the discussion of types begun in the last chapter. We now turn to the structured types, that is, types that are built up as collections of other types: sets, arrays, strings, and records. Another structured type, the object, is left for Chapter 11.

5.1 Strings

A string, or text string, is a sequence of characters. Strings are used in virtually every program, because most programs interact with people and people read and write strings of characters. Sometimes strings are used just to label output. At other times, the primary purpose of a program may be to perform complicated transformations on strings. Many programming languages represent strings as arrays of characters, but in Modula–3, there is also a special string type called TEXT. (TEXT is actually a reference type, and storage for strings is dynamically allocated; see page 92.)

The simplest way of using a TEXT value is to write it as a literal, as shown on page 18. For example, the statement

```
Wr.PutText(Stdio.stdout, "This is a string.\n")
```

writes out a string containing 17 printing characters followed by a newline character (\n). The second argument to PutText has type TEXT, which is the type of string literal. You can also declare constants and variables of type TEXT.

Example 5–1

The following procedure uses a string constant and a string variable to print either The answer is TRUE or The answer is FALSE, depending on the value of the single Boolean parameter.

Text Type

```
┌──────────┐
│ TextType │
└──────────┘
     └────────────▶────── TEXT ────────▶
```

Literal values: "string of chars"

Binary operators: &

Built-in functions: *none*

Statements: assignment

Built-in Interface: Text (Cat, Equal, GetChar, Length,
                      Empty, Sub, SetChars, FromChar,
                      FromChars)

plus all operations defined for reference types

```
PROCEDURE PrintAnswer(b: BOOLEAN) =
    CONST Prefix = "The answer is ";
    VAR answer: TEXT;
    BEGIN
      IF b THEN
        answer := "TRUE";
      ELSE
        answer := "FALSE";
      END;
      Wr.PutText(Stdio.stdout, Prefix);
      Wr.PutText(Stdio.stdout, answer);
    END PrintAnswer;
```

Unlike many other programming languages, Modula–3 allows a TEXT variable to hold a string consisting of any number of characters, with no fixed limit. A particular Modula–3 implementation might impose a limit on the length of a TEXT value, but you can expect it to be extremely large—more than 65,000 characters—and Modula–3 will check that you don't exceed the limit. The length of a single string literal might be further limited to a few hundred characters, and exceeding that limit would be detected when your program is compiled. A string containing no characters is called the *empty string* and can be written "".

Example 5–2

The following procedure copies a text file by reading the contents of the file into a TEXT variable and then writing it out to a new file. (The I/O procedures are described beginning on page 278.)

```
IMPORT FileStream, Wr, Rd;
...
PROCEDURE CopyFile(oldFile, newFile: TEXT) =
    VAR contents: TEXT;   (* the entire input file *)
    BEGIN
        WITH
            input = FileStream.OpenRead(oldFile),
            output = FileStream.OpenWrite(newFile),
            fileLength = Rd.Length(input)
        DO
            contents := Rd.GetText(input, fileLength);
            Wr.PutText(output, contents);
            Rd.Close(input);
            Wr.Close(output);
        END;
    END CopyFile;
```

5.1.1 Operations on TEXT

Most of the operations on type TEXT are provided by a library module, Text, which you can import into your Modula–3 program. The Text interface is shown in Listing 5–1.

The single operator on strings that is built into the language is the catenation operator, which is the same as the function Text.Cat. If A and B are TEXT values, then A & B is the TEXT value consisting of the characters from A followed by the characters from B. The same result is produced by Text.Cat(A, B).

```
INTERFACE Text;
TYPE T = TEXT;   (* Text.T is the same as TEXT *)
PROCEDURE Cat (t, u: T): T;
PROCEDURE Equal (t, u: T): BOOLEAN;
PROCEDURE GetChar (t: T; i: CARDINAL): CHAR;
PROCEDURE Length (t: T): CARDINAL;
PROCEDURE Empty (t: T): BOOLEAN;
PROCEDURE Sub (t: T; start, length: CARDINAL): T;
PROCEDURE SetChars (VAR a: ARRAY OF CHAR; t: T);
PROCEDURE FromChar (c: CHAR): T;
PROCEDURE FromChars (READONLY a: ARRAY OF CHAR): T;
END Text.
```

Listing 5–1   The Text interface.

Example 5–3

In Example 5–1 on page 87, the two statements

```
Wr.PutText(Stdio.stdout, Prefix);
Wr.PutText(Stdio.stdout, answer);
```

could have been combined into the single statement

```
Wr.PutText(Stdio.stdout, Prefix & answer);
```

5.1.2 Strings and Characters

You can use the Text.Length and Text.Empty functions to determine the number of characters in a string str:

Text.Length(str)	returns the number of characters in str
Text.Empty(str)	returns TRUE if Text.Length(str) = 0

The *position* of a character in a string is represented by a CARDINAL value. The first character has position 0, the second has position 1, etc. If Text.Length(str) is n ($n > 0$), then the last character in t has position $n - 1$. If you know the position of a character in a string, the function Text.GetChar will retrieve the character:

Text.GetChar(str, i)	returns the character that occupies position i in string str; an error occurs if i >= Text.Length(str) or if i < 0.

There are several procedures that are used to create strings:

Text.FromChar(c)	returns a string containing the single character c
Text.Sub(str, pos, len)	returns a string consisting of the len characters starting at position pos in str

The Text.Sub function has several special cases:

1. It is an error if pos < 0 or len < 0.
2. Text.Sub returns the empty string if pos >= Text.Length(str) or if len = 0.
3. If t does not contain enough characters [i.e., if pos + len > Text.Length(str)], then Text.Sub returns the remaining characters in str, as if len were Text.Length(str) – pos.

Finally, there are two procedures for converting between strings and arrays of characters. In both cases, arr must be a designator for a variable of type ARRAY T OF CHAR, for some index type T:

Text.SetChars(arr, str)	fills array arr with characters from str, until arr is full or str is exhausted. If str does not fill arr, the remaining elements in arr are unmodified. arr must be a writable designator.
Text.FromChars(arr)	returns a text string consisting of the characters from the array arr.

5.1.3 Relational Operations

You can determine if two strings contain the same characters with the Equal function:

Text.Equal(s, t)   returns TRUE if strings s and t contain the same characters

One of Modula–3's few traps awaits you here! The equality operators = and # *can* be applied to TEXT values, but they do *not* test if the strings contain the same characters. Rather, they test if both operands are identical references (pointers). As a result, the expression

("abc" & "def") = "abcdef"

will (probably) have the value FALSE. The expression "abc" = "abc" might be TRUE or FALSE, depending on details of the Modula–3 implementation. (Reference types are discussed in Chapter 6; the equality operator is discussed on page 179.) Always use Text.Equal to test if two strings contain the same characters.

Modula–3 does not specify functions that test for "less than" or "greater than" on strings. In normal situations, "less than" probably refers to the "dictionary order" of strings, but even that concept is not universal. Therefore, you will have to write your own comparison functions.

Example 5–4

Write a LessThan function for strings. The first character that is not the same in the two strings determines the order according to the order relation for type CHAR. If the strings have different lengths and all characters match up to the end of the shorter string, then the shorter string is "less than" the longer string.

Solution We must scan down both strings, comparing pairs of characters:

```
PROCEDURE LessThan(a, b: TEXT): BOOLEAN =
  (* Returns TRUE if a is less than b, using the ordering relation
  between individual characters. *)
  BEGIN
    WITH
        aLen = Text.Length(a),
        bLen = Text.Length(b)
    DO
      FOR i := 0 TO MIN(aLen, bLen) – 1 DO
        WITH
            aChar = Text.GetChar(a, i),
            bChar = Text.GetChar(b, i)
        DO
          IF aChar # bChar THEN
              RETURN aChar < bChar;
          END;
        END;
      END (* FOR *);
      RETURN aLen < bLen;
    END;
  END LessThan;
```

5.1.4 TEXT is a Reference Type

As mentioned earlier, type TEXT is really a reference type. That is, TEXT objects are represented as references (pointers) to dynamically allocated storage. Readers not yet familiar with reference types (they are presented in Chapter 10) can skim the rest of this section, which contains some additional details about TEXT.

The TEXT type is predefined as an opaque reference type, a subtype of REFANY, as if it were declared:

```
TYPE TEXT <: REFANY;
```

This means that TEXT is some kind of pointer. (See page 188.) The Text interface provides a synonym for this type, Text.T.

You use procedures in the Text interface to create TEXT objects. Once created, the value of a TEXT object never changes—the Text interface contains no procedures that change the contents of a TEXT object. Therefore, TEXT objects can be shared without worrying that someone will change the value through an alias. The garbage collector reclaims the storage used by TEXT objects when they are no longer needed.

Since TEXT is a reference type, NIL is a member of type TEXT. However, it is a checked run-time error to pass NIL to any procedure in the Text interface that expects a string, so NIL must be considered an improper value of type TEXT. In particular, NIL does not represent the empty string.

The Modula–3 language makes no assumptions about the semantics of = applied to TEXT objects, other than what is applicable to any reference type. If s and t have type TEXT, and s = t, then certainly Text.Equal(s, t) is true. However, if s # t, then Text.Equal(s, t) might be true or false.

5.2 Sets

A *set* is an unordered collection of objects, or *elements*. By unordered we mean that it doesn't matter which object in the set was added first or which was added last; it only matters which objects are in the set. Also, it makes no sense to talk about an element being in a set more than once. For example, we might talk about "the set of all prime numbers less than ten," which is the set {2, 3, 5, 7}. (Braces are customarily used to enclose elements of a set.) We could write the same set as {7, 5, 2, 3}—the order of the elements doesn't matter. Sets can also contain *no* elements; { } is the *empty set*, containing no values.

The set is the simplest structured data type in Modula–3. By *structured type* we mean types that are built using other types; in this case, sets are built from the element type. In Modula–3, the elements of a set must be members of an ordinal type— integer, enumeration, or subrange. So, if you want a variable whose values are sets of positive integers less than 5, you can write

```
VAR s: SET OF [1..4];
```

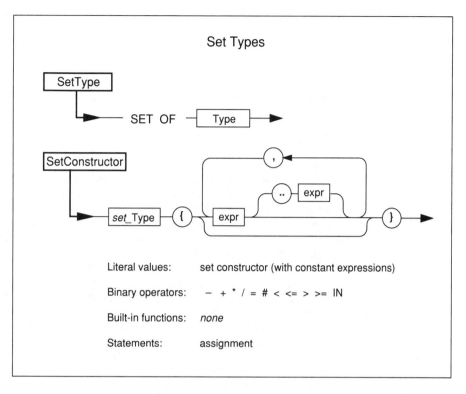

The 16 possible values of this set are {}, {1}, {2}, {3}, {4}, {1,2}, {1,3}, {1,4}, {2,3}, {2,4}, {3,4}, {1,2,3}, {1,2,4}, {1,3,4}, {2,3,4}, and {1,2,3,4}. The initial value of s after the declaration could be any of these, since no initial value was specified.

Example 5–5

If you want cs to be a set of colors defined by an enumeration type, you can write

```
TYPE
    Color = {Blue, Green, Red, Yellow, Black, White};
    ColorSet = SET OF Color;
VAR
    cs: ColorSet;
```

cs can assume the values {Color.Blue}, {Color.Blue, Color.Black, Color.White}, {}, etc.

Sets can be large objects. If an ordinal type T contains n values, each variable of type SET OF T will require at least 2^n bits of storage. (Each bit specifies if one of the n elements is in the set or not.) For practical reasons, Modula–3 implementation may impose a reasonable limit on the size of sets. You can assume at least that sets of not more than 256 elements will be supported, because that is usually necessary to represent SET OF CHAR. However, the type SET OF INTEGER is likely to be rejected by most Modula–3 compilers.

Living Without Sets

The set type is present in Pascal and Modula–2, but it is missing from Ada, C, and C++. In Ada, sets can be simulated with boolean arrays. That is, the type SET OF [0..n–1] is written in Ada as

ARRAY (0..n – 1) OF BOOLEAN

The Modula–3 set union expression S+T is written S OR T in Ada. Ada's operators on boolean arrays, coupled with the ability to represent such arrays using one bit per element, allows most set operations to be conveniently and efficiently simulated with arrays.

   C and C++ do not have a set type, but they have an extensive set of bit operations on integers. Integers are often used to simulate small sets. If there are 32 bits in each integer, then an integer can represent a set of up to 32 different elements. The integer is treated as an array of 32 1-bit (boolean) elements. Set operations can be translated to bit operations. For example, the set containing only the i'th element can be written 1<<i, which is the result of shifting a single bit i places to the left.

   The C implementation of sets is efficient but it uses more operators, is rather more confusing to read and maintain, and is somewhat machine dependent. Furthermore, if the number of potential elements exceeds the number of bits per integer, the C implementation becomes much more complicated. (In C++, this complication can be largely hidden from users of sets.) C programmers can fall back on the simpler boolean array implementation of sets, but the arrays will always occupy at least one character per element because the character is the smallest data type in C.

5.2.1 Set Constructors

A value of a set type is written using a *set constructor*, consisting of the set type followed by the elements enclosed in braces. For example, to set cs from Example 5–5 to the set containing Red, Yellow, and Black, you could write

```
cs := ColorSet{Color.Red, Color.Yellow, Color.Black};
```

The empty ColorSet is written ColorSet{}. Since the values of the element type are ordered (even though the set is not), you can also specify ranges inside the set constructor. For example:

```
VAR
   threeColors := ColorSet{Color.Red .. Color.Black};
   allColors := ColorSet{FIRST(Color) .. LAST(Color)};
```

The values inside the set constructor do not have to be constants, although they happen to be constants in the examples so far. It is a checked run-time error for a set constructor to contain a value that is not in the set's element type.

Example 5–6

> The procedure SingleSet takes an argument of type Color and returns a set (of type ColorSet) containing the single color that was supplied as an argument:
>
> ```
> PROCEDURE SingleSet(c: Color): ColorSet =
>    BEGIN
>        RETURN ColorSet{ c };
>    END SingleSet;
> ```

5.2.2 Set Operations

Four binary arithmetic operators (+, −, *, /) are defined for sets. Both operands must be sets of the same type and the result is also of that type.

> s + t   returns the *union* of s and t: a set containing the elements in s or in t (or in both)
>
> s − t   returns the *difference* of s and t: a set containing those elements in s but not in t
>
> s * t   returns the *intersection* of s and t: a set containing the elements in both s and t
>
> s / t   returns the *symmetric difference* of s and t: a set containing the elements in either s or t but not both

Example 5–7

> The procedure Complement returns the complement of its argument set, which is of type SET OF CHAR. That is, Complement returns a set containing those characters that are not in the argument set.
>
> ```
> PROCEDURE Complement(s: SET OF CHAR): SET OF CHAR =
>    CONST AllChars = SET OF CHAR {FIRST(CHAR) .. LAST(CHAR)};
>    BEGIN
>        RETURN AllChars − s;   (* equivalently: AllChars / s *)
>    END Complement;
> ```

5.2.3 Relational Operations on Sets

The IN operator is defined only for sets. It is used to determine if an element is a member of a set:

> e IN s   returns TRUE if the value of the expression e is in the set s

In the expression e IN s, the type of e must be assignable to the element type of s. However, it is not an error if the value of e is not in the element type of s; rather, the value of the expression is simply false. That is, if the type of S is SET OF [1..4], then the expression (10 IN S) is always false, but it is not an error.

The following relational operators take two sets as operands and test certain relationships between the sets. The sets must be of the same type.

s = t   returns true if sets s and t contain the same elements (i.e., if they are the same)

s # t   same as (NOT s = t)

s <= t   returns true if all the elements in s are also in t

s < t   same as s <= t AND s # t

s >= t   same as t <= s

s > t   same as t < s

Following customary mathematical terminology, if s <= t, we say that s is a *subset* of t; if s < t, we say that s is a *proper subset* of t.

Example 5–8

If ElemType is an integer subrange, write a procedure, PrintSet, that takes an argument of type SET OF ElemType and prints it using customary set notation. That is, if the argument contains the integers 5 and 1, then the output should be

{1, 5}

Solution   The only way to determine what elements are contained in a set is to individually test for each value of the element type. The FirstName variable is used to avoid printing a comma before the first name in the output list:

```
PROCEDURE PrintSet( set: SET OF ElemType ) =
    VAR firstName := TRUE;
    BEGIN
        Wr.PutText(Stdio.stdout, "{");
        FOR i := FIRST(ElemType) TO LAST(ElemType) DO
            IF i IN set THEN
                IF NOT firstName THEN
                    Wr.PutText(Stdio.stdout, ", ");
                ELSE
                    firstName := FALSE;
                END;
                Wr.PutText(Stdio.stdout, Fmt.Int(i));
            END
        END;
        Wr.PutText(Stdio.stdout, "}\n");
    END PrintSet;
```

5.2.4 Assignment of Sets

A value can be assigned to a set variable only if the value and variable have the same set type. For example, given these declarations,

```
VAR
    a: SET OF [2..5];
    b: SET OF [1..10];
    c: SET OF [0..3];
```

none of the variables can be assigned to one another because they have different types. It does not matter that b's element type includes c's type, or that the sets a and c have the same number of elements.

Example 5–9

Suppose we have a set of experimental observations. Because the equipment is faulty, some of the observations will be invalid, which we can determine by seeing if they are outside some range. We'll store the data as an array of N floating-point numbers, and will create and use a "validity" set—a set that indicates which array elements represent valid data.

```
CONST N = 100;
TYPE
    DataIndex = [0..N − 1];
    DataArray = ARRAY DataIndex OF REAL;
    ValiditySet = SET OF DataIndex;
```

The procedure CreateValid accepts a data array and a range and returns the validity set:

```
PROCEDURE CreateValid(READONLY data: DataArray; low, high: REAL)
    : ValiditySet =
    VAR valid := ValiditySet{};   (* start with empty set *)
    BEGIN
        FOR i := FIRST(data) TO LAST(data) DO
            IF data[i] >= low AND data[i] <= high THEN
                valid := valid + ValiditySet{i};   (* Add this element to the set *)
            END
        END;
        RETURN valid;
    END CreateValid;
```

The procedure Average returns the average of all the valid data points:

```
PROCEDURE Average(READONLY data: DataArray; valid: ValiditySet): REAL =
    VAR
        sum := 0.0;   (* sum of valid points *)
        n := 0;   (* number of valid points *)
    BEGIN
        FOR i := FIRST(data) TO LAST(data) DO
            IF i IN valid THEN
                sum := sum + data[i];
                INC(n);
            END;
        END;
        RETURN sum / FLOAT(n);
    END Average;
```

5.3 Arrays

An *array* is an ordered collection of individual variables, called the *elements* of the array. Each of the elements occupies some position or *index* within the array and can hold a value of the *element type*. Typically, the position is an integer value, but it can also be an enumeration.

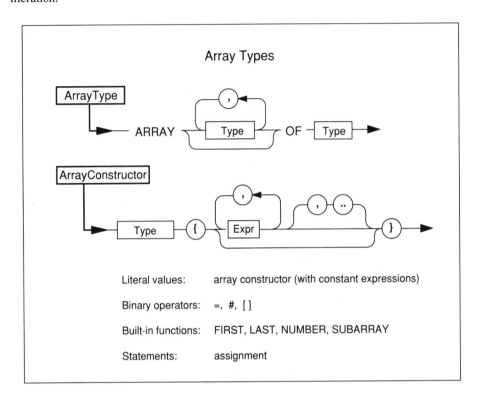

A real-world analogy to an array is a set of mailboxes in a post office. Each post office has a set of numbered boxes which can hold mail. If you want to get mail out of a box or send mail to a box, you just specify, for example, "Box 23 in the Oakland Post Office." In Modula–3, you would say, in effect, "element 23 of Oakland," where Oakland is an array variable.

Like a set, an array is a structured type. In this case, it is built from two other types: the element type and the index type. For example, the array type

```
ARRAY [1..10] OF REAL
```

specifies an array of 10 elements, numbered 1 through 10, each of which can hold a REAL value. The index type is the integer subrange [1..10], and the element type is REAL.

The index type can also be an enumeration type or enumeration subrange, in which case the individual elements are indexed by enumeration values rather than by integers.

Example 5–10

Here are some array type and variable declarations:

```
TYPE Automaker = {Ford, Chevrolet, Chrysler};
VAR
    averageFuelMilage: ARRAY Automaker OF REAL;
    yearlySalesInDollars: ARRAY Automaker OF INTEGER;
    chiefCompetitor: ARRAY Automaker OF Automaker;
```

In Modula–3, it is possible to omit the index type, using what is known as an *open array type*. Open arrays are discussed on page 102 and page 180; until then, we will use only *fixed array types*.

5.3.1 Array Constructors

A value of an array type can be written as an array constructor. Array constructors resemble set constructors, but an array type is specified instead of a set type. For example, here is a declaration and initialization of an array variable, classScores.

```
TYPE TenIntegers = ARRAY [1..10] OF INTEGER;
VAR classScores := TenIntegers{1, 2, 3, 4, 5, 6, 7, 8, 9, 10};
```

The elements of an array constructor do not have to be constants. Here is a procedure that returns an array all of whose elements are initialized to the specified value:

```
PROCEDURE ConstantArray(v: INTEGER): TenIntegers =
    BEGIN
        RETURN TenIntegers{v, v, v, v, v, v, v, v, v, v};
    END ConstantArray;
```

Since it is common for array constructors to use a repeated value, especially at the end of the array, Modula–3 allows an array constructor to end with two periods (..) to signify that the last element of the constructor is to be replicated as many times as necessary to fill out the array. Thus, the procedure ConstantArray above could have used the following return statement with the same effect:

```
RETURN TenIntegers{v, ..}
```

There is a slight difference between using .. and repeating the initializer. When using .., the expression before the .. is evaluated only once. If the initialization expression is repeated, it is evaluated as many times as it appears. This difference may matter if the expression has a side effect.

5.3.2 Subscripting Arrays

The most common operation on an array is subscripting—designating an individual element of the array by specifying the element's index enclosed in square brackets. For example, consider the arrays A and B declared below:

```
TYPE
    Size = {Small, Medium, Large};
VAR
    a: ARRAY [1..4] OF INTEGER;
    b: ARRAY Size OF REAL;
```

The four elements of a are denoted a[1], a[2], a[3], and a[4]. The three elements of b are denoted b[Size.Small], b[Size.Medium], and b[Size.Large]. Although this example used constant expressions for the subscripts, most of the power of arrays comes from using general expressions as indices. Indexing expressions must be assignable to the index type of the array. Using an index outside the range of the index type is a checked run-time error.

Example 5–11

Array scores is defined like this:

```
VAR scores: ARRAY [1..100] OF REAL;
```

Write a procedure that computes and returns the average of all the elements in scores.

Solution   To compute the average we must sum all the scores and then divide by the number of scores (100). We will use a loop to iterate over the elements of the array. The scores array is already declared outside the procedure, so we don't pass it as a parameter.

```
PROCEDURE AverageOfScores(): REAL =
    VAR sumOfScores := 0.0;
    BEGIN
        FOR i := 1 TO 100 DO
            sumOfScores := sumOfScores + scores[i];
        END;
        RETURN sumOfScores / 100.0;
    END AverageOfScores;
```

There are many ways to program with arrays, and some programming styles result in clearer and more general programs. The index types of arrays deserve special attention, for index ranges often change as a program is modified. Using suitable parameters for the index range can greatly improve program maintainability.

Example 5–12

Suppose we have been running an experiment and have collected some integer data points, each in the range [1..10]. Write a procedure, Classify, that accepts some test data in the form of an array of 100 data points and returns an array of 10 integers. In the returned array, the i'th element is to be the number of times the value i occurred in the test data.

Solution The first problem is to determine what array types are needed in the problem. We'll call the input array type TestData and the output type ClassData. We could just define these in a straightforward fashion:

```
TYPE
    TestData = ARRAY [1..100] OF [1..10];
    ClassData = ARRAY [1..10] OF [0..100];
```

However, the constant values 1, 10, and 100 do not suggest any meaning, and could easily be confused by a reader. Furthermore, the most likely things to change in the problem would be the number of data points (NumberOfPoints) and the range of the individual measurements (DataRange). Therefore, we'll write declarations that are based on these parameters:

```
CONST
    NumberOfPoints = 100;
    DataMax = 10;
    DataMin = 1;
TYPE
    DataRange = [DataMin .. DataMax];
    TestData = ARRAY [1 .. NumberOfPoints] OF DataRange;
    ClassData = ARRAY DataRange OF [0 .. NumberOfPoints];
```

The Classify procedure itself is easy once you see that you have to use values from the input array to select an element of the output array to increment. You also have to declare and initialize an output array, output, to hold the classified data as they are collected; with an array constructor, this can be done in a single operation.

```
PROCEDURE Classify(input: TestData): ClassData =
    VAR output := ClassData{0,..};
    BEGIN
        FOR point := 1 TO NumberOfPoints DO
            INC(output[input[point]]);
        END;
        RETURN output;
    END Classify;
```

5.3.3 Operations on Arrays

You can use the = and # operators to test two arrays for equality:

a = b	returns TRUE if the corresponding elements of arrays a and b are equal
a # b	same as NOT (a = b)

The types of the two arrays being compared must be assignable. Assignability of arrays is discussed on page 103, but in brief it means that the arrays must have the same element type and their lengths must be the same. (Their index types can be different, however.)

There are three useful built-in functions on arrays that can be used to keep programs relatively independent of the index types.

FIRST(a)	returns the index of the first element of array a
LAST(a)	returns the index of the last element of array a
NUMBER(a)	returns the number of elements in array a

These functions can take either an array expression or an array type as a parameter. The values returned by FIRST and LAST have the same type as the index type of the array. The result of NUMBER has type CARDINAL. FIRST and LAST are especially useful in loops that iterate over all elements of an array.

Example 5–13

In the following procedure, the only way to be sure the loop is iterating over all elements of array is to locate the type declaration for Array and verify that the bounds of the index type match the bounds of the loop.

```
CONST Max = 10;
TYPE Array = ARRAY [1 .. Max] OF INTEGER;
...
PROCEDURE Sum(array: Array): INTEGER =
  VAR sum := 0;
  BEGIN
    FOR i := 1 TO Max DO
      INC(sum, array[i])
    END;
    RETURN sum;
  END Sum;
```

In a larger program this would be a lot of work. By writing the loop using FIRST and LAST, a reader knows for sure that the whole array is being scanned, without having to check the type declaration:

```
PROCEDURE Sum(array: Array): INTEGER =
  VAR sum := 0;
  BEGIN
    FOR i := FIRST(array) TO LAST(array) DO
      INC(sum, array[i])
    END;
    RETURN sum;
  END Sum;
```

5.3.4 Open Array Parameters

When you try to generalize a program that uses arrays, it is particularly good to keep the program independent of particular array index types. Modula–3 provides a different kind of array type, the *open array*, that can be used in formal parameters so that arrays with any index type can be passed as an argument. An open array type expression looks like a fixed array expression without the index type (e.g., ARRAY OF INTEGER).

Since the argument passed to an open array parameter could be an array with any index type, Modula–3 maps all the argument arrays to a standard form. An INTEGER array argument with n elements (whether indexed by integers or enumerations) is seen in the procedure as if it had the type ARRAY $[0..n-1]$ OF INTEGER. This is the type of the open array parameter as far as the procedure is concerned.

Open arrays can have more than one dimension; see page 105. Open arrays cannot be used as the type of a variable in a VAR declaration, although references to open arrays can; see page 181.

Example 5–14

Here is a procedure that sums arrays of integers. It takes a single open array parameter, and FIRST and LAST are used to determine the index bounds. (Actually, FIRST(array) is always 0, but using FIRST makes the procedure more readable.)

```
PROCEDURE Sum(array: ARRAY OF INTEGER): INTEGER =
   VAR sum := 0;
   BEGIN
      FOR i := FIRST(array) TO LAST(array) DO
         INC(sum, array[i]);
      END;
      RETURN sum;
   END Sum;
```

Here is how this function can be used to compute the sum of various arrays:

```
TYPE Fruit = {Apple, Orange, Banana};
VAR
   bigArray: ARRAY [1..1000] OF INTEGER;
   smallArray: ARRAY [–1..1] OF INTEGER;
   enumArray: ARRAY Fruit OF INTEGER;
   bigSum, smallSum, enumSum : INTEGER;
BEGIN
   (* Fill arrays: *)
   …
   (* Compute sums: *)
   bigSum := Sum(bigArray);
   smallSum := Sum(smallArray);
   enumSum := Sum(enumArray);
END
```

Within the Sum procedure, bigArray becomes ARRAY [0..999] OF INTEGER, smallArray becomes ARRAY [0..2] OF INTEGER, and enumArray becomes ARRAY [0..2] OF INTEGER.

5.3.5 Assignment of Arrays

Modula–3 allows one array to be assigned to another if both arrays have the same element type and the same size (i.e., the same number of dimensions and the same number of elements in each dimension). If one or both of the arrays is an open array type, there will be a run-time check to ensure that the sizes are the same.

Example 5–15

Here is an example that shows some legal and illegal array assignments:

```
MODULE Main;
TYPE Veggy = {Tomato, Cucumber, Squash, Carrot, Lettuce};
VAR
   a: ARRAY [1..5] OF INTEGER;
   b: ARRAY Veggy OF INTEGER;
   c: ARRAY [1..5] OF CARDINAL;
   d: ARRAY [1..10] OF INTEGER;
```

```
PROCEDURE Example( p: ARRAY OF INTEGER ) =
  BEGIN
    a := b;  (* OK *)
    a := c;  (* Illegal; element types different *)
    a := p;  (* OK if p has 5 elements; otherwise, a checked run-time error *)
    d := a;  (* Illegal; sizes are different *)
    p := d;  (* OK if p has 10 elements; otherwise, a checked run-time error *)
  END Example;

BEGIN
  Example(a);  (* OK *)
  Example(d);  (* OK *)
  Example(c);  (* Illegal; element types different *)
END Main.
```

The example of assigning to an open array parameter in the procedure (e.g., p:=d) is a bit subtle. The open array parameter p can accept an argument of any size when the procedure Example is called. However, p is treated like a fixed array during the execution of the procedure, and therefore only arrays with the same size as the actual parameter can be assigned to p.

5.3.6 Subarrays

It is often useful to be able to work with only a part of an array—more than a single element but less than the entire array. The part is called a *subarray* or *slice* and the built-in function SUBARRAY can be used to designate the part of the array.

> SUBARRAY(a, p, m)   designates the m elements of array a that begin after the first p elements.

The expressions p and m must have type CARDINAL. Like open array parameters, the SUBARRAY function treats all *n*-element arrays as if their index type were $[0..n-1]$.

Example 5–16

For example, if these declarations are given:

```
TYPE Size = {S, M, L, XL};
VAR
  scores: ARRAY [1..10] OF REAL;
  inventory: ARRAY Size OF INTEGER;
  num := 5
```

then, SUBARRAY(scores, 2, num) refers to the five elements scores[3] through scores[7], and SUBARRAY(Inventory, 0, 2) refers to the two elements Inventory[Size.S] and Inventory-[Size.M].

SUBARRAY is a designator if the array expression is a designator, and is writable if the array is writable. Therefore, SUBARRAY can be used as the LHS expression in an assignment statement.

Example 5–17

Suppose that a and b are INTEGER arrays of possibly different lengths and index types. Show how to assign b to a, ignoring the extra elements of the longer array.

Solution   The number of elements that will be assigned is the number of elements in the shorter array. We assume that the assignment is to start at the beginning of the arrays. The assignment could be done by looping over the elements of the two arrays, but this would be cumbersome since the arrays might have different index types. By using SUBARRAY we don't have to worry about the index types.

```
WITH
    commonLength = MIN(NUMBER(a), NUMBER(b))
DO
    SUBARRAY(a, 0, commonLength) := SUBARRAY(b, 0, commonLength);
END;
```

5.3.7 Multidimensional Arrays

All the arrays discussed so far have had a single dimension—they were linear sequences of elements. However, Modula–3 allows you to define arrays with any number of dimensions and assign each dimension its own index type. A two-dimensional array of numbers is sometimes called a *matrix*.

Example 5–18

Suppose your manufacturing company wants to track sales by product and by day within a year. You could keep the information in the array dataFor1990:

```
TYPE
    Product = {Thingys, Whatsits, Gadgets};
    Month = {Jan,Feb,Mar,Apr,May,Jun,Jul,Aug,Sep,Oct,Nov,Dec};
    DayOfMonth = [1..31];
    SalesData = ARRAY Product, Month, DayOfMonth OF REAL;
VAR
    dataFor1990 : SalesData;
```

The array contains 1,116 REAL elements (1,116 is 3*12*31). With these declarations, the sales for Whatsits on February 20, 1990 would be represented by the value of

dataFor1990[Product.Whatsits, Month.Feb, 20]

Example 5–19

Given the declarations in Example 5–18, write a function, MonthlyTotals, that accepts an array of type SalesData and returns a singly dimensioned array indexed by type Month. The entry in the output array for each month should be the total sales for all products in that month.

Solution Each element *m* in the output array represents the sum of all elements in the other two dimensions, holding *m* constant. The use of the READONLY mode for the input parameter is not necessary but is somewhat more efficient, since only a pointer to the array is passed as the argument:

```
PROCEDURE MonthlyTotals(READONLY data: SalesData )
  : ARRAY Month OF REAL =
  VAR totals := ARRAY Month OF REAL { 0.0, .. };
  BEGIN
    FOR month := FIRST(Month) TO LAST(Month) DO
      FOR product := FIRST(Product) TO LAST(Product) DO
        FOR day := FIRST(DayOfMonth) TO LAST(DayOfMonth) DO
          totals[month] := totals[month] + data[product, month, day];
        END;
      END;
    END;
    RETURN totals;
END MonthlyTotals;
```

There is no difference in effect between writing an array type as

```
ARRAY S, T, ... U OF E
```

and as

```
ARRAY S OF ARRAY T OF ... ARRAY U OF E
```

The types are the same under the usual structural equivalence rules. Similarly, A[i, j, ..., k] is shorthand to A[i][j]...[k].

Open arrays   Open arrays can be multiply dimensioned. For example,

```
VAR openArray: REF ARRAY OF ARRAY OF INTEGER;
```

is a reference to a two-dimensional open array. Open arrays cannot be elements of fixed arrays, but fixed arrays can be elements of open arrays. The functions FIRST(a), LAST(a), and NUMBER(a) only return the information for the first dimension of a multiply dimensioned array, a. To determine the bounds of the second dimension, you have to write FIRST(a[0]), LAST(a[0]), and NUMBER(a[0]).

Assignment of multiply dimensioned arrays is permitted, but the arrays must agree in the element type, the number of dimensions, and the length of each dimension. The SUBARRAY built-in function applies only to the top-level array of a multiply dimensioned array. There is no built-in way to obtain a "slice" of an array along any other dimension.

Example 5–20

Using the SalesData array type defined in Example 5–18, write a function ProductData that accepts a SalesData array and a product name, and returns a two-dimensional array that holds the sales for that product by month and day.

Solution The problem is to return a two-dimensional slice of a three-dimensional array, specified by a value in the third dimension. The only way to do this is to copy each element individually into the output array.

```
TYPE ProductSlice = ARRAY Month, DayOfMonth OF REAL;
PROCEDURE ProductData(data: SalesData; p: Product): ProductSlice =
VAR slice : ProductSlice;
BEGIN
    FOR month := FIRST(Month) TO LAST(Month) DO
        FOR day := FIRST(DayOfMonth) TO LAST(DayOfMonth) DO
            slice[month, day] := data[p, month, day];
        END
    END;
    RETURN slice;
END ProductData;
```

5.4 Records

Like an array, a *record* contains within it a number of component variables. Unlike an array, the elements of the record (called *fields*) can be of different types and are referenced by name rather than by an index value. Records are important abstraction tools; use them when you want to group together several related pieces of information.

Example 5–21

If you are writing a graphics program, you might want to define the abstraction of a "point," represented by its (x,y) coordinates and its color. In this declaration, Point has three fields, named x, y, and color:

```
TYPE
    Color = {Red, Blue, Green, White, Black};
    Point = RECORD
        x,y: REAL;
        color: Color
    END;
```

The fields in a record type definition may have constant initialization expressions. Whenever a variable of that record type is allocated, the fields will be initialized to the indicated values. When no initialization expressions are present, the fields are initialized to an arbitrary value of their type.

You can declare variables of record types and use values of the record type much the same as arrays or sets. Values of record types may be written with record constructors, much like set and record constructors are written. The values enclosed in braces represent values of the individual fields (not all of which must be included in the constructor). When you use a record constructor to provide an initial value for a record variable, you can omit the type of the variable since the type is evident in the constructor:

```
VAR point := Point{ 0.0, 0.0, Color.White };
```

When using records with many fields, record constructors can be large enough to be confusing to the reader. In that case, it may help to include the record field names in the constructor. Here is another way to write the declaration of point.

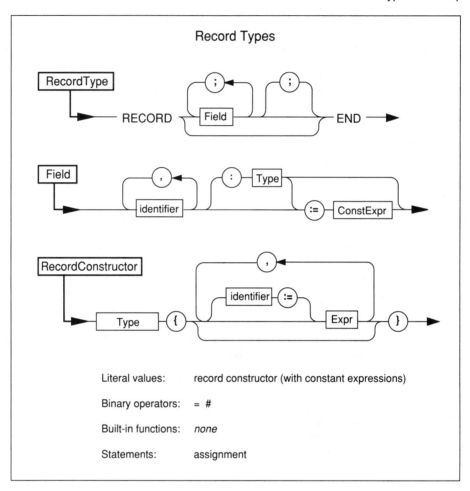

Record Types

Literal values: record constructor (with constant expressions)

Binary operators: = #

Built-in functions: *none*

Statements: assignment

```
VAR point := Point{y:=0.0, color := Color.White, x := 0.0};
```

Positional and named record bindings may be mixed in constructors just as they can in procedure parameters. See page 121.

5.4.1 Operations on Records

The most common operation on records is the selection of individual fields. For example, if point is a record of type Point, the expressions point.x and point.color are designators for two fields within point. Here is how point might be declared and initialized field by field:

```
VAR point: Point;
...
point.x := 0.0;
point.y := 1.0;
point.color := Color.Green;
```

Example 5–22

Write a function, Reflect, that takes a point as an argument and returns the corresponding point on the other side of the origin: that is, the point with its coordinates negated.

Solution You could declare a new Point variable inside Reflect, set its fields individually, and return it. However, using a record constructor is more compact:

```
PROCEDURE Reflect(p: Point): Point =
    BEGIN RETURN Point{–p.x, –p.y, p.color}; END Reflect;
```

Example 5–23

A polygon is a closed, *n*-sided figure. A polygon can be represented by the coordinates of each of its vertices. Define a record type to represent polygons with up to 10 sides and then write a function that computes the circumference (the sum of the side lengths) of a polygon.

Solution   The record type must be capable of holding up to 10 points, each of which is presumably an (x, y) pair of numbers. This suggests using an array of points. We will also need to hold the actual number of vertices of the polygon. The following declaration of Polygon will work:

```
TYPE
    Point = RECORD x,y: REAL END;
    VertexNumber = [1..10];
    Polygon = RECORD
        lastVertex: VertexNumber;
        vertices: ARRAY VertexNumber OF Point;
    END;
```

The function must take a Polygon argument and sum the length of the sides. The length of a line from (x_1, y_1) to (x_2, y_2) is given by the formula $\sqrt{(x_2 - x_1)^2 + (y_2 - y_1)^2}$. Modula–3 has no exponentiation operator, but a square root function can be found in interface Math, as can a hypot function that computes $\sqrt{a^2 + b^2}$. The Math functions operate on arguments of type LONGREAL; see page 287. The following version of Circumference also works reasonably, if we define the circumference of a point to be zero and the circumference of a line to be twice its length:

```
IMPORT Math;
...
PROCEDURE SideLength(p: Polygon; v0, v1: VertexNumber): REAL =
    (* Returns the length of the side from p.v0 to p.v1. *)
    BEGIN
        WITH
            p0 = p.vertices[v0],
            p1 = p.vertices[v1],
            deltaX = FLOAT(p1.x – p0.x, LONGREAL),
            deltaY = FLOAT(p1.y – p0.y, LONGREAL)
        DO
            RETURN FLOAT(Math.hypot(deltaX, deltaY), REAL);
        END;
    END SideLength;
```

```
PROCEDURE Circumference( p: Polygon) : REAL =
  VAR
     circum:= 0.0;
  BEGIN
     IF p.lastVertex = FIRST(p.vertices) THEN RETURN 0.0; END;
     FOR v := FIRST(p.vertices) + 1 TO p.lastVertex DO
        circum := circum+ SideLength(p, v − 1, v);
     END;
     (* Add in the length from the last vertex to the first. *)
     circum := circum + SideLength(p, p.lastVertex, FIRST(p.vertices));
     RETURN circum;
  END Circumference;
```

Variant Records

Modula–3 does not include variant records, as do C, Pascal, Modula–2, and Ada. Variant records can be unsafe, and object types (Chapter 11) give you roughly the same benefits with absolute safety. The problem? In the Modula–2 declaration below, Shape is a variant record containing either two integers or a real number, depending on the value of the kind field:

```
TYPE   (* Modula–2 *)
   Figure = (Rectangle, Circle);
   Shape = RECORD
      CASE kind: Figure OF
         Rectangle: length, height: [0..100] |
         Circle: radius: REAL
      END
   END;
```

This declaration allows two logically different records—a "rectangle shape" and a "circle shape"—to exist within a single record type, Shape. If you write a procedure to operate on a Shape parameter, for instance, you can pass either variant as an argument. The danger is that you might reference the "wrong" variant by mistake. That is, after writing

```
VAR s: Shape;
...
s.kind := Rectangle;   (* s is a Rectangle shape *)
s.length := 3; s.height := 5;
```

you might inadvertently change the field in the Circle variant:

```
s.radius := 3.14159265;
```

Since different variants share the same storage, changing s.radius will also change s.length and s.height, giving them values outside their declared range and leading to unpredictable behavior later.

5.4.2 Other Operations on Records

The = and # operators may be used to test whether two records of the same type are equal:

r = s   is true if the corresponding elements of records r and s are equal
r # s   same as NOT (r = s)

Example 5–24

> For example, if p and q have type Point (page 107), the expression p = q is the same as
>
> p.x = q.x AND p.y = q.y AND p.color = q.color

5.4.3 Assignment of Records

Two records can be assigned if they have fields with the same names, the same types, and if those fields are in the same order. The presence or absence of default initializers in the types does not affect assignability.

Example 5–25

> For example, suppose the following declarations were given:
>
> ```
> TYPE
>     R1 = RECORD a, b: INTEGER END;
>     R2 = RECORD a: INTEGER; b: INTEGER := 0 END;
>     R3 = RECORD b, a: INTEGER END;
>     R4 = RECORD a: INTEGER; b: [0..100] END;
> ```
>
> The types R1 and R2 are the same, but type R3 is different because the names of the fields are in a different order, and type R4 is different because the type of field b is different.

5.5 Exercises

Answers to the exercises marked "[A]" appear in Appendix D.

1. Which of the following statements about Modula–3 are true?   [A]
   a. Two strings have the same type only if their maximum lengths are the same.
   b. If A and B are strings, A = B is the same as Text.Equal(A, B).
   c. If A and B are strings, A & B is the same as Text.Cat(A, B).
   d. The expression str[i] is a designator for the i'th character in TEXT object str.
   e. Implementations may restrict the size of sets to N elements, where N is the number of bits used to represent type INTEGER.
   f. The element type of a set need not be a subrange.
   g. If s is a SET OF S and t is a SET OF T, then s := t is legal if NUMBER(S) = NUMBER(T).
   h. The number of elements in array A is LAST(A) – FIRST(A) + 1.
   i. An open array can be used as a formal parameter type but not the type in a VAR declaration.
   j. The value of SUBARRAY can be a writable designator.
   k. A record field can have an initializer only if the initializer is a constant expression.

2. Determine what is wrong with the following procedure, and fix it.

```
PROCEDURE Is_Yes(t:TEXT): BOOLEAN =
(* Returns TRUE if t is the string "YES". *)
BEGIN
    RETURN (t = "YES");
END Is_Yes;
```

3. Given the following declarations, what is the value of each of the indicated expressions?   [A]

```
VAR
    s := "comes before t";
    t := "comes after s";
```

   a. s # t

   b. Text.Length(s & t)

   c. Text.Sub(t, 1, 5)

   d. Text.GetChar(s, 5)

4. Consider the following declarations, where N is a constant value that is not shown.

```
TYPE Writer = {Pen, Pencil, Crayon};
VAR
    a: ARRAY Writer OF REAL;
    b: ARRAY [1..N] OF REAL;
```

   a. For what value(s) of N would the assignment a := b be legal and not cause a run-time error?

   b. For what values(s) of K would the expression SUBARRAY(b, 0, K) be legal and not cause a run-time error? (K can depend on N.)

   c. For what value(s) of P would the expression SUBARRAY(a, 2, P) be legal and not cause a run-time error?

5. Given the following declarations, what are the values of the indicated expressions?   [A]

```
TYPE Set = SET OF [1..4];
VAR
    s1 := Set{1..2};
    s2 := Set{1, 3};
```

   a. s1 + s2

   b. s1 − s2

   c. s1 * s2

   d. s1 / s2

   e. s1 <= s2

   f. s2 < Set{1..4}

   g. 3 IN s2

6. Write a function CARDINALITY that returns the number of elements in a set. The function should have the signature

```
PROCEDURE Cardinality(s: SET OF E): CARDINAL;
```

7. If s has type SET OF E and k is an element of E, write a Modula–3 expression whose value is the union of s and $\{k\}$.

8. Identify the error(s), if any, in each of the following declarations: [A]

    a. VAR a: ARRAY 1..10 OF INTEGER;

    b. TYPE Iota = [0..5]; CONST powers = ARRAY Iota OF INTEGER{1, 2, 4, 8, 16, 32};

    c. TYPE Sub = 1..10;

    d. TYPE Record = RECORD rate: REAL := CurrentRate(); END;

    e. TYPE List = RECORD elements: ARRAY OF INTEGER END;

9. In Example 5–17 on page 105, SUBARRAY was used to assign two arrays (a and b) of unequal length and index types. We remarked that the alternative—looping over the elements—was cumbersome. To see how much more cumbersome it is, try writing the assignment as a loop. Your solution should be independent of the index types of a and b. As a check, test your solution on these arrays: [A]

```
TYPE Size = {S, M, L, XL};
VAR
    a : ARRAY Size OF INTEGER;
    b : ARRAY [1..6] OF INTEGER;
```

6

Procedures

Procedures are the most common—and probably the most important—abstraction mechanisms in programming languages. They provide a convenient way to encapsulate a set of statements, generalizing them as an abstract "operation" and controlling their communication with other parts of the program.

In Modula–3, you can declare procedures, procedure types, and procedure variables. You can call procedures, store them in arrays and records, and associate them with objects as methods.

6.1 Procedure Declarations

Procedure declarations have been used throughout this book in examples, so you should be somewhat familiar with them. A procedure can be declared anywhere a declaration is allowed. When the declaration appears at the top level of a module or interface, it is called a *top-level procedure*. Otherwise, the procedure is called a *nested*, or *local procedure*. A procedure can be called from anywhere its name is visible.

A procedure declaration comes in four pieces: the keyword PROCEDURE, the procedure's *name*, its *signature*, and its *body*. (See "Procedure Declarations" on page 116.) The body—a block—is omitted only when the procedure declaration appears in an interface. In that case, the procedure must be redeclared with a body in some module exporting the interface, as discussed in Chapter 8 (Interfaces and Modules).

The procedure signature specifies the formal parameters, the result type (if any), and the set of exceptions raised by the procedure (if any). Each formal parameter declaration specifies the parameter's name, its mode, its type, and optionally a default value. A procedure that returns no value is referred to as a *proper procedure*. A procedure that returns a value—and therefore can be called in expressions—is called a *function procedure*, or simply *function*.

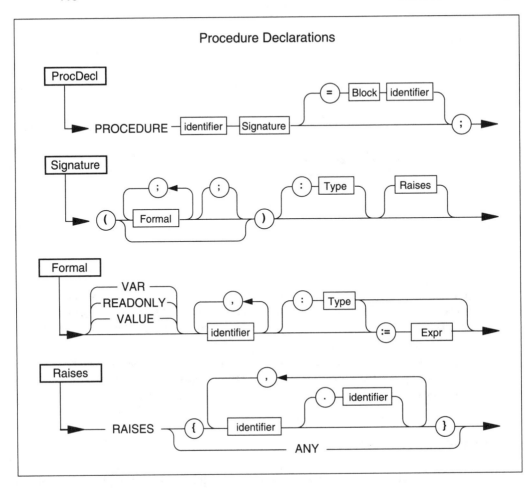

A procedure accesses information outside itself in two ways: through its parameters, and by referring to declarations that appear outside the procedure. In general, it is better not to reference variable declarations outside a procedure. If you have many such *global data references*, it can be difficult to discover how the procedure and program operates. Procedures usually operate on data through their formal parameters.

6.2 Formal Parameters

Formal parameters are a channel though which data is passed into and out of a procedure. During a procedure or function call, the *actual arguments* supplied in the call are matched with the formal parameters declared in the procedure. Some of the rules for matching arguments and parameters were discussed in Chapter 3 when procedure calls were introduced. The rest of this section will discuss procedure parameters in more detail. A procedure does not have to have any formal parameters. If there are none, you still have to include an empty set of parentheses after the procedure name in a declaration and when calling the procedure.

6.2.1 Parameter Types and Modes

Each formal parameter has a type and a mode. The type is like the type of a variable—it determines what values the parameter can take on and what operations can be performed on those values. The type appears in the procedure's signature in the declaration. For example, the procedure declared as

```
PROCEDURE P(x, y: INTEGER; z: SET OF [0..5]) =
   BEGIN
      ...
   END P;
```

has three formal parameters: x and y have type INTEGER and z has type SET OF [0..5].

A parameter's mode determines how an argument appearing in a call is "passed" or "connected" to the corresponding formal parameter. The parameter passing process is also called *binding*. The three possible modes are VALUE, VAR, and READONLY, with VALUE being assumed if no mode is specified.

VALUE mode   VALUE parameters use a *call by value* parameter passing mechanism. Each value parameter is treated like a variable local to the procedure, and is initialized to the value of the actual argument by actually copying the value into the variable, just as if an assignment statement were performed. Once the procedure begins to execute, any changes made to the parameter are strictly local to the procedure.

Example 6–1

The function Square returns the square of its argument. Both the function and a sample call are shown below:

```
PROCEDURE Square(x: REAL): REAL =
   BEGIN
      x := x * x;
      RETURN x;
   END Square;
...
VAR
   a := 8.0;
   r: REAL;
BEGIN
   r := Square(a); ...
END;
```

This call of Square will return the value 64.0. The argument, a, is not changed even though the formal parameter x was assigned the value 64.0 inside the procedure. During the binding of arguments to Square, the parameter, x, was created as a separate variable and the value of variable a was copied into it (see Figure 6–1 on page 118). When the function was executed, x was changed but not a. After Square returned, x was discarded.

Figure 6–1   Binding **VALUE** parameter x to
argument a by copying.

VAR mode   A VAR parameter, unlike a VALUE parameter, is *aliased* to its actual
argument, a parameter passing mechanism termed *call by reference*. The formal parameter
becomes another name (an alias) for the actual argument, and therefore changes to the formal parameter affect the argument immediately. The argument to a VAR parameter must
be a writable designator; that is, it must be an expression that could appear on the left side
of an assignment.

Example 6–2

Here is a procedure that squares its argument rather than returning the squared value. It is
used to square the value of the variable A:

```
PROCEDURE SquareArg(VAR x: REAL) =
    BEGIN
        x := x * x;
        RETURN;
    END SquareArg;
...
VAR a := 8.0;
BEGIN
    SquareArg(a); ...
END;
```

After the procedure is executed, a has the value 64.0. Figure 6–2 shows the relationship between the argument a and the parameter x. Both names refer to the same variable.

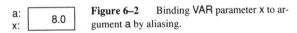

Figure 6–2   Binding VAR parameter x to argument a by aliasing.

VAR parameters give programmers an important tool, but it is one that can easily be
misused. In general, VAR parameters make a program less easy to understand, because
changes to the formal have potentially far-reaching effects on the distant argument. Try to
use VAR parameters sparingly and in ways that a reader might expect. Try not to use VAR
parameters in functions, because readers often assume that returning a value is a function's
only effect.

READONLY mode   A parameter with READONLY mode differs from parameters
with the other modes in that it cannot be modified. Modula–3 prohibits any attempt to assign a value to the read-only parameter inside the procedure. Since its value can't be
changed, it doesn't really matter if the argument is bound using the call-by-value or call-
by-reference mechanisms, and Modula–3 does not specify which should be used. In practice, call-by-value is generally used for read-only parameters whose types are fairly small,
while call-by-reference is used for larger types (e.g., arrays and records) because it is more
efficient in those cases.

Ins and Outs: Parameter Modes

Parameter modes have evolved somewhat since the early programming languages. FORTRAN passes all parameters by reference. Pascal provides by-value and by-reference modes, corresponding to Modula-3's VALUE and VAR. Some Modula–2 implementations add READONLY as a way to speed up the passing of large array and record parameters. A "by-name" parameter mode was present in Algol 60 (the mother of all block-structured languages), but it turned out to be only a curiosity.

Ada has a more rational mode scheme. Parameters may have modes IN, OUT, or INOUT, depending on whether the procedure reads, writes, or reads and writes the actual argument. The decision of whether to pass a parameter by reference or by value (with copy-out in the case of OUT and INOUT parameters) is left up to the Ada compiler. This tends to make Ada programs more readable.

C passes all parameters by value. By-reference parameters can be simulated by explicitly passing a pointer to an argument. C++ has added a general reference mode for types, which can be used in parameter declarations and elsewhere.

6.2.2 Default Values

If a parameter's mode is VALUE or READONLY, it may be declared with a *default value*— a value for the parameter that will be used if the corresponding argument is omitted in the call. The default value must be a constant expression whose value is a member of the parameter's type. When you call the procedure and omit the argument for such a parameter, the parameter is assigned the default value. This can shorten the argument list to a procedure and therefore make it clearer. The next section discusses how you can designate an argument as missing in a call.

Default values also provide a shortcut in the procedure declaration. If a default value is present for a formal parameter, you can omit the parameter's type. In this case, the type of the parameter is taken from the type of the default value.

Example 6–3

What are the types of parameters x, y, and z in the declarations below?

```
TYPE Sub = [1..5];
PROCEDURE A(x: Sub := 5);
PROCEDURE B(y := 5);
PROCEDURE C(READONLY z := ARRAY Sub OF INTEGER {1, 2, 3, 4, 5});
```

Solution   The type of x is Sub, as declared. The type of y is INTEGER (i.e., the type of 5). The type of z is ARRAY [1..5] OF INTEGER.

6.3 Procedure Calls and Arguments

This section discusses several aspects of procedure calls: how to be sure arguments and formal parameters are compatible, how to use default parameter values, and how to use named arguments in a call.

6.3.1 Argument Compatibility

The arguments supplied in a procedure call must be compatible with the types and modes of the corresponding formal parameters. The rules were discussed in Chapter 3, but are repeated here:

1. For VALUE and READONLY parameters, the argument must be assignable to a variable of the parameter's type.

2. For VAR parameters, the argument must have the same type as the parameter and, in addition, it must be a writable designator. For VAR array parameters, the actual does not need to have the same type; it only needs to be assignable to the formal.

The rules are stricter for VAR parameters because both argument and formal must have precisely the same memory layout. In general, Modula–3 allows different types (e.g., INTEGER and [1..10]) to be placed in memory differently. Minor layout differences can be accommodated during the copy involved in an assignment to a VALUE parameter. The relaxed rules for VAR array parameters allow mixing open and fixed arrays as formals and arguments, provided that their shape and element type are compatible.

Example 6–4

Suppose we have the declarations listed below:

```
VAR
    a: [1..5];
    b: INTEGER;
CONST
    C: CARDINAL = 0;
PROCEDURE P1(x: INTEGER);
PROCEDURE P2(VAR y: INTEGER);
PROCEDURE P3(READONLY z: INTEGER);
```

Which of the six expressions a, b, C, 12, –4.0, and b+5 would be permitted as arguments to P1, P2, and P3?

Solution   All of the expressions except –4.0 can be arguments to P1 because their types are assignment compatible with x's type (INTEGER). The expression –4.0 has type REAL and is not compatible with INTEGER. For P2, only b can be an argument; a, C, and –4.0 have different types (not INTEGER), and C, –4.0, and b+5 are not writable designators. P3 accepts all the arguments that P1 does; mode READONLY does not impose additional restrictions over those required by the VALUE mode.

6.3.2 Using Default Arguments

Modula–3 procedure declarations can specify default values for their formal parameters. If a procedure defines such defaults for its last few parameters, and if those defaults are acceptable, you can simplify the procedure call by leaving off the corresponding arguments. Unless you use named arguments—as we'll describe in the next section—you can only omit the final argument(s) in a call. You can't omit an argument at the beginning or in the middle of an argument list. Default arguments can be used in functions as well as proper procedures.

Example 6–5

Here is a simulation of the INC statement for REAL variables. It includes a default value for parameter n:

```
PROCEDURE Inc(VAR v: REAL; n: REAL := 1.0) =
    BEGIN v := v + n; END Inc;
```

You could call this procedure as Inc(a, 10.0) to add 10.0 to a, or you could default the second argument by writing just Inc(a), thus adding 1.0 to a.

6.3.3 Named Arguments

Long argument lists on procedure calls can be confusing to both the programmer and the reader of the program. ("Is that third argument the acreage of the zoo or the weight of the elephant?") With Modula–3, you can reduce the confusion by prefixing the arguments with their formal parameter names. When arguments are given names this way, they can be specified in any order. If you want to mix named and positional (i.e., unnamed) arguments, the positional arguments must come first and must match the first formal parameters.

Example 6–6

In Example 6–5 we defined the Inc procedure with signature

```
PROCEDURE Inc(VAR v: REAL; n: REAL:= 1.0);
```

The call Inc(a, 10.0); could also be written in any of these ways:

```
Inc(v:=a, n := 10.0);
Inc(n := 10.0, v := a);
Inc(a, n := 10.0);
```

The last version shows mixed positional (a) and named (n := 10.0) parameters. Here are some illegal variations:

```
Inc(10.0, v := a);   (* First positional argument doesn't match first parameter *)
Inc(v := a, 10.0);   (* Positional argument is not first *)
```

6.3.4 Using Named and Default Parameters

You can use both named and default arguments in the same call, although it can get a bit confusing when you are omitting some arguments, rearranging others, and so on. Here is the algorithm that Modula–3 uses to match arguments and parameters and determine if the call is legal:

1. If there are *n* positional arguments in the call, change them to named arguments by adding the names of the first *n* formal parameters. Now, all the arguments in the call will be named arguments.
2. If there are any formal parameters with default values that are not in the argument list after step 1, add them as named arguments, using their default values.

After performing these two steps, there must be exactly one named argument for each formal parameter. If any are missing, or if any are duplicated, the call is in error and Modula–3 will reject it.

Example 6–7

Suppose P is a procedure with signature

PROCEDURE P(a: INTEGER; b: INTEGER := 0; c: INTEGER := 5; d: INTEGER);

and you see the call P(4, d := 6, b := 9). Is the call legal, and what values will each parameter receive?

Solution   After naming the positional parameter, we get

P(a := 4, d := 6, b := 9);

After adding parameters with default values, and rearranging the arguments so they match the order of the formals, we get

P(a := 4, b := 9, c := 5, d := 6);

This call is legal because there is one argument for each formal parameter. On the other hand, after rewriting the call

P(1, 2, b := 0, d := 0);

becomes, after rewriting,

P(a := 1, b := 2, b := 0, c := 5, d := 0);

This is an illegal call because parameter b appears twice in the argument list.

6.4 Nested Procedure Declarations

Most procedures are declared at the top level of modules, but in fact you can declare a procedure in any block. When a procedure declaration appears inside another procedure, we call it a *local* or *nested procedure*. Nested procedures can access the local declarations in all surrounding blocks.

Whether or not you use nested procedures is mostly a matter of style. (The C and C++ languages disallow nested procedures, but the Pascal family has always allowed them.) There are two advantages to using nested procedures. First, nesting limits the scope of the inner procedure. If you know that a procedure will be called only from within another procedure, it makes sense to declare the first procedure inside the second. The second reason is that it can be easier to write the inner procedure if it can access the local variables and the formal parameters of the surrounding procedure.

Example 6–8

> Example 5–23 on page 109 concerned computing the circumference of a polygon. The solution procedure, Circumference, made use of a smaller procedure, SideLength. Since Side-Length is used only within Circumference, we can rewrite this solution and make SideLength a nested procedure. This will also let us remove the parameter p from SideLength, since Circumference's formal parameter can be accessed directly. Compare the following solution with the original in Example 5–23.

```
PROCEDURE Circumference( p: Polygon) : REAL =

    PROCEDURE SideLength(v0, v1: VertexNumber): REAL =
    (* Returns the length of the side from p.v0 to p.v1. *)
    BEGIN
        WITH
            p0 = p.vertices[v0],   p1 = p.vertices[v1],
            deltaX = FLOAT(p1.x − p0.x, LONGREAL),
            deltaY = FLOAT(p1.y − p0.y, LONGREAL)
        DO
            RETURN FLOAT(Math.hypot(deltaX, deltaY));
        END (*WITH*)
    END SideLength;

VAR
    circum := 0.0;
BEGIN (*Circumference*)
    IF p.lastVertex = FIRST(p.vertices) THEN RETURN 0.0; END;
    FOR v := FIRST(p.vertices) + 1 TO p.lastVertex DO
        circum := circum+ SideLength(v − 1, v);
    END;
    (* Add in the length from the last vertex to the first. *)
    circum := circum + SideLength(p.lastVertex, FIRST(p.vertices));
    RETURN circum;
END Circumference;
```

There are also some disadvantages to nested procedures. When nested procedures make many references to declarations in the surrounding procedure, it can be quite confusing. Large nested procedures also tend to push the outer procedure's statements away from its own declarations, making the outer procedure harder to read. If you find yourself using a collection of nested procedures which share a lot of information, it may be better to generalize them and place them in their own interface and module.

6.5 Procedure Types, Values, and Variables

When you declare a procedure in Modula–3, you are actually declaring a procedure *constant*, that is, a constant value of procedure type. Just as the declaration

```
CONST Four = 4;
```

establishes Four as having type INTEGER and the value 4, so the declaration

```
PROCEDURE Add(x, y: INTEGER): INTEGER =
  BEGIN
    RETURN x + y;
  END Sum;
```

establishes Add as having type

```
PROCEDURE (x, y: INTEGER): INTEGER
```

and having as its value the code that returns the sum of its arguments. Carrying the analogy further, just as we can declare an integer variable

```
VAR numberSold: INTEGER;
```

so we can declare a procedure variable

```
VAR integerBinaryOp: PROCEDURE (x, y: INTEGER): INTEGER;
```

The procedure type is written almost exactly like a procedure declaration—with a signature, return type, and raises set. Only the name of the procedure and its body are omitted. You can assign values to procedure variables; here is how you would assign the procedure Add to the variable IntegerBinaryOp:

```
integerBinaryOp := Add;
```

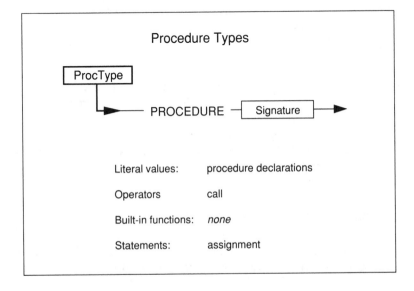

Procedure Types

ProcType

PROCEDURE — Signature

Literal values:	procedure declarations
Operators	call
Built-in functions:	*none*
Statements:	assignment

Procedure values can be passed as arguments and returned as values from other procedures. They can also be stored in arrays, records, and objects.

6.5.1 Operations on Procedure Values

Procedure values can be called just like procedure constants. For example, if integerBinaryOp is a procedure variable whose value is the procedure Add, then these two statements are equivalent:

```
sum := integerBinaryOp(a, b);
sum := Add(a, b);
```

Procedure values can be used in expressions, procedure call statements, and EVAL statements just like procedure constants.

Example 6–9

Suppose you are asked to write a Modula–3 program that sums the value of the expression x^2-x for $x = 1, 2, ..., 10$. Rather than write a program that computes just this value, you could generalize the problem to compute the sum of any integer function f of one integer argument. Begin by writing a function, Sigma, that takes three arguments: a, b, and the function f. Sigma must evaluate f for all values from a to b and sum the results. Then, write a specific function $f(x) = x^2 - x$ and arrange to call Sigma with the parameters 1, 10, and f.

Solution

```
MODULE Main;
IMPORT Wr, Stdio, Fmt;
TYPE ArgumentFunction = PROCEDURE (x: INTEGER): INTEGER;

PROCEDURE Sigma(a, b: INTEGER; f: ArgumentFunction): INTEGER =
   VAR Sum := 0;
   BEGIN
      FOR k := a TO b DO INC(Sum, f(k)); END;
      RETURN Sum;
   END Sigma;

PROCEDURE F(x: INTEGER): INTEGER = BEGIN  RETURN x * x – x; END F;

BEGIN
   Wr.PutText(Stdio.stdout, "The value of Sigma(1, 10 ,x * x – x) is "
      & Fmt.Int(Sigma(1, 10, F))
      & "\n");
END Main.
```

By the way, you might wonder why parameter names are included in procedure types, that is, why we write

```
VAR integerBinaryOp: PROCEDURE (x, y: INTEGER): INTEGER;
```

instead of simply, say,

```
VAR integerBinaryOp: PROCEDURE (INTEGER, INTEGER): INTEGER;
```

There are several reasons. First, having the names makes it slightly easier to write the signature when there are multiple parameters of the same type (as in the example). Second, the parameter names provide convenient handles for documenting the type:

```
TYPE IntToReal = PROCEDURE (x: INTEGER) : REAL;
(* x should be a prime number *)
```

Finally, the parameter names can be used to name the arguments when calling procedure values (page 121).

6.5.2 Assignment of Procedures

We indicated before that procedure values can be assigned to procedure variables and passed as parameters, but we did not discuss precisely when such assignments are legal. For example, suppose p and q are defined as

```
VAR
    p: PROCEDURE (x: INTEGER ): INTEGER;
    q: PROCEDURE (y: INTEGER := 3): INTEGER;
```

Are the types of p and q the same? No. Are the assignments p := q and q := p legal? Yes, they are.

For a procedure value e to be assignable to a procedure variable V (of type T_V), e must be a member of T_V, which in turn means that either e must be NIL—the value NIL is a member of all procedure types—or e must be a top-level procedure and the signature of e must be *covered* by the signature of T_V. *Cover* here means:

1. Both signatures must have the same number of parameters with the same types and modes.
2. The result types must be the same, or neither must have a result type.
3. The exceptions raised by T_V (its raises set) must include all the exceptions in the raises set of e (page 133).

The only flexibility is in choosing the names of the parameters, the default values, and the raises set. Since these are the only difference in the declarations of p and q above, the signatures cover each other and the assignment is legal. However, if r were declared as

```
VAR r: PROCEDURE (x: CARDINAL): INTEGER;
```

then neither p := r nor r := p would be legal, since neither signature covers the other. A procedure value can be passed to a formal procedure parameter as long as the value would be assignable to the type of the formal. The formal can have any mode. Although parameter names and default values do not affect type compatibility, they are important when calling a procedure, as the following example illustrates.

Example 6–10

Consider the following declarations:

```
PROCEDURE Ident(x: INTEGER := 1): INTEGER = BEGIN RETURN x; END Ident;

VAR
    a: PROCEDURE (a: INTEGER): INTEGER := Ident;
    b: PROCEDURE (b: INTEGER := 3) : INTEGER := Ident;
```

The names Ident, a, and b now all refer to the same procedure, but calls on that procedure behave somewhat differently depending on which name is used. The calls Ident(6), a(6), and b(6) all return the value 6, as expected. However, while the value of Ident() is 1, the value of b() is 3 because b's type has a different default value for its parameter, and a() would be illegal because it has no default parameter value. The call a(a:=1) is legal, but the call b(a:=1) is not—the name of the parameter of the b procedure is b, so the call must be written b(b:=1).

One additional point: For safety reasons, you can assign only top-level procedures to procedure variables. To see the danger of assigning a local procedure, consider the following example.

Example 6–11

This example demonstrates the problems that could result if local procedures could be assigned to procedure variables.

```
MODULE Main;
VAR p: PROCEDURE ();

PROCEDURE Outer() =
    VAR outerVar: INTEGER := 10;
    PROCEDURE Inner() = BEGIN INC(outerVar); END Inner;
    BEGIN
        ... p := Inner; (* Illegal! *) ...
    END Outer;

BEGIN
    Outer();
    p();
END Main;
```

Procedure Inner is nested inside procedure Outer, and it increments one of Outer's local variables, outerVar. Outer assigns procedure Inner to the top-level variable p. Everything in this example is legal except the fact that Inner is not a top-level procedure. Consider what happens if this assignment were allowed: The program begins by calling outer, which assigns Inner to p. After Outer returns, p is called, causing control to be transferred to Inner. However, when Inner is called, its environment (i.e., Outer) does not exist! The local variable outerVar has not been allocated, and the behavior of INC(outerVar) is unpredictable. Modula–3 does not wish to permit such an unchecked run-time error, and therefore disallows the assignment of Inner.

Although local procedures cannot be assigned, they can be passed as parameters. Because procedure calls obey a "last-in, first-out" discipline, any local procedure that could passed as a parameter (i.e., was namable and hence existed) will remain valid during the procedure call.

6.6 Exercises

Answers to the exercises marked with "[A]" appear in Appendix D.

1. Which of the following statements are true?   [A]

   a. Two procedure types are not the same if their parameters' default values are different.

   b. If the signature of procedure P covers the signature of procedure Q, then the raises set of P is a subset of the raises set of Q.

   c. An argument of type [1..5] can be passed to a READONLY formal parameter of type INTEGER.

   d. If the statement P := Q is legal, then Q cannot be a nested procedure.

   e. If the expression P(Q) is legal, then Q cannot be a nested procedure.

   f. Any argument that could be passed to a VALUE parameter could be passed to a READONLY parameter of the same type.

   g. If P is a procedure variable and Q is a procedure value, then P := Q is legal if P's signature covers Q's signature, or vice versa.

   h. If a read-only designator is used as an argument to a VAR formal parameter, then the value of the argument is copied to a temporary variable which is then aliased to the parameter.

2. The WITH statement can be thought of as a way to introduce parameters into a program without using a procedure. In the following example, what are the "modes" of X, Y, and Z?   [A]

```
PROCEDURE P(READONLY a: INTEGER) =
VAR
    b: ARRAY [1..5] OF INTEGER;
BEGIN
    ...
    WITH
        X = a,
        Y = b[3],
        Z = a + 4
    DO
        ...
    END (*WITH*)
END P;
```

3. Given the following procedure declaration, which of the calls on the procedure are legal?

```
PROCEDURE Salary(rate: REAL; hours: INTEGER := 40): REAL;
```

   a. Salary(5.50)

   b. Salary(rate := 5.50)

   c. Salary(hours := 40)

   d. Salary(40, rate := 5.50)

   e. Salary(5.50, hours := 40)

   f. Salary(5.50, 40)

   g. Salary()

4. Several procedure types are shown below. Which signatures cover which other signatures?

   a. PROCEDURE ()

   b. PROCEDURE (x: INTEGER) RAISES {E1, E2}

   c. PROCEDURE (y: INTEGER): INTEGER

   d. PROCEDURE () RAISES {E1}

   e. PROCEDURE (y: INTEGER)

   f. PROCEDURE (x: [1..10]) RAISES {E1, E2}

   g. PROCEDURE (x: INTEGER): CARDINAL

   h. PROCEDURE (READONLY y: INTEGER)

5. The following program is complete except that the parameter mode in procedure P is missing. What value will the program print if the mode is VALUE? What if it is VAR? What if it is READONLY?   [A]

```
MODULE Main;
TYPE Array = ARRAY [1..10] OF INTEGER
VAR array := Array {0, ..};
PROCEDURE P(mode a: Array) =
   BEGIN
      FOR i := FIRST(a) + 1TO LAST(a) DO
         a[i] := a[i − 1] + 1;
      END;
   END P;
BEGIN
   P(array);
   Wr.PutText(Fmt.Int(array[10]));
END Main.
```

6. What parameter mode(s) can result in a formal parameter being an alias for the actual parameter?

7. Write a procedure, ForAllElements, that invokes a supplied procedure on each element of an integer array. The supplied procedure will take as arguments the value of the array element and the index of the array element. The signature of ForAllElements should be

```
PROCEDURE ForAllElements(
   READONLY array: ARRAY OF INTEGER;
   proc: Proc);
```

where

```
TYPE Proc = PROCEDURE (index: CARDINAL; value: INTEGER);
```

After writing ForAllElements, use it to implement procedure Largest, which returns the index of the largest element in an array (or LAST(CARDINAL) if the array is empty):

```
PROCEDURE Largest(READONLY array: ARRAY OF INTEGER): CARDINAL;
```

8. When can two different procedures in the same module have the same name?

7

Exceptions

It is important that programs be reliable. This means more than simply taking care to minimize mistakes as you write code. It means that programs should operate in a well behaved fashion even if unexpected circumstances arise:

- if input data is in the wrong format or is missing
- if writing a file fails because there is no more space on the disk holding the file
- if an arithmetic overflow occurs because data values are larger than expected
- if the user stops program execution by typing an interrupt character at the keyboard

For each of these situations, you must plan in advance how to detect the problem and what action to take when it occurs. Simply allowing the system to terminate your program is usually not a good response—at the very least the program should print an informative message that will help an operator or user correct the problem. More complicated programs may have to take specific recovery actions to ensure that communication links or databases are not corrupted by a sudden stop. A critical, embedded application may have to reset, reconfigure, or restart itself automatically.

Modula–3 cannot help you plan error recovery, but it can help in detecting problems and in invoking appropriate actions. Detection is aided by the language design and the run-time checking, which quickly detects and contains errors. Recovery is addressed by the exception mechanism.

An *exception* generally is any error or other situation that causes an interruption in normal program control flow. When the situation occurs, we say that an exception is *raised*. Control is immediately given to a designated *handler* for the exception, which can undertake recovery actions. When the handler is finished, the program continues at a predetermined location.

For the most part, programmers declare and use specific exceptions to represent situations that are meaningful to their applications, such as passing nonsensical arguments to

---

Error Handling in Other Languages

Many older languages, such as C and Pascal, do not have exception handling mechanisms. In those languages, errors may be handled by using special error codes or by calling library routines. In C, for example, library functions that encounter errors either return a special failure code or set a special global variable, errno, with an appropriate error code. You must check errno after every call that might fail:

```
errno = 0;   /* reset error flag */
x = sqrt(y);
if (errno != 0) {   /* Check global error flag */
    /* handle error */
}
/* continue normal logic */
```

This way of detecting errors is very cumbersome: it requires a lot of checking code; it interrupts the normal "no errors" logic of the program with the error handling; and it is difficult to propagate errors up to the calling function. In fact, the method is so cumbersome that many C programs lack adequate error checking. When an error causes an exception to be raised, however, you can't ignore it and allow the program to continue.

Library procedures such as C's setjmp() and longjmp() can sometimes simulate exceptions by forcibly returning control to a calling procedure. However, these mechanisms are difficult to understand if not used with great discipline.

The Ada language includes an exception mechanism similar to Modula–3's, except that Ada exceptions don't have parameters. Exceptions are being added to C++ and the ISO revision of Modula–2.

---

a procedure or exceeding the capacity of some internal table. However, other exceptions may be built into Modula–3 implementations and available to all applications. For example, some implementations might raise predefined exceptions when an arithmetic calculation overflows or when dynamic storage is exhausted. The Modula–3 language does not require all implementations to deal with run-time errors in this fashion, so depending on these predefined exceptions may make your programs less portable. (The SRC Modula–3 system does not have such predefined exceptions.)

7.1 Exception Declarations

Before an exception is used it must be declared. You can declare exceptions much like you declare variables or types, although the declarations can appear only at the top level of interfaces and modules—never inside procedures or blocks. (This restriction simplifies the rules a bit and is not at all burdensome.) When you declare an exception, you must choose a name for it and decide if the exception is to have a parameter. For example, this declaration defines Disk_Full to be an exception that has no parameter, and IOError to be an exception that takes a text string as a parameter:

```
EXCEPTION
  Disk_Full;
  IOError(TEXT);
```

An exception's parameter is used to piggyback additional information with the exception. This information could be used to discriminate between different variations of the exception, or it might simply provide a message to be printed. Parameters can have any type except an open array, and it's possible to pass any amount of information by using a suitable record or object type as the parameter. However, an exception can have at most one parameter.

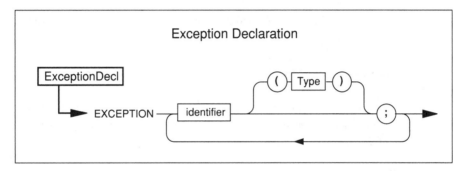

After declaring an exception, you can raise it when the appropriate situation arises and you can handle it in appropriate places. The next section discusses how to raise exceptions and Section 7.3 discusses handlers.

7.2 Raising Exceptions

You use the RAISE statement to raise an exception. If the exception has a parameter, you must supply a value for the parameter at the same time. For example, the statement

```
RAISE OutOfStorage;
```

raises the OutOfStorage exception, and the statement

```
RAISE IOError("Output device full");
```

raises the IOError exception with the string "Output device full" as its argument.

Raising an exception E causes control to pass immediately to the innermost exception handler in the current procedure that lists exception E. (Handlers are discussed in the next section.) If there is no such handler, the current procedure is terminated and the search for a handler continues at the point where the procedure was called. This action is

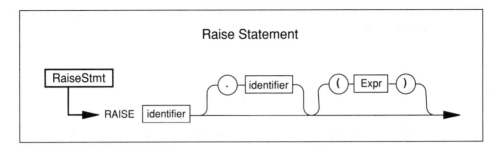

called *propagating* the exception. In this way, procedure calls are continually "unwound" until:

1. a suitable handler is found,
2. the procedure being terminated is not permitted to propagate the exception, or
3. there are no more calls to unwind

In the last two cases the Modula–3 run-time system will stop the program and issue a suitable error message.

A procedure is "permitted" to propagate an exception when the procedure has a *raises set* that includes the exception. Raises sets are part of the declaration of a procedure or procedure type. If you include the clause

RAISES { e_1, e_2, ..., e_n }

in such a declaration, then the listed exceptions can be propagated out of the procedure. It is a checked run-time error for any other exception to propagate out.If you omit the raises set or if you write RAISES {}, then no exceptions can propagate out of the procedure. If you wish to allow all exceptions to propagate out of a procedure, you must write RAISES ANY.

Example 7–1

Suppose you are writing a simple function, Volume, which takes the radius and height of a cylinder as parameters and returns the volume of the cylinder according to the formula $V = \pi \cdot r^2 \cdot h$. The parameters and result will all be of type REAL. However, what should the function do if one or both input parameters are not positive numbers? You might decide to treat those conditions as errors and raise an appropriate exception, in which case you could write the function like this:

```
EXCEPTION BadParameters;
...
PROCEDURE Volume(r, h: REAL): REAL RAISES {BadParameters} =
BEGIN
    IF r <= 0.0 OR h <= 0.0 THEN RAISE BadParameters; END;
    RETURN 3.1415926536 * r * r * h;
END Volume;
```

Since the Volume function itself does not contain any exception handlers, Modula–3 will terminate the Volume procedure when BadParameters is raised and will search for a handler from the point at which Volume was called.

The computation of $\pi \cdot r^2 \cdot h$ might overflow, which is a checked run-time error. If an overflow did occur, the program would halt, either because that is the normal way such errors are handled, or because the Modula–3 run-time system converted the overflow to an exception which was not listed in the raises set.

When a function procedure's execution is cut short by raising an exception, it gets no chance to return a value. However, changes that any procedure makes to global data or VAR parameters before the exception is raised will remain. You should think about whether you want to change global data before or after possibly raising an exception.

7.3 Exception Handlers

If you anticipate that an exception might be raised in a section of code, you can use the TRY-EXCEPT statement to supply a handler that will deal with that exception. (A second kind of handler statement, TRY-FINALLY, is discussed in Section 7.4.1.)

The TRY-EXCEPT statement is somewhat complicated. (See the diagram "Try-Except Statement" on page 136.) In brief, it has two parts: a sequence of statements which are "guarded" by some handlers, and the handlers themselves:

```
TRY
    guarded_statements
EXCEPT
    exception_handlers
END
```

Any exception raised within the guarded statements can be intercepted by the handlers. Any exceptions raised in procedures called from the guarded statements can also be intercepted, if they were not handled at a lower level.

The individual exception handlers are preceded by | (vertical bar) characters. You can omit the | before the first handler, but keeping it probably improves the readability of the statement. Handlers begin with the name of the exception(s) to be handled and include a list of statements. For exceptions that take a parameter, a handler usually has the form

```
exception_name(v) => handler_stmts
```

where v is an identifier. Like the identifier in a FOR statement, v is implicitly declared as a variable and is initialized to the actual argument specified when the exception was raised. The scope of the identifier is the statements in its handler.

If the exceptions to be handled do not take parameters—or if you don't care what the parameter values are—you can write the handler as

```
exception_name, exception_name, ... => handler_stmts
```

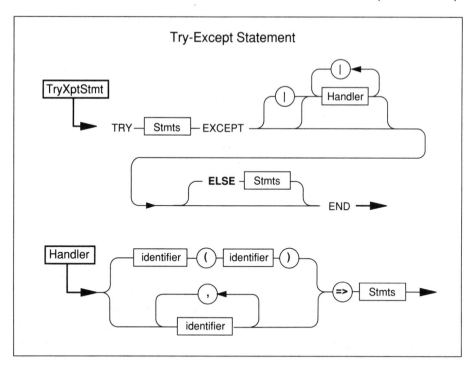

in which case the statements apply to any of the listed exceptions.

It's also possible to include a handler for "all exceptions" by adding the clause

```
ELSE  handler_stmts
```

at the end of the TRY-EXCEPT statement. Any exception not explicitly listed in the preceding handlers is intercepted by the ELSE handler (if present). The actual exceptions handled by the ELSE handler can have parameters, but the parameters cannot be accessed in the ELSE handler.

When an exception is intercepted by a handler, and all the statements of the handler have been executed, control passes to the statement following TRY-EXCEPT. There is no returning to the place where the exception was raised. (That is, there is no "retrying" of the code that raised the exception.)

Example 7–2

Suppose we want to call a procedure, Process, which may fail by raising exception Process_-
Failure. If the procedure does fail, we want to call Reject(); otherwise, we want to call Accept(). A sequence of statements that does this is listed below:

```
TRY
    Process();
    Accept();
EXCEPT
|   Process_Failure => Reject();
END
```

Notice that it would be wrong to place Accept() after the TRY-EXCEPT statement, because then it would be called after Reject() if an exception were raised.

Example 7–3

Complicating Example 7–2, suppose that Process_Failure took a parameter that indicated the severity of the problem, for example,

```
EXCEPTION Process_Failure(Severity);
TYPE Severity = {QuiteBad, NotSoBad};
```

Let's change the code so that Accept is called even for failures that are not so bad:

```
TRY
    Process();
    Accept();
EXCEPT
|   Process_Failure(severity) =>
        IF severity = Severity.NotSoBad THEN Accept(); ELSE Reject(); END;
END
```

Example 7–4

Finally, if Process might also raise other fatal exceptions, you could use an ELSE clause to catch them:

```
TRY
    Process();
    Accept();
EXCEPT
|   Process_Failure(severity) =>
        IF severity = Severity.NotSoBad THEN Accept(); ELSE Reject(); END;
ELSE Reject();
END
```

7.4 Exception Propagation

When an exception is raised, the Modula–3 run-time system attempts to find an appropriate handler for the exception. It does this by looking in the current procedure for the innermost TRY-EXCEPT statement that is guarding the code that raised the exception. If that statement has a handler for the exception, it is used. Otherwise, the search continues in the current procedure for another TRY-EXCEPT guarding the first TRY-EXCEPT, and so forth.

If no handler is found in the current procedure, the exception is *propagated*. That is, the search for a handler continues in the procedure that called the current one, beginning at the location of the call. In this way, procedure calls are progressively "unwound" until a handler is found, until a procedure not listing the exception in its raises set is about to be unwound, or until no more calls remain. If no handler is found, the Modula–3 run-time system will halt the program with a suitable error message.

Example 7–5

The body of module Main below calls procedure P, which calls procedure Q. Q raises one of four exceptions. Where is each exception handled?

```
MODULE Main;
EXCEPTION Exc_A; Exc_B; Exc_C; Exc_D;
PROCEDURE Q() RAISES ANY =
   BEGIN
      TRY
         ... (* Raise Exc_A, Exc_B, Exc_C, or Exc_D *) ...
      EXCEPT
      |   Exc_A => ...
      END;
   END Q;

PROCEDURE P() RAISES ANY=
   BEGIN
      TRY
         Q();
      EXCEPT
      |  Exc_A => ...
      |  Exc_B => ...
      END;
   END P;

BEGIN
   TRY
      P();
   EXCEPT
   |  Exc_A => ...
   |  Exc_B => ...
   |  Exc_C => ...
   END;
END Main.
```

Solution   The module initialization code calls P, which calls Q. Exc_A is intercepted by the handler within Q. Since that handler names only Exc_A, all other exceptions propagate to the caller, P. Procedure P handles Exc_B since Exc_A was handled within Q. All other exceptions (Exc_C and Exc_D) propagate out of P to the body of Main. Main handles Exc_C; Exc_A and Exc_B don't get out that far. Raising Exc_D in Q will cause a run-time error, since there is no handler for Exc_D in the program. An ELSE clause in any of the handlers would serve to catch Exc_D.

Exception handling code can itself raise an exception, either directly or because an exception propagates out of a procedure called from the handling code. In this case, the original exception is abandoned and the search for a handler for the new exception begins just outside the current TRY-EXCEPT statement. That way, you can't get stuck in a loop processing and reprocessing the same exception in the same handler. For example, the TRY-EXCEPT statement below has no noticeable effect since it propagates the Error exception just as if no handler had been present:

```
EXCEPTION Error;
...
TRY
   ...
EXCEPT
|   Error => RAISE Error;
END
```

However, this does not mean that a Modula–3 program can be processing only one exception at a time. The statements in a handler can call procedures that raise and handle any number of exceptions. When the procedures finally return normally, the original handler completes.

7.4.1 TRY-FINALLY

An exception can cause several layers of procedure calls to be unwound as control passes from the site of a raise to a procedure that handles the exception. In some cases, the intermediate procedures—those between the raise and the handler—will want to know that their processing is being aborted. This lets them clean up their data structures as they would have if their processing had completed normally. For this kind of task, Modula–3 provides the TRY-FINALLY statement, which contains two sequences of statements—guarded and finalization:

```
TRY
   guarded-stmts
FINALLY
   final-stmts
END
```

If no exceptions are raised in *guarded-stmts*, the *final-stmts* are executed after the *guarded-stmts*. However, if an exception is raised in the *guarded-stmts*, control is transferred immediately to the *final-stmts*. After the *final-stmts* are executed, the original exception is reraised. As you can see, TRY-FINALLY allows you to briefly delay a propagating exception on its way to a handler.

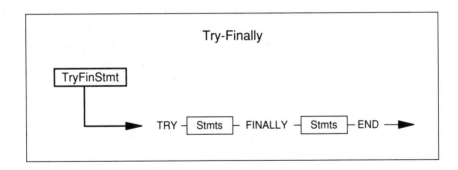

Example 7–6

Suppose you are writing a database application. The procedure Acquire gains access to the database, Get_Records retrieves some records, Change performs local changes on the records, Commit() makes all the changes permanent, and Release relinquishes the database. All the procedures signal failure by raising the exception DB_Failure. The procedure Work, below, calls each of the database procedures and signals errors by allowing the DB_Failure exception to propagate out to callers. However, procedure Work takes care to call Release even when a failure occurs during processing.

```
PROCEDURE Work() RAISES {DB_Failure} =
  BEGIN
     Acquire();
     TRY
       Get_Records();
       Change();
       Commit();
     FINALLY
       Release();
     END;
  END Work;
```

The call to Acquire is outside the TRY-FINALLY statement because we don't want to call Release if Acquire fails.

If an exception is raised and propagated out of the *final-stmts*, that exception is propagated out of the TRY-FINALLY statement and the original exception (if any) is lost.

7.4.2 RETURN and EXIT Exceptions

The RETURN and EXIT statements in Modula–3 are defined in terms of exceptions. Their description in Chapter 3 (Statements) was simplified since exceptions had not been discussed.

The RETURN statement behaves as if it raised a special exception, called the *return exception*. You cannot name this exception in a TRY-EXCEPT statement. This exception has no parameter in proper procedures, but in functions it has a parameter whose type is the function return type. Every procedure body acts as if it contained a handler for this exception at the outermost level; the handler terminates the procedure and handles the return value (if any) properly.

In a similar way, the EXIT statement behaves as if it raised a special *exit exception*. Each loop statement behaves as if it included a handler for this exception around the loop. The handler does nothing except return control to the statement following the loop.

These definitions of RETURN and EXIT would be academic if it were not for TRY-FINALLY, which does intercept the return and exit exceptions.

Example 7–7

In the following code fragment, the procedure Stop_It will be called when the RETURN statement inside TRY-FINALLY is executed. However, the Flush_It procedure will not be called; Do_It will return after the call to Stop_It.

```
PROCEDURE Do_It() =
BEGIN
    Start_It();
    TRY
        ... RETURN; ...
    FINALLY
        Stop_It();
    END;
    Flush_It();
END Do_It;
```

For another example of why it is good that TRY-FINALLY intercepts RETURN and EXIT exceptions, see the LOCK statement on page 242.

The ELSE clause of a TRY-EXCEPT statement will also catch the return and exit exceptions. This is a much less useful feature in Modula–3. In fact, it can be quite dangerous. Once in the ELSE handler, you cannot re-raise the return or exit exceptions, which means that EXIT won't really exit and RETURN won't really return.

Example 7–8

The loop in the procedure below won't terminate because the RETURN statement will be thwarted by the enclosing TRY-EXCEPT statement.

```
PROCEDURE Forever=
VAR done := FALSE;
BEGIN
    LOOP
        TRY
            ... IF done THEN RETURN; END; ...
        EXCEPT
        ELSE Wr.PutText(Stdio.stderr, "Exception ignored.\n");
        END;
    END;
END Forever;
```

7.4.3 Exceptions and Threads

Threads are discussed in Chapter 12. You can skip this subsection if you are unfamiliar with them.

Exception propagation and handling is local to each thread. That is, a raised exception is always handled in the current thread; it can't cross over to another thread. It is a checked run-time error for no handler to be present. A thread can be rescheduled during exception propagation; this is normally invisible to the programmer.

7.5 Expecting Exceptions

Some exceptions may be raised automatically by the Modula–3 run-time environment. You may not be able to predict when or where these exception will be raised. For example, if your Modula–3 implementation causes the exception DivideByZero to be raised when division by zero is attempted, then that exception could be raised as a side effect of executing the statement

```
quotient := dividend / divisor;  (* raises exception if Divsr = 0 *)
```

However, the exception could not be raised by statements that did not perform division.

Other exceptions can be raised at any time. For example, if your Modula–3 system maps a keyboard interrupt to an exception (say, Terminal.Interrupt), then that exception could be raised at any time or place in the program. By placing handlers at the very beginning of a program, you can catch exceptions raised anywhere. These handlers provide a good "backstop" for exceptions that are not caught at a lower level. However, since they are far away from the site of the error, they can seldom do anything except stop the program gracefully.

Example 7–9

The Main module below includes a handler at its top level to intercept exceptions:

```
MODULE Main;
IMPORT Terminal, Wr, Stdio;
... (* Other declarations *)
BEGIN
    TRY
        ...(* Main program processing *)
    EXCEPT
    |   Terminal.Interrupt => Wr.PutText(Stdio.stderr, "Interrupt; quitting...\n");
    ELSE
        Wr.PutText(Stdio.stderr, "Error; quitting...\n");
    END;
END Main.
```

7.6 Exercises

Answers to the exercises marked "[A]" appear in Appendix D.

1. Which of the following statements are true?   [A]
   a. The name of an exception can be any nonreserved identifier.
   b. An exception parameter cannot have type ARRAY OF CHAR.
   c. An exception parameter must have a scalar type.
   d. A RAISE statement cannot appear in an exception handler.
   e. A TRY-FINALLY statement can cause an EXIT statement to be ignored.
   f. If an exception handler completes normally, the exception that triggered the handler is forgotten.
   g. Unhandled exceptions are likely to cause the Modula–3 program to terminate.
   h. Modula–3's exception mechanism is an example of "exceptions with retry."
2. In the ELSE handler of a TRY-EXCEPT statement, can you:
   a. Determine the name of the exception being handled?   [A]
   b. Propagate the exception to enclosing handlers?   [A]

3. If your programming language doesn't support exceptions, you may have to use return codes to signal the success or failure of your procedures. Rewrite the procedure Work in Example 7–6 on page 140 without exceptions, assuming the database routines return TRUE if they succeed and FALSE if they do not.

4. Change the Bad Parameters exception in Example 7–1 on page 134 so that it takes a parameter to indicate which of the two parameters was faulty. Then change procedure Volume to supply the proper argument to the exception.   [A]

5. Many programmers don't check for errors, whether they are indicated by return codes or by exceptions. Is the programmer who doesn't write exception handlers any better or worse off than the programmer who doesn't check return codes?

6. The procedure Send() attempts to send a message over a communication line. If it fails, it raises the exception Send_Failure. Because transmission errors can be transient, Send() might succeed if called again after a failure. Write a procedure, SendWithRetry, that retries the Send up to n times (a parameter to SendWithRetry). Only if the n'th call to Send fails should SendWithRetry raise Send_Failure.

7. If procedure P can raise exception Exc_P and procedure Q can raise Exc_Q, what should be the raises sets of A and B in the program fragment below?   [A]

```
PROCEDURE A() =
  BEGIN
      TRY B(); P(); EXCEPT Exc_P => (* empty *) END;
  END A;

PROCEDURE B() =
  BEGIN
      TRY Q(); FINALLY (*empty*) END;
  END B;
```

8. Some implementations of exception handling unwind the call stack (i.e., pop off procedure call frames) as they are searching for an appropriate handler. Others find the handler first and then unwind the stack appropriately. With which implementation would it be easier to debug uncaught exceptions (raised exceptions with no handlers)? Why?

9. Modula–3 allows you to list several exceptions in the same handler, if the exceptions do not have formal parameters:

TRY ... EXCEPT E_1, E_2, E_3=> stmts END

Suppose you allow this for exceptions with parameters, for example,

TRY ... EXCEPT $E_1(v_1)$, $E_2(v_2)$, $E_3(v_3)$ => stmts END

What restrictions would you have to put on the E_i and v_i?

8

Interfaces and Modules

If you are writing a small program, you can keep all of the declarations and procedures together in a single file. However, as your program becomes larger, you may encounter problems:

1. You may find it hard to keep track of so many declarations and procedures without some higher-level organization.

2. It may take a long time to compile all those procedures every time you make the simplest change.

3. You may want to divide the program into pieces that different people can work on independently.

4. You may want to reuse parts of the code in other programs.

Interfaces and modules address all of these problems. The key concept here is separating a *specification* (interface) from an *implementation* (module). A specification describes what something does; an implementation describes how it does it. In Modula-3, you simplify programs by carving them into pieces with explicit interfaces. When the interface is complete, you have all you need to write code that uses the interface; there is no need to look at the implementation. In fact, many people use Modula-3 as a design language, developing interfaces in detail and only sketching out selected parts of modules. Such designs are not executable, but the interfaces can be checked for consistency by a Modula-3 compiler.

8.1 Interfaces, Modules, and Clients

Interfaces declare abstract facilities or services that can be used by modules and by other interfaces. *Modules* implement these facilities and services by providing bodies for procedures declared in interfaces. Each module and each interface is typically contained in its own file and is compiled individually, a technique called *separate compilation*.

For example, a module Mod or an interface Int can *import* another interface Server and thus gain access to Server's declarations. In that case, Mod and Int are called *clients* of Server. A module (also typically named Server) can implement interface Server by *exporting* Server. These relationships are shown graphically in Figure 8–1. Notice the differently styled boxes that are used to represent modules and interfaces, and the differently styled arrows that are used to show import and export relationships.

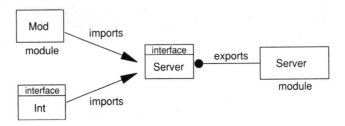

Figure 8–1   Mod and Int import (are clients of) interface Server; module ServerImpl exports (implements) Server.

8.2 Import Statements

An interface consists of a series of declarations. A module or another interface can gain access to these declarations by using an IMPORT statement to make the declared names visible. The IMPORT statement comes in two forms. The statement

    IMPORT Math, Fmt;

grants access to interfaces Math and Fmt and makes the names Math and Fmt visible. Then, you can refer to items declared in these interfaces by qualifying the item names with the interface name. For example, if interface Math declares a procedure Sqrt, you can refer to that procedure as Math.Sqrt in the client, but not simply as Sqrt. It doesn't matter if you list several interfaces in the same IMPORT statement or if you use a separate IMPORT statement for each interface. An IMPORT statement including the AS keyword is called a *renamed import* and is discussed in Chapter 9 (Generics).

The second way of importing an interface eliminates the need to qualify the imported names. The statement

    FROM Math IMPORT Sin, Cos;

makes the names Sin and Cos declared in interface Math visible, but does not make the name Math itself visible. That is, you can use the names Sin and Cos, but you cannot refer to Sin as Math.Sin, nor can you refer to another name Sqrt declared in Math as Math.Sqrt.

You can mix both kinds of import statements, and the same interface can be imported in both ways. For example, writing the statements

```
FROM Math IMPORT Sin, Cos;
IMPORT Math;
```

allows you to use the names Sin, Cos, Math.Sin, Math.Cos, and Math.Sqrt (or Math.T for any name T declared in Math).

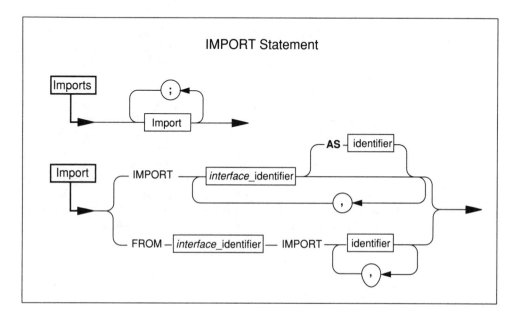

Actually, many experienced programmers try to avoid the FROM form of IMPORT, because they don't want to mix names from interfaces with names declared in the client. By carefully naming interfaces and items you can make qualified names read naturally.

Example 8–1

Suppose you have an interface that provides operations on "boxes," and one of these operations is "create a new box." A good approach is to name the interface Box and the operation New, which makes for clear and concise code in clients using qualified names:

```
IMPORT Box; ... aBox := Box.New(); ...
```

In contrast to this, other programmers choose names like BoxFunctions for the interface and NewBox for the operation. With this choice of names, the use of qualified names is unwieldy [e.g., BoxFunctions.NewBox()], and the other form of import is needed:

```
FROM BoxFunctions IMPORT NewBox; ... aBox := NewBox(); ...
```

8.2.1 Name Conflicts

You must not import a name more than once. For example, the statements

Modules and Imports

Modula–3's module and import mechanisms are taken largely from Modula–2, with some generalizations (e.g., interfaces) and some restrictions (e.g., no internal modules). Turbo Pascal and Ada also include the ability to use separate modules and import names from other modules.

Turbo Pascal extends standard Pascal by adding the ability to divide programs into separate *units*, each with a specification part and an implementation part. Both parts must be in the same file and are compiled together. When a unit is imported, all public names in the unit become directly visible; there is no qualified naming. This makes it difficult to avoid name clashes when you have a large number of units.

Ada and Modula–3 have similar module structures. Ada programs are divided into package bodies (modules) and package specifications (interfaces), which are compiled separately as in Modula–3. The Ada clause "WITH Math" corresponds to Modula–3's "IMPORT Math." Public names from package specifications can be referenced using qualified names (e.g., Math.-Sqrt). However, Ada also permits the programmer to write "USE Math," which makes *all* the names in interface Math visible. A debate rages among Ada programmers over whether the USE clause is good or not. To make only a few names visible from a package specification, the Ada programmer must employ "renaming declarations," which are more cumbersome.

```
FROM Bibiography IMPORT Math, Science;
IMPORT Math;  (* Illegal! *)
```

are illegal because the declared name Math in Bibliography is the same as the interface name Math. It doesn't even matter if the two occurrences of the name refer to the same object. For example, the statement

```
IMPORT Math, Math;  (* Illegal! *)
```

is illegal because it imports the interface name Math twice. Although this violation may seem harmless, Modula–3's simple rule makes it easier to understand more complex examples.

Imported names must also be distinct from names declared at the top level of the client module or interface. For example, the following module is illegal because the imported name Sin from interface Math is the same as the name of a declared type:

```
MODULE Client;
FROM Math IMPORT Sin;
TYPE Sin = INTEGER;  (* Illegal! *)
...
END Client.
```

Problems like this one can often be solved by removing the FROM-style import and using qualified names.

8.3 Interfaces

An interface is a top-level program unit which exists independently of other interfaces and modules. An interface consists of a series of declarations that are subject to two restrictions:

1. Variable declarations (if any) can only have constant initializers.

2. Procedure declarations (if any) must not include bodies.

As usual in Modula-3, the declarations can appear in any order. Every interface must have a name that is distinct from all other interfaces in a program, and this name is used in IMPORT statements by clients of the interface. The UNSAFE keyword is used to specify an unsafe interface (page 261).

Example 8–2

A *rational number* in mathematics is a number that can be expressed as the quotient p/q of two integers p and q ($q > 0$). Here is an interface that defines a rational data type and some operations on it:

```
INTERFACE Rational;
TYPE T = RECORD p: INTEGER := 0; q: CARDINAL := 1; END;
PROCEDURE New(p: INTEGER; q: CARDINAL:=1) : T;
PROCEDURE Plus(x, y: T): T;
PROCEDURE Minus(x, y: T): T;
PROCEDURE Times(x, y: T): T;
PROCEDURE Divide(x, y: T): T;
END Rational.
```

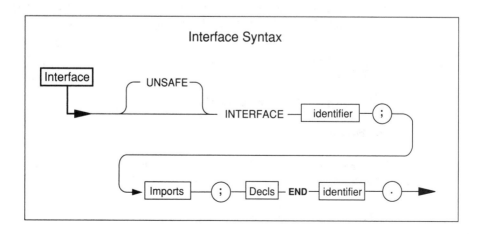

Interface Syntax

The Rational interface could be used by a client to define a function that squares rational numbers:

```
MODULE Rational_Client;
IMPORT Rational;

...

PROCEDURE Square(r: Rational.T) : Rational.T =
    BEGIN
        RETURN Rational.Times(r, r);
    END Square;

...

END Rational_Client.
```

8.3.1 Interface Limitations

An interface A can itself be a client of another interface B, but names from B are not available to clients of A (Figure 8–2) unless the clients explicitly import B.

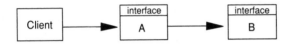

Figure 8–2   Client can access names from A, but not from B.

For example, consider the Box interface:

```
INTERFACE Box;
FROM DiskIO IMPORT Location;

...

PROCEDURE Find(): Location;
END Box.
```

Although the imported name Location is defined inside the interface, it is not available—qualified or unqualified—to clients who only import Box. To use Location, a client would have to import DiskIO in addition to Box. For example:

```
MODULE BoxClient;
IMPORT Box, DiskIO;

...

VAR diskLocation: DiskIO.Location := Box.Find();

...

END BoxClient.
```

Actually, if the only use of Location was in this variable declaration, you could avoid importing DiskIO. By writing the declaration as

```
VAR diskLocation := Box.Find();
```

you would get the right type for diskLocation without ever explicitly naming that type. Put another way, the abstract *type* always exists whenever it is needed; it is just a particular *name* for the type (e.g., Location) that may not be visible at the moment.

A second limitation on interfaces is that you cannot write two interfaces that import each other, either directly or in a cycle through other interfaces (Figure 8–3a). However, two modules can import each other's exported interfaces (Figure 8–3b). This does not generate a cycle.

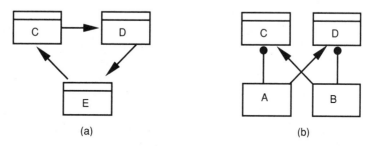

(a)   (b)

Figure 8–3   Illegal import cycle (a) and legal alternative (b).

8.4 Modules

A module consists of a set of declarations and some executable code. Except for the initialization of variables (page 30), the order of declarations doesn't matter.

Names declared within the module are not visible outside it. Like interfaces, each module exists as a top-level entity in the program, and has a name which must not duplicate the name of any other module in the program. (A module name can duplicate an interface name.) A module can import interfaces that declare other names. The UNSAFE keyword is used to specify an unsafe module (page 261).

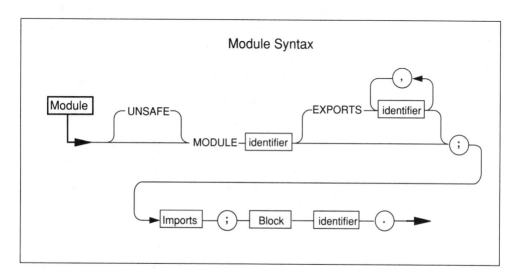

Modules exist to "complete" interfaces by suppling bodies for the procedures declared in those interfaces. If you look at a module, however, you'll typically see more than just those procedure bodies. A module often makes use of additional types, procedures, variables, etc., in the course of implementing the interface procedures. These additional declarations are sometimes called *private declarations*, since they are not needed by (nor are they available to) interface clients.

8.4.1 Exporting Interfaces

Modules and interfaces can both import interfaces, but only a module can *export* an interface. A module exports an interface by listing the interface's name after the EXPORTS keyword in the module declaration. Every module must export at least one interface; if you omit the EXPORTS clause, Modula-3 assumes that you are exporting a single interface with the same name as the module. That is, the module

MODULE M (* *No EXPORTS list* *) ; ... END M.

is taken to be an abbreviation for

MODULE M EXPORTS M; ... END M.

By exporting an interface, a module declares that it is "responsible" for the interface—that it is the implementor of the facilities in the interface. This has two effects. First, all the names in an exported interface become directly visible in the module—no qualification is needed. Second, the module is permitted to redeclare any procedure in the interface, thus supplying a body for the procedure—in effect "implementing" it. The procedures do not have to be in any particular order within the module.

Example 8–3

The Rational interface developed earlier needs a module to supply bodies for the interface procedures. The interface and a suitable module are shown below. The module could import other interfaces or define additional procedures, but we have not shown any.

```
INTERFACE Rational;
TYPE T = RECORD p: INTEGER := 0; q: CARDINAL := 1; END;
PROCEDURE New(p: INTEGER; q: CARDINAL := 1) : T;
PROCEDURE Plus(x, y: T): T;
PROCEDURE Minus(x, y: T): T;
PROCEDURE Times(x, y: T): T;
PROCEDURE Divide(x, y: T): T;
END Rational.

MODULE Rational EXPORTS Rational;
PROCEDURE New(x, y: T): T = BEGIN ... END New;
PROCEDURE Plus(x, y: T): T = BEGIN ... END Plus;
PROCEDURE Minus(x, y: T): T = BEGIN ... END Minus;
PROCEDURE Times(x, y: T): T = BEGIN ... END Times;
PROCEDURE Divide(x, y: T): T = BEGIN ... END Divide;
END Rational.
```

8.4.2 Name Visibility and Conflicts

When a module exports an interface, all the names declared in that interface—but not names imported into the interface—become directly visible. You must take care that these visible names do not conflict with any imported names or with any declarations at the top level of the module (except when redeclaring procedures, of course).

Example 8–4

> Consider the interface Set and module SetModule below:
>
> ```
> INTERFACE Set;
> FROM Word IMPORT Size;
> TYPE T = SET OF [0..Size];
> PROCEDURE Empty(): T;
> END Set.
>
> MODULE SetUnion EXPORTS Set;
> CONST Size = 32;
> PROCEDURE Empty(): T = BEGIN ... END Empty;
> END SetUnion.
> ```

Within SetModule, the exported names T and Empty are visible. Size (from Word) is not visible because it is not declared directly within Set, and therefore SetModule's declaration of (a different) Size is legal. The declaration of Empty in SetModule is all right since it is taken to be a redeclaration of the exported procedure Empty. However, consider what happens if an import is added to SetModule:

```
MODULE SetModule EXPORTS Set;
FROM Set IMPORT Empty;
CONST Size = 32;
PROCEDURE Empty(): T = BEGIN ... END P;
BEGIN ...
END SetModule.
```

Now, the introduction of the imported name Empty conflicts with both the exported name Empty and the redeclaration of Empty. It doesn't matter that all the Empty's refer to the same procedure.

8.4.3 Procedure Redeclarations

A procedure P in an exported interface can be redeclared in a module only to supply a body. The redeclaration of P does not have to be precisely identical to the exported declaration; what is required is that the exported declaration *cover* the redeclaration in the module. This means:

1. Both declarations must specify the same number of parameters with the same types and modes.

2. Both declarations must specify the same return type, or both must omit a return type.

3. The raises set in the exported declaration must include all the exceptions in the raises set of the module's redeclaration.

Reading between the lines, this means that the formal parameter names may be different in the two declarations, and that the module's declaration of P may omit some exceptions that were listed in the interface's declaration of P. These rules are the same as those used for procedure types and variables (page 126).

If the redeclaration changes the formal parameter names, which names do you use in keyword calls? You must use the module's formal names within the module and the interface's formal names within clients.

As for the raises set, the subset declared with the procedure body is used to determine which exceptions can be propagated.

Example 8–5

In the code below, the procedure P has different formal names in the interface and module, and the raises set is different:

```
INTERFACE M;
PROCEDURE P(VAR x: REAL) RAISES {Error, Overflow};
...
END M.

MODULE M;
PROCEDURE P(VAR y: REAL) RAISES {Error} = BEGIN ... END P;
...
END M.
```

Inside M, a call on P with argument e could be written P(y := e), whereas outside M—in a client that imported M—calls would be written P(x := e). If exception Overflow is raised within P, it will cause a run-time error because Overflow is not in the raises set for the implementation of P (although it is in the raises set of the interface declaration).

8.4.4 Exporting Multiple Interfaces

There is usually a one-to-one correspondence between modules and exported interfaces. However, it is possible for a module to export several interfaces—or for an interface to be exported by several modules—as long as there are no name conflicts and every exported procedure is redeclared exactly once in some module, i.e., as long as every interface procedure is assigned a body exactly once. If an interface is exported by only one module, that module must supply bodies for all the procedures declared in the interface. If more than one module exports the same interface, each module can redeclare some of the procedures and ignore others. This is one way to break a large implementation into several modules of manageable size.

Example 8–6

Interface A's procedures are implemented by two modules, A_1 and A_2:

```
INTERFACE A;
TYPE T = INTEGER;
PROCEDURE P1(x: T);
PROCEDURE P2(): T;
END A.
```

```
MODULE A_1 EXPORTS A;
PROCEDURE P1(x: T) = BEGIN ... END P1;
END A_1.


MODULE A_2 EXPORTS A;
PROCEDURE P2(): T = BEGIN ... END P2;
END A_2.
```

There are also situations in which a module needs to export more than one interface. Most modules export a single interface which is used by all clients. Sometimes, however, certain "trusted" clients may need access to additional information or to operations that are hidden from ordinary clients. Thus, we need both an "ordinary" interface (say, Basic) and a "friendly" interface (Friendly) from the same module.

When exporting several interfaces, you have to be careful not to violate the name conflict rules. For example, a new programmer might imagine that the Friendly interface should contain all the declarations in Basic, plus some extra ones. This doesn't work because the duplicated declarations would result in name conflicts when both interfaces were exported by the same module (Figure 8–4).

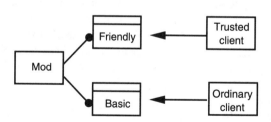

Figure 8–4   An incorrect way to provide alternate interfaces.

The solution is to declare in Friendly only the supplementary facilities needed by trusted clients. It's likely that Friendly will need access to some common declarations in Basic, so Friendly will have to import Basic. Ordinary clients will import only Basic, while trusted clients will import both Basic and Friendly (Figure 8–5).

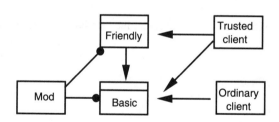

Figure 8–5   Providing a friendly interface for trusted clients.

Example 8–7

Suppose we wanted to give trusted clients of the Rational interface a Normalize function. We would create a RationalF interface that contained Normalize. RationalF would have to import Rational to gain access to the data type.

```
INTERFACE Rational;
... (* type T and procedures Plus, Minus, Times, Divide, as before *)
END Rational.

INTERFACE RationalF;
FROM Rational IMPORT T;
PROCEDURE Normalize(r:T): T;
END RationalF.

MODULE Rational EXPORTS Rational, RationalF;
PROCEDURE Normalize(x:T):T = BEGIN ... END Normalize;
... (* other procedures for Plus, Minus, Times, and Divide, as before *)
END Rational.
```

8.4.5 Module Initialization Code

The statements in the block at the end of a module form what is called *initialization code*. When your Modula-3 program starts, the initialization code in every module is executed automatically. The order in which modules are initialized depends on the import/export structure of the program. The basic rule is that if module Imports_C imports interface C and module Exports_C exports C, then Exports_C will be initialized before Imports_C (Figure 8–6). This ensures that each module gets a chance to initialize itself before any cli-

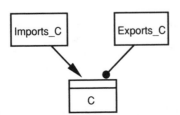

Figure 8–6   Initialization order: C (constant), then Exports_C, then Imports_C.

ents try to use its services through an interface. (Initializations in the interface C must be constant, so they can be done before the program starts.) The last module initialized in a program is the topmost, or "main" module—the module that exports the system-dependent Main interface. The main module's initialization code is, in effect, the program's starting point.

When several modules export the same interface, the relative order in which those modules are initialized is not specified.

```
MODULE A_Client;
    IMPORT A, Wr, Fmt, Stdio;
BEGIN
    Wr.PutText(Stdio.stdout, "top is " & Fmt.Bool(A.top) & "\n");
END A_Client;
```

```
INTERFACE A;
VAR top, bottom: BOOLEAN := FALSE;
END A;

MODULE A_1 EXPORTS A;
BEGIN
   top := NOT bottom;
END A_1;

MODULE A_2 EXPORTS A;
BEGIN
   bottom := NOT top;
END A_2;
```

8.5 Building a Program with Modules

Modules and interfaces are distinct Modula-3 program structures which can be compiled separately. All the modules and interfaces making up a program must be compiled by a Modula-3 compiler as part of the process of building the program. In fact, many Modula–3 systems (including SRC Modula–3) require each module and interface to be in a separate file and be compiled individually. For this reason, interfaces and modules are sometimes called *compilation units*, or simply *units*. We'll use the term *unit* when we mean either a module or an interface.

8.5.1 The Main Module

The *main module* in a Modula-3 program is the module whose initialization code is executed last. The designation of a main module is not defined in the language, but it is suggested that main modules be required to export a built-in interface, Main, whose contents are implementation-dependent. This is the approach taken by SRC Modula-3. The main module can be named Main, but it need not be. In SRC Modula-3 the Main interface is empty, and therefore the main module does not have to provide any procedures. The module's initialization code is effectively the program's starting point.

8.5.2 Finding Out Which Units Go Into a Program

Starting with the main module, you can find out what interfaces and modules are needed in the program. Start with all the interfaces imported by the main module, and add all the modules that export those interfaces. Then look for interfaces imported by those modules, and so forth. (See "Algorithm for Finding Units" on page 158.)

Some Modula-3 systems may be able to determine the set of needed units automatically. Others may require you to explicitly list all the units. In SRC Modula-3, you must list all the files containing the compiled units. The system will verify that the list is complete, but you have to correct any errors manually.

Algorithm for Finding Units

The interfaces and modules that make up a program can be determined by using this algorithm, which makes use of two lists of units, A and B:

1. Start with list B empty and list A containing just the module that exports the predefined interface Main. This module is the starting point of the program.

2. Select a unit from list A, but don't remove it yet; we'll call this unit X.

3. Add to list A all interfaces imported or exported by X that are not already on either list A or list B. (If an imported interface is part of a built-in library, place it on list B instead of list A.)

4. If X is an interface (not a module), add to list A the module (or modules) that export X.

5. Remove X from list A and add it to list B.

6. If list A is not empty, go back to step 2. If list A is empty, then list B contains all the units making up the program.

8.5.3 Units and Files

The Modula-3 language works entirely in terms of module and interface names, which are normal Modula-3 identifiers. However, your units will actually be stored in files, whose names are arbitrary and vary from computer to computer. In general, compilers associate units with files in one of two ways. Some require you to use file names that are related to the unit names; for example, a module named Fred might have to be stored in a file named Fred.m3. Others allow you to use any name, but require you to compile each file once manually; after that, the system keeps track of the correspondence between files and units. (There are procedures to follow when you change file names, of course.)

8.5.4 Dependencies and Compilation Order

When a unit A imports or exports an interface B, the information in B is used when A is compiled. If B were changed, A might compile differently, or even become illegal. There-fore, we often say that the compilation of A *depends on* B, or simply "A depends on B". Dependencies are transitive: If A depends on B and B depends on C, then A also depends on C. Dependencies are only directed to interfaces: If module M exports interface C, then M depends on C but neither C nor anyone importing C (e.g., B) depends on M for their compilation Figure 8–6).

Example 8–8

Suppose you have a program consisting of modules ModA, ModB, and Main. Modules ModA and ModB export interfaces A and B, respectively. Interface A also imports interface B, and Main imports A. Which units depend (directly or indirectly) on A and B?

Solution   The program in this example is displayed graphically in Figure 8–8.

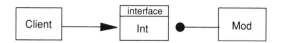

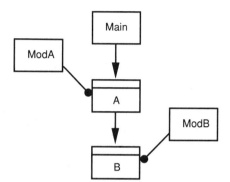

Figure 8–7   Client and Mod depend on Int, but Client does not depend on Mod.

Figure 8–8   ModA and Main depend on A, and all three modules and interface A depend on B.

When unit A depends on interface B, it generally makes good sense to compile B before A. You have to compile both sooner or later, and it's easier and faster to discover errors in B by compiling it alone. Furthermore, some Modula–3 compilers require you to follow this policy because of the way they are programmed. With these compilers, you must compile each interface before you compile any unit that depends on it. If you change interface A, you must recompile A and all the units that depend on A.

For this reason, we sometimes say that the dependencies among units impose a *compilation order* on the units in a program. The compilation order is the order in which individual units should be compiled so that each interface is compiled before any unit that depends on it is compiled. It is always possible to determine such an order, because Modula-3 doesn't allow two interfaces to depend on each other, either directly or indirectly. In general, however, there is usually some freedom in choosing when to compile a unit. For example, if A and C both depend on B, and if there are no other dependencies, then A and C must be compiled after B but it doesn't matter if the compilation order is B, A, C or B, C, A. If you add new units to the program, or if you change IMPORT and EXPORT declarations in the program, the compilation order may change.

Example 8–9

Consider the program consisting of the modules Main, ModA, and ModB, and the interfaces A and B as described in Example 8–8. Which of the following compilation orders are permissible for this program?

1. A, B, ModA, ModB, Main

2. Main, B, ModB, A, ModA.

3. B, ModB, ModA, A, Main.

4. B, ModB, A, ModA, Main.

5. B, A, Main, ModA, ModB.

Solution   Interface B must be compiled before A, and once both have been compiled, the modules can be compiled in any order. (Strictly speaking, ModB can be compiled before A is compiled.) Therefore:

1. is incorrect, since B must precede A.

2. is incorrect, because A must precede Main.

3. is incorrect, because A must precede ModA.

4. and 5. are both allowable.

8.5.5 Version Skews

A problem arises when you violate the compilation order and use different versions of the same interface in the same program. For example, suppose that a program consists of a module Main which imports interface Int and a module ExportsInt which exports Int:

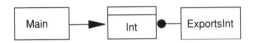

Now, suppose you do the following:

1. You compile interface Int.
2. You compile unit Main.
3. You change interface Int and recompile it.
4. You compile unit ExportsInt.
5. You attempt to build a program that includes units Main, Int, and ExportsInt.

The problem here is that units Main and ExportsInt have been compiled with different versions of interface Int. We don't know what might have changed in Int, but it's possible that unit Main, which was compiled with the old version of Int, will not work correctly with the new implementation of Int as compiled into ExportsInt. (For example, the signature of one of the procedures in Int may have changed.)

Modula-3 systems must be able to detect this kind of problem, which is called a *version skew*. Some skews, like the one in Example 8–9, might only be detected when you try to link the final program. Each of the compilations, considered in isolation, seems all right; it's only when the pieces are put together that the problem is discovered. Other skews may be detected during compilation. For example, if unit M imports A and B, and if A and B are each compiled with a different version of a third interface, C, then the Modula-3 compiler will probably detect this version skew when M is compiled.

To avoid version skews, you must keep track of changes made to interfaces and be sure to properly recompile *all* dependents after a change. Some Modula-3 systems can help you do this automatically, and in other cases you can use programs such as UNIX's make to keep your compilations up-to-date.

8.6 Exercises

Answers to the exercises marked "[A]" appear in Appendix D.

1. Which of the following statements are true?   [A]
   a. The total number of modules in a program must be at least as great at the total number of interfaces.
   b. Each interface must be exported by some module.
   c. Changing a module will require at most a recompilation of those interfaces exported by the module.
   d. If two modules export the same interface and implement the same interface procedure, which implementation is used is not defined by Modula–3.
   e. If a module has the same name as an interface, it can export only that interface.
   f. If a "friendly" interface is available, it can be used instead of the standard interface.
   g. The starting point in a Modula–3 program is the module with the name Main.
   h. Once all the interfaces in a program have been compiled successfully, the modules can be compiled in any order.

2. The order in which variables are declared at the top level of a module or in a block can affect the initialization of those variables. However, the order of declarations in an interface cannot affect initializations. Why?

3. An interface and module are shown below. Which of the names T, X, Y, r, B.T, C.X, C.Y, Z, and B.Z are visible in AMod's initialization code?   [A]

```
INTERFACE A;
    IMPORT B, C;
    FROM C IMPORT X, Y;
    TYPE T = B.T;
    VAR r: INTEGER := X + Y;
END A.

MODULE AMod EXPORTS A;
    FROM B IMPORT Z;
BEGIN
    ... (* Initialization code: what names are visible here? *)
END AMod.
```

4. Consider the interface A containing the procedure declaration P:

```
INTERFACE A;
    PROCEDURE P(VAR x: INTEGER; y: REF INTEGER): REAL;
END A;
```

Which of the following procedure declarations would be legal redeclarations of P if they appeared in a module exporting A? Note: The type REF INTEGER is a subtype of REFANY.
   a. PROCEDURE P(x: INTEGER; y: REF INTEGER): REAL = ...;
   b. PROCEDURE P(VAR x: INTEGER; y: REFANY): REAL = ...;
   c. PROCEDURE P(VAR x: INTEGER; y: REF INTEGER := NIL): REAL = ...;
   d. PROCEDURE P(VAR y: INTEGER; x: REF INTEGER): REAL = ...;

5. A program consists of the modules Main, ModA, ModB, and ModC. Main is the main module. ModA exports interface A, ModB exports interface B, and ModC exports interface C. ModB im-

ports C, Main imports A and C, and A imports B. There are no other imports or exports. Answer the following questions:

   a. Which units (interfaces and modules) must be compiled before compiling ModA? Which before ModB? Which before ModC? Which before Main?

   b. Specify a compilation order for all units in the program such that ModB is compiled as soon as possible.

   c. The program has been compiled correctly, but then you make a change to interface C. What units have to be recompiled?

6. Will module A_Client below print TRUE or FALSE for the value of A.top? Why? Can this situation exist in a program if each interface is exported by no more than one module?   [A]

```
MODULE A_Client;
    IMPORT A, Wr, Fmt, Stdio;
BEGIN
    Wr.PutText(Stdio.stdout, "top is " & Fmt.Bool(A.top) & "\n");
END A_Client;

INTERFACE A;
VAR top, bottom: BOOLEAN := FALSE;
END A;

MODULE A_1 EXPORTS A;
BEGIN top := NOT bottom;
END A_1;

MODULE A_2 EXPORTS A;
BEGIN bottom := NOT top;
END A_2;
```

7. A "harmless" change to a program is one that cannot affect the program's legality or meaning. For example, changing a comment is harmless. Suppose you add to an interface the declaration

```
CONST Harmless = 5;.
```

Is this change harmless? Assume that the addition causes no name conflicts within the interface, and that no other changes are made to the (working) program.

9

Generics

Many features in programming languages are designed to let you avoid writing the "same thing" more than once. Formal parameters allow you to write procedures that can operate on different data without being rewritten. Open array parameters allow you to write procedures that operate on arrays of any length.

However, these features do not solve all the problems. In particular, although the strong typing of Modula–3 promotes clarity and safety, you sometimes have to duplicate code that looks "mostly the same." As a trivial example, suppose you were writing a function that determined if one integer was larger than another:

```
PROCEDURE Bigger(a, b: INTEGER): BOOLEAN =
   BEGIN
      RETURN a > b;
   END Bigger;
```

Now, suppose you wanted a similar procedure that compared two floating-point numbers. The procedure would look identical except for the type of its parameters and perhaps its name:

```
PROCEDURE BiggerR(a, b: REAL): BOOLEAN =
   BEGIN
      RETURN a > b;
   END BiggerR;
```

This sort of code duplication—when applied to less trivial programs—is bothersome. Not only is it more work, but there is always the chance of introducing an error in one of the duplicate procedures. Modula–3's solution is to provide a mechanism for the creation of "generic" code that can be adapted to different situations without duplication.

9.1 Renamed Imports

Before discussing the generic facility, we'll take a short detour to discuss a feature of the IMPORT statement that was postponed in Chapter 8: *renamed imports*. An import statement of the form

    IMPORT A AS N;

is known as a *renamed import*. It has the effect of importing interface A but calling it by the name N. That is, if A declares the names U and V, then this statement allows you to refer to U and V as N.U an N.V. The name A is not made visible. The name N must not duplicate any other imported names. Although it is confusing, the statement

    IMPORT A AS N, N AS A;

is permitted, and has the effect of swapping the names A and N. That is, it makes any name U in interface A available as N.A and any name T in interface N available as A.T. Of course, you must not rename two different interfaces to be the same name (i.e., it is illegal to write IMPORT A AS N, B AS N). The statement IMPORT A AS A is allowed for completeness (rather than utility) and is the same as IMPORT A.

The renaming of interfaces takes effect before any FROM...IMPORT statements, even if the FROM...IMPORT precedes the renamed import statement. For example, the statements

    FROM N IMPORT U, V;
    IMPORT A AS N;

cause U and V to be imported from interface A. In this case—since no other interface is renamed to A—you could get the same effect by writing

    FROM A IMPORT U, V;
    IMPORT A AS N;

In both cases, the order of the statements doesn't matter.

We will see shortly how renamed imports are useful in implementing generics. However, renamed imports are occasionally useful by themselves when an imported interface name collides with an existing name in a module or interface. They can also help when you switch between alternate interfaces for a common service, as illustrated by the following example.

Example 9–1

Suppose you are writing a module that will make use of a "table" interface. Checking in the local libraries, you find two interfaces that provide different implementations of the table. One interface, TableWithArrays, implements tables as arrays, and the other, TableWithLists, implements tables as lists. The operations declared by each interface are the same. You're not sure which implementation will be best one to use, so you expect to try out both. How could you use renamed imports to minimize your work when you switch interfaces?

Solution You don't want to edit every use of the table facilities when you switch interfaces. [You don't want to change TableWithArrays.Lookup(...) to TableWithLists.Lookup(...), for example.] Therefore, write all uses of the table facilities using a neutral interface name, such as Table [e.g., Table.Lookup(...)]. Then, include either of the following import statements, depending on which interface you want:

```
IMPORT TablesWithArrays AS Table;   (* or *)
IMPORT TablesWithLists AS Table;
```

9.2 Generic Units

Now we return to generics. A *generic interface* is a kind of template. It defines variables, types, procedures, etc., based on a set of sample imported interfaces called the *formal imports*. An actual interface is created by *instantiating* the generic interface by supplying actual imported interfaces for the formal imports. Generic modules are defined in the same way, and are instantiated to create modules that export the instantiated generic interfaces.

The syntax for generic interfaces and modules is shown on page 166. A generic interface has this general form:

```
GENERIC INTERFACE GenInt(F, G, H );
IMPORT R, S, T;
...declarations...
END GenInt.
```

The identifier GenInt is the name of the generic interface. F, G, and H are the formal imports, which are used in the interface declarations as if the statement

```
IMPORT F, G, H;
```

had been written. (However, F, G, and H do not appear in actual import statements, and they do not have to name actual interfaces.) The interfaces R, S, and T are nonformal imports, which are used just as in nongeneric interfaces. The declarations in the generic interface can use names from F, G, and H as well as R, S, and T.

A generic module has the form

```
GENERIC MODULE GenMod(J, K, L);
IMPORT U, V, W;...
...declarations...
BEGIN
    ...statements...
END GenMod.
```

As with generic interfaces, the names J, K, and L are the formal imports and U, V, and W are the nonformal imports. The formal imports in the generic module will usually be the same as those in the generic interface, although this is not required. Notice that the generic module cannot have an EXPORTS clause or an UNSAFE keyword; we'll see how these are supplied later.

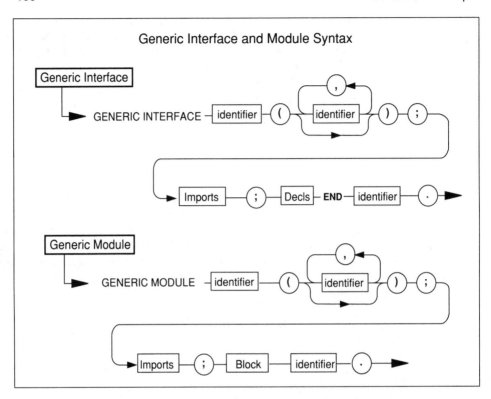

Generic Interface and Module Syntax

Example 9–2

Below is a generic interface, ArrayServices, with a single formal import, Element. The SRC
Modula–3 interface Wr is also imported, but it is not a formal import.

```
GENERIC INTERFACE ArrayServices(Element);
IMPORT Wr;
EXCEPTION EmptyArray;
PROCEDURE Max(READONLY anArray: ARRAY OF Element.T): Element.T;
    (* Return the largest element of the array *)
PROCEDURE Write(wr: Wr.T; READONLY anArray: ARRAY OF Element.T);
    (* Write out all elements of the array *)
END ArrayServices.
```

Accompanying this generic interface would be a generic module such as the following. (This
implementation is correct but has some deficiencies that are discussed later.)

```
GENERIC MODULE ArrayServices(Element);
IMPORT Wr, Fmt;
```

```
PROCEDURE Max(READONLY anArray: ARRAY OF Element.T)
    : Element.T RAISES {EmptyArray} =
    VAR biggest := FIRST(Element.T);
    BEGIN
      IF NUMBER(anArray) = 0 THEN RAISE EmptyArray; END;
      FOR i := FIRST(anArray) TO LAST(anArray) DO
        IF anArray[i] > biggest THEN biggest := anArray[i]; END;
      END;
      RETURN biggest;
    END Max;

PROCEDURE Write(wr: Wr.T; READONLY anArray: ARRAY OF Element.T)
    RAISES {EmptyArray} =
    BEGIN
      IF NUMBER(anArray) = 0 THEN RAISE EmptyArray; END;
      FOR i := FIRST(anArray) TO LAST(anArray) DO
        Wr.PutText(wr, Fmt.Int(i) & " " & Element.Format(anArray[i]) & "\n");
      END;
    END Write;
BEGIN
END ArrayServices.
```

9.3 Instantiations

A generic unit cannot be included in a program directly. It must be converted into a normal interface or module by a two-step process known as instantiation. In instantiation, you first locate or write "actual" interfaces to use in place of the formal imports. Then, you create an instantiated interface by naming the generic unit and supplying the actual interfaces.

The syntax for generic instantiations is shown on page 168. Let's start with the generic interface GenInt:

```
GENERIC INTERFACE GenInt(F, G, H );
IMPORT R, S, T;
...declarations...
END GenInt.
```

An instantiation of GenInt looks like this:

```
INTERFACE NewInt = GenInt(A, B, C) END NewInt.
```

The name of the new interface is NewInt. The new interface is formed from the generic interface GenInt by substituting the actual interfaces A, B, and C for the formal imports F, G, and H. This substitution is accomplished with renamed imports. That is, the net effect of the above instantiation is the same as if you had inserted some renamed imports into a copy of GenInt:

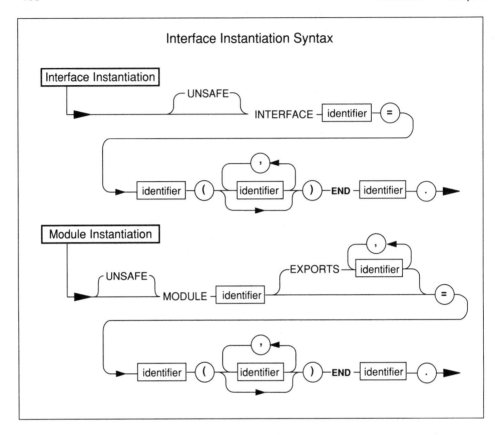

```
INTERFACE NewInt;
IMPORT A AS F, B AS G, C AS H;   (* Added *)
IMPORT R, S, T;   (* Copied from GenInt *)
(* Declarations copied from GenInt *)
END NewInt.
```

Modules can also be instantiated, like this:

```
MODULE NewMod EXPORTS NewInt = GenMod(A,B,C) END NewMod.
```

This instantiation creates module NewMod from the generic module GenInt as if by copying GenInt and renaming the formal imports J, K, and L to be A, B, and C. (If the EXPORTS clause is omitted, EXPORTS NewMod would be assumed.)

In general, generic interfaces and modules are instantiated in pairs, so that each new interface is matched by a module that exports it. A single generic interface and module can be instantiated any number of times in the same program. Each newly instantiated unit is given a new name, and is treated just like a nongeneric unit in the program.

Example 9–3

The generic ArrayServices units from Example 9–2 can be instantiated to provide services on integer arrays in the following fashion. First, you must create an actual interface—IntegerElement, say—to replace Element in the generic. By inspecting the generic units, you can see that the following declarations are used from Element:

Element.T   the array element type

Element.Format   a procedure that returns the string representation of an element

This suggests that the IntegerElement interface would have to include at least the following items. (It could include other declarations that don't happen to be used by ArrayServices.)

```
INTERFACE IntegerElement;
TYPE T = INTEGER;
PROCEDURE Format(a: INTEGER): TEXT;
END IntegerElement.
```

Once the IntegerElement interface is in place, you can instantiate the generic interface.

```
INTERFACE IntegerArrayServices = ArrayServices(IntegerElement)
END IntegerArrayServices.
```

Finally, we need modules to implement both IntegerArrayServices and IntegerElement. IntegerArrayServices can be built by instantiation:

```
MODULE IntegerArrayServices = ArrayServices(IntegerElement)
END IntegerArrayServices.
```

However, the **IntegerElement** module would have to be written

```
MODULE IntegerElement;
IMPORT Fmt;
PROCEDURE Format(a: T): TEXT =
    BEGIN
        RETURN Fmt.Int(a);
    END Format;
END IntegerElement.
```

The generic and instantiated units are shown in Figure 9–1.

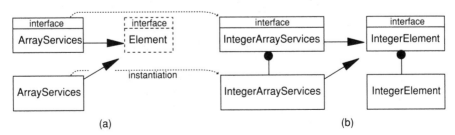

Figure 9–1   Generic units (a) and after instantiation (b).

9.4 Using Generics

The Modula–3 generic facility may seem somewhat cumbersome for simple generics. In the ArrayServices example, you only want to change the array element type and provide a single output procedure, but you have to create a special interface and module (IntegerEle-ment) for the instantiation. The compensation for this burden is that the Modula–3 facility is very straightforward and general. It is easy to parameterize generic modules with any set of declarations: constants, procedures, types, exceptions, etc.

When writing a generic unit, keep in mind the possible instantiations that might be attempted. It is all too easy to write the generics in a way that works for some instantiations and not others. For example, the ArrayServices generic from Example 9–2 on page 166 works fine when the element type is an ordinal or floating-point type. However, what would happen if Element.T were a record or reference type? In that case, the module instantiated from the ArrayServices generic would fail to compile because:

1. The built-in FIRST function used in the initialization of biggest is not applicable to record or reference types.

2. The > relational operator used in the loop is not applicable to record or reference types.

To fix these problems, the Element interface must provide type-independent versions of FIRST and >.

Example 9–4

A better version of ArrayServices will assume that the Element interface also contains Great-er(a, b), a procedure that returns TRUE if the first element is greater than the second; and First(), a procedure that returns the smallest value of type Element.T. Here is a version of the ArrayServices generic module that uses these new functions:

```
GENERIC MODULE ArrayServices(Element);
IMPORT Wr, Fmt;

PROCEDURE Max(READONLY anArray: ARRAY OF Element.T): Element.T =
    VAR biggest := Element.First();
    BEGIN
        FOR i := FIRST(anArray) TO LAST(anArray) DO
            IF Element.Greater(anArray[i], biggest) THEN biggest := anArray[i]; END;
        END;
        RETURN biggest;
    END Max;

PROCEDURE Write(wr: Wr.T; READONLY anArray: ARRAY OF Element.T) =
    BEGIN
        FOR i := FIRST(anArray) TO LAST(anArray) DO
            Wr.PutText(wr, Fmt.Int(i) & " " & Element.Format(anArray[i]) & "\n");
        END;
    END Write;
BEGIN
END ArrayServices.
```

Then, here are the new versions of IntegerElement:

```
INTERFACE IntegerElement;
TYPE T = INTEGER;
PROCEDURE Greater(a, b: T): BOOLEAN;
PROCEDURE First(): T;
PROCEDURE Format(a: T): TEXT;
END IntegerElement;

MODULE IntegerElement;
IMPORT Fmt;
PROCEDURE Greater(a, b: T): BOOLEAN =
    BEGIN
        RETURN a>b;
    END Greater;

PROCEDURE First(): T =
    BEGIN
        RETURN FIRST(INTEGER);
    END First;

PROCEDURE Format(a: T): TEXT=
    BEGIN
        RETURN Fmt.Int(a);
    END Format;

BEGIN
END IntegerElement.
```

9.5 Exercises

Answers to the exercises marked "[A]" appear in Appendix D.

1. Which of the following statements about the renamed import "IMPORT A AS B" are true?   [A]
   a. A and B cannot be the same name.
   b. The name A cannot be used at the top level of the enclosing interface or module as a variable name.
   c. The name B cannot be used at the top level of the enclosing interface or module as a variable name.
   d. The effect of the import "FROM B IMPORT N" is not changed by "IMPORT A AS B."
   e. The import "FROM B IMPORT N" would have a different meaning depending on whether it preceded or followed "IMPORT A AS B."
   f. It would be illegal to also include the import "IMPORT B AS A."
   g. It would be illegal to also include the import "IMPORT A AS C."
   h. It would be illegal to also include the import "IMPORT C AS B."
   i. It would be illegal to also include the import "FROM C IMPORT A."

2. Which of the following statements about generic units are true? Some questions refer to this declaration: [A]

```
GENERIC INTERFACE Table(F);
IMPORT Z;
...
END Table.
```

   a. It would be illegal to instantiate Table with an actual interface named F.
   b. It would be illegal to instantiate Table with an actual interface named Z.
   c. Instantiations of interface Table cannot export a top-level variable named F.
   d. If N is a name defined in F, then a generic module Table could refer to F.N without including F as one of its formal imports.
   e. If a generic module does not contain an EXPORT clause, it is assumed to export a generic interface of the same name.
   f. An instantiation of a generic module can export a nongeneric interface.
   g. An instantiation of a generic interface can be exported by a nongeneric module.
   h. A generic interface cannot export anything.
   i. If a generic interface has no formal imports, it can be instantiated only once in a single program.
   j. A generic interface or module must be compiled before it is instantiated.

3. Instantiate a version of ArrayServices interface (Example 9–2 on page 166) to work on arrays of TEXT; assume the generic module in Example 9–4 on page 170. Write the TextElement interface and module, and write the appropriate instantiations.

4. Here is a type declaration and three procedures for a type Complex whose real and imaginary components are of type REAL. Construct a generic interface and module for type Complex so that the interface can be instantiated to use any of the floating-point types as the component type.

```
IMPORT Math;   (* see Listing B–9 on page 290 *)

TYPE Complex = RECORD
    real := 1.0;
    imag:= 0.0;
END;

PROCEDURE New(real, imag: REAL): Complex RAISES {NaN}=
    BEGIN
        RETURN Complex{real := real, imag := imag};
    END New;

PROCEDURE Plus(x, y: Complex): Complex =
    BEGIN
        RETURN Complex{real := x.real + y.real, imag := x.imag + y.imag}
    END Plus;

PROCEDURE Abs(x: Complex): REAL =
    BEGIN
        WITH K = x.real * x.real + x.imag * x.imag DO
            RETURN FLOAT(Math.sqrt(FLOAT(K, LONGREAL)), REAL);
        END;
    END Abs;
```

5. Below is a simple linear search procedure. Rewrite it as a generic procedure, allowing the client to choose both the Key and DataRecord types. Do not assume that DataRecord must be a record. Also write a sample generic actual interface to show what the client must provide to instantiate the generic.

```
TYPE
  Key = INTEGER;
  DataRecord = RECORD
    value: TEXT;
    key: Key;
  END;

PROCEDURE Search(k: Key; READONLY table: ARRAY OF DataRecord)
  : CARDINAL =
BEGIN
  FOR i := 0 TO LAST(table) DO
    IF k = table[i].k THEN RETURN i; END;
  END;
  RETURN NUMBER(table);
END Search;
```

10

Dynamic Programming

Dynamic programming refers to the set of language facilities and programming techniques which support the use of data structures that are allocated at run time (i.e., dynamically). Almost all large programs use dynamic allocation because it permits a program to adapt to the changing demands of different problems and input data.

A single program typically runs on computers of different sizes and handles problems of different sizes. A compiler, for example, will be called upon to compile both very small programs and very large programs. Some users of the compiler will have computers with lots of memory and others will have computers with limited memory. Without dynamic allocation in your programs, you have to declare variables capable of handling the largest problems you ever expect while not exceeding the resources of the smallest computer. With dynamic allocation, you expand your resources to match the problem—until the resources of the underlying computer are truly exhausted.

Although useful, dynamic programming comes with its own problems. The concepts involved can be confusing to new programmers, and dynamic programs are subject to a number of different kinds of bugs. Happily, Modula–3's dynamic programming facilities are both flexible and safe.

10.1 Basic Concepts

As we said earlier, a *variable* is an area in the computer's memory that can hold a set of values. The values are determined by the variable's *type*. All the variables we have used so far have been *declared* and given *names*. For example, the declaration

```
VAR x: INTEGER := 17;
```

creates an integer variable and gives it the name x and an initial value of 17. Wherever x is used in the program—subject to the name scoping rules—it stands for the declared variable. Figure 10–1 depicts this situation.

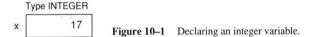

Figure 10–1   Declaring an integer variable.

When a variable declaration appears at the top level of a module or interface, it exists throughout the execution of the program. (Some books refer to these top-level variables as *static*.) All other declared variables are *local*—they are declared inside procedures and they exist only while the enclosing procedure is executing. New *instances* of local variables are created each time the procedure is called and are discarded each time the procedure returns.

You don't declare dynamic variables. Instead, you *allocate* them by calling the built-in function NEW. NEW allocates (creates) the new variable and returns a *reference* (sometimes called a *pointer*) to it. References are like other data values in Modula–3: They have a type—a *reference* type—and can be used in expressions and stored in variables. A reference to a dynamic INTEGER variable, for example, has type REF INTEGER. The reference type is, in fact, the argument that is passed to NEW in order to allocate the new variable: NEW(REF INTEGER) allocates a new INTEGER variable and returns a reference to it.

In Modula–3, a dynamic variable comes into existence when NEW is called, and remains in existence until no more references to it exist. It is then discarded automatically and the memory it occupied is made available for other uses, a process called *automatic garbage collection*. NEW performs the same default initializations that would occur if the new variable were declared instead of allocated.

Example 10–1

> The declaration below creates a reference variable, P, and initializes it to a reference to a newly allocated floating-point variable. The type of P, which is taken from the type of the initialization expression, is REF REAL. The result of the declaration is also depicted graphically:

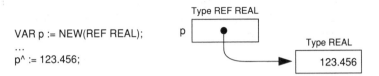

```
VAR p := NEW(REF REAL);
...
p^ := 123.456;
```

Whereas declared variables are accessed by writing their names, dynamic variables are used by applying the dereferencing operator (^, up-arrow or caret) to their references. If P is an expression whose value is a reference to an integer variable, then P^ refers to the integer variable, called P's *referent*. There is a special reference value, NIL, which references no variable; an attempt to apply ^ to a NIL value is a checked run-time error. When using dynamic variables, be sure to understand when you are manipulating references and when you are manipulating referenced objects.

Example 10–2

Here is a typical sequence of operations on references and dynamic variables. After each set of operations we show the results graphically. First, we allocate two reference variables, alpha and beta, and assign to each a reference to a newly allocated INTEGER variable:

VAR
    alpha := NEW(REF INTEGER);
    beta := NEW(REF INTEGER);

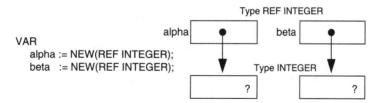

The INTEGER variables allocated above are uninitialized, so now we'll give them values:

BEGIN
    alpha^ := 17;
    beta^ := –34;

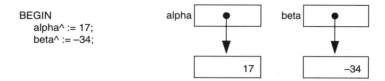

We can assign the value of the variable referenced by alpha to the variable reference by beta:

beta^ := alpha^;

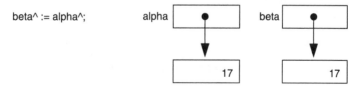

We can also assign the reference alpha to beta. Now we can refer to the same variable as either alpha^ or beta^. Notice that this leaves the variable formerly referenced by beta with no active references, so it can be discarded:

beta := alpha

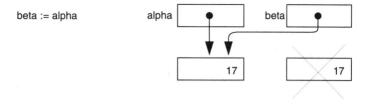

Finally, we set beta to NIL. Any attempt to reference beta^ will now cause an error:

beta := NIL;

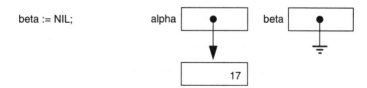

10.2 Reference Types

A reference type usually has the form REF T for some type T. The values of the reference type are references to variables of type T, which is called the *referent type*. There is also a built-in type, REFANY, which contains all references.

The complete story is more complicated. Modula–3 reference types can be either *traced* or *untraced*. The REF T types are the traced types, and REFANY—another traced type—contains all traced references. Traced reference types are monitored at run time by the garbage collector; when no traced references to an object remain, the garbage collector reclaims the object's storage. Untraced references, which include the built-in type AD-DRESS and the types UNTRACED REF T, are ignored by the garbage collector. (See the discussion beginning on page 258.) Object types are also classified as reference types, and can be traced or untraced (see Chapter 11). Finally, a reference type may be *branded* (see page 188). The complete, nonobject reference type syntax is summarized in the box below. The remainder of this section is concerned with the traced, nonobject reference types.

10.2.1 Operations with Reference Types

A value of type REF T is either NIL or a reference to some variable of type T. We've already seen examples of REF INTEGER, REF REAL, etc. Since different reference types cannot be mixed in operations, it's important to remember that the types REF T1 and REF T2 are the same only if T1 is the same type as T2 (page 60). The types REF [10..20] and REF INTEGER, for example, are different reference types.

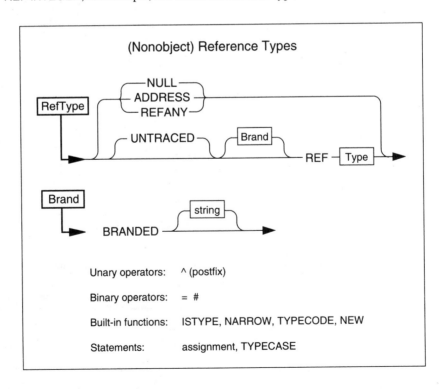

There are several operations you can use with reference types:

NEW(RT)   NEW returns a reference to a newly allocated variable of type T.
                  RT must be a reference type REF T. If T is an open array or record
                  type, NEW can take additional arguments.

^   Applied to a reference of type REF T, the postfix dereference op-
                  erator (^) returns a writable designator to a variable of type T. It is
                  a checked run-time error to apply ^ to NIL.

=, #   Two reference values are equal only if they refer to the same vari-
                  able, or are both NIL.

.   If P is a reference to a record, then P.f is shorthand for P^.f.

[ ]   If P is a reference to an array, then P[i] is shorthand for P^[i].

Both operands of = and # must be of the same reference type, or one must be REFANY
(page 183).

Example 10–3

Here are some declarations involving reference types:

```
VAR
    p0: REF INTEGER;
    p1 := NEW(REF INTEGER);
    p2 := NEW(REF INTEGER);
    p3 := p1;
    p4, p5 : REF INTEGER := NIL;
    p6 := NEW(REF REAL);
    p7 := NEW(REF RECORD a:=10; END);
```

Given these declarations, the following expressions have the indicated values and types:

p0	(* contains either NIL or a reference to some integer variable *)
p1	(* a reference to an integer variable; type REF INTEGER *)
p1^	(* designates an integer variable *)
p1 = p2	(* FALSE; p1 and p2 refer to different variables *)
p0 = p1	(* FALSE, p0 could not refer to the same variable as p1 *)
p1^ = p2^	(* may be TRUE or FALSE;
	p1^ and p2^ have not been given values *)
p1 = p3	(* TRUE *)
p1^ = p3^	(* TRUE always since p1=p3 *)
p1 = p4	(* FALSE *)
p4 = p5	(* TRUE *)
p1 = p6	(* illegal! can't mix different reference types *)
p4^	(* causes a run-time error because p4 is NIL *)
p7.a	(* a record field designator, with current value 10 *)

The only other interesting operation on fixed reference types is assignment. If both
the left-hand side (LHS) and the right-hand side (RHS) of an assignment are fixed reference types, they must be the same type for assignment to be permitted. The effect is to
copy the RHS reference into the LHS variable; the former reference stored in the LHS

variable is discarded. We will see in Section 10.4 on page 183 that fixed reference types and the open REFANY type can be mixed in assignments.

10.2.2 References to Records

You can create records dynamically and use them like declared records. Modula–3 includes some shortcuts to make dynamic records as convenient as declared ones. For example, here is how you would create two Point variables, one allocated on the stack and one allocated dynamically:

```
TYPE Point = RECORD radius, theta: REAL END;
VAR
    point1: Point;
    point2 := NEW(REF Point);
```

You can set the fields of a dynamic record when you create it, by adding the field assignments to the call on NEW. The following declarations create two Point variables with the same initial values:

```
VAR
    point1 := Point{ radius := FLOAT(Math.sqrt(2.0D0)), theta := Math.Pi/2.0 };
    point2 := NEW(REF Point,
        radius := FLOAT(Math.sqrt(2.0D0)),
        theta := Math.Pi / 2.0
```

You can also use fields in a dynamic record just as in a declared record. You don't have to use the dereference operator:

```
point1.radius := point2.radius;   (* same as point1.radius := point2^.radius *)
```

However, you must be aware that point2 is really a reference, and use the ^ operator if you want to refer to the whole record instead of the reference. For example, here is how you would copy the point1 record into the point2 record:

```
point2^ := point1;   (* the ^ is required *)
```

10.2.3 References to Arrays

You can also create arrays dynamically and use them like declared arrays. Here are two array variables, one of which is allocated dynamically:

```
TYPE HoursWorkedPerDay = ARRAY [1..31] OF REAL;
VAR
    fredsHours: HoursWorkedPerDay;
    sallysHours := NEW(REF HoursWorkedPerDay);
```

You cannot set the elements of a dynamic array in the call to NEW, as you can for records. Instead, you must use an assignment statement:

sallysHours^ := HoursWorkedPerDay{0.0, ..};

You can subscript a dynamic array without dereferencing it, but other uses of the array (such as in calls to FIRST or LAST) must include the ^ operator:

```
VAR totalHours := 0.0;
...
FOR day := FIRST(sallysHours^) TO LAST(sallysHours^) DO
    totalHours := totalHours + sallysHours[day];   (* same as sallysHours^[day] *)
END;
```

10.2.4 Using Dynamic Open Arrays

A very useful data structure in Modula–3 is a reference to an open array. When you declare a fixed array variable, you must know at compile time the number of elements that the array will hold. That is, if currentLength were a variable, you could not declare an array as, say,

```
VAR vector: ARRAY [1..currentLength] OF INTEGER;   (* Illegal! *)
```

Open arrays are the solution. We saw on page 102 how open array parameters can adapt to different sizes of arguments, but the argument arrays themselves were always assumed to be fixed (or to be other open array parameters). To create arrays whose bounds are determined at run time, you must dynamically allocate an open array. For example, you could declare the vector array above like this:

```
TYPE Vector = REF ARRAY OF INTEGER;
...
VAR vector := NEW(Vector, currentLength);
```

The call to NEW creates a reference to an array whose index type is [0..currentLength–1]. The second argument to NEW must be the length of the array to allocate.

More generally, if RefOpenArray is a reference to an array with k open dimensions, a new array can be allocated by calling the NEW function in this way:

```
NEW(RefOpenArray, n1, n2,..., nk)
```

The integer values $n_1, n_2,..., n_k$ are the sizes of the new array in each of its k open dimensions. You must supply a size for all open dimensions when allocating an open array reference. As with other open arrays, the index values in the open dimension range from 0 through n–1, where n is the size of the dimension. (n can be zero, but not negative.)

Example 10–4

> A baseball scorekeeper keeps a tally of how many runs, hits, and errors each player had in each of his team's games during a week. The information is kept in an $N_P \times N_G \times 3$ array, where N_P is the number of players and N_G is the number of names. The WeeklyStats function returns an array of the correct size for the week: The SetStats procedure stores the statistics for one player in one game in the array.

```
TYPE
    Stat = {Runs, Hits, Errors};
    Stats = ARRAY Stat OF CARDINAL;
    StatArray = ARRAY OF ARRAY OF Stats;

PROCEDURE WeeklyStats(nGames, nPlayers: CARDINAL): REF StatArray =
    BEGIN
            RETURN NEW(REF StatArray, nGames, nPlayers);
    END WeeklyStats;

PROCEDURE SetStats(
    stats: REF StatArray;
    game, player, runs, hits, errors: CARDINAL) =
    BEGIN
        stats[game, player] := Stats{runs, hits, errors};
    END SetStats;
```

10.3 A List Example

A declared array contains a compile-time-constant number of elements. Using references to open arrays, you can construct arrays of dynamic size, but you must know the needed size before you store elements in the array, and that size is fixed. In many programming situations, you are presented with the problem of holding data items without knowing beforehand how many there will be. The data may come and go during program execution. For this problem, it is better to hold the data in a *linked list,* or, simply, a *list.*

A list is a fundamental dynamic data structure that can contain any number of elements. There are many ways to implement such lists. The scheme we will discuss builds the list out of *cells,* one for each element stored in the list. Each cell holds a data item and a reference to the next element on the list. The entire list is represented by a reference to the first cell. The last cell in the list has NIL for its next-cell reference. The first element in the list is sometimes called the *head,* and the list after removing the first element is often called the *tail.* A diagram of this kind of list—with integers as the elements—is shown in Figure 10–2. Typical operations defined on lists include: add a value to the front (or back) of the list; find a value in a list; delete a value in a list, etc. In the following example, the List type doubles as the cell type.

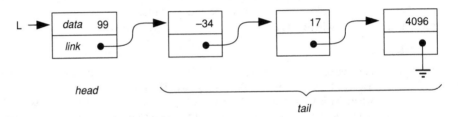

Figure 10–2 Linked list.

```
TYPE List = REF RECORD
    head: INTEGER := 0;                    (* Value of this cell *)
    tail: List := NIL;                     (* Rest of the list *)
END;
```

Notice that List was used in its own declaration. This is permitted because List is a reference type.

The empty list will be represented by a NIL pointer. The function used to build a list is Cons, which adds an element item to the front of list L and returns the new list. Because List is a record type, we can initialize the elements when calling NEW:

```
PROCEDURE Cons(item: INTEGER; list: List): List =
BEGIN
    RETURN NEW(List, head := item, tail := list);
END Cons;
```

The Length procedure determines the length of a list, visiting each cell and incrementing a counter.

```
PROCEDURE Length(list: List): CARDINAL =
VAR len: CARDINAL := 0;
BEGIN
    WHILE list # NIL DO INC(len); list := list.tail; END;
    RETURN len;
END Length;
```

Finally, Insert adds a new element in a list that is sorted in ascending order. Whereas the Length procedure used iteration over the list elements, Insert uses recursion. Which technique you use is largely a matter of personal preference. Iteration can be more efficient, but recursion is often simpler:

```
PROCEDURE Insert(item: INTEGER; list: List): List =
(* The elements of L are assumed to be sorted into ascending order. This procedure adds item
in its proper place on L, returning the new list. *)
    BEGIN
        IF list = NIL OR list.head >= item THEN
            list := Cons(item, list);  (* add to front *)
        ELSE
            list.tail := Insert(item, list.tail);
        END;
        RETURN list;
    END Insert;
```

10.4 The REFANY Type

The built-in type REFANY contains all traced reference types. That is, REFANY variables can contain values of any REF T type, including NIL. In Modula–3, REFANY is type-safe, which means that if you store a value of type REF INTEGER in a variable of type REFA-NY, the value is still identifiable as type REF INTEGER. When NEW is called with a traced reference type as its argument, NEW tags the newly created variable with a permanent indication of its *allocated type*. This type tag can be tested at run time by the Modula–3 system (Figure 10–3).

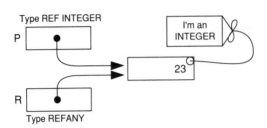

Figure 10–3 Run-time type tags on dynamic variables.

The type REFANY is a subtype of REF T, and the two types are assignable to each other. If the LHS of the assignment is a REFANY variable, the RHS can be any REFANY or REF T value. If the LHS is a REF T type and the RHS is REFANY, then a run-time check will occur to be sure the value assigned is actually a REF T.

Example 10–5

Consider the following declarations:

```
VAR
    any1: REFANY;
    any2: REFANY := NEW(REF REAL);
    fixed1: REF INTEGER;
```

Given these declarations, here are some possible assignment statements:

```
any1 := NEW(REF REAL);          (* OK *)
any1 := NEW(REF INTEGER);       (* OK *)
fixed1 := any1;                  (* OK, because any1 now holds
                                   a REF INTEGER *)
fixed1 := any2;                  (* Legal, but causes a run-time error
                                   because any2 is not a REF INTEGER*)
```

Similarly, the operands of the equality operators (= and #) can be REF T and REF-ANY types. Two references are equal if they refer to the same variable (or both are NIL). You cannot use the ^ (dereferencing) operator with REFANY values, since they have no referent type. However, you can use the built-in functions ISTYPE and NARROW, and the TYPECASE statement, to test the allocated types of REFANY values and convert them to fixed references:

ISTYPE(any, RT)   returns TRUE if the reference any is a member of the reference type RT (i.e., REF T, for some T).

NARROW(any, RT)   returns the reference any as a value of type RT (REF T), after checking to be sure that any is in fact a member of RT.

It is typical for the reference value any in the functions above to be a REFANY value. (The name NARROW refers to that function's ability to narrow down to a single type a value that could be of any reference type.) It is legal for the value of any to be NIL, but remember that NIL is a member of all reference types, so ISTYPE(NIL, RT) is always TRUE, for any reference type RT.

Example 10–6

Suppose we want to represent a list of integers and floating-point (REAL) values. One choice is to use an array whose element type is REFANY, storing in the array references to the integers and floating-point values. Here is a function that accepts such an array and returns the sum of all the elements as a REAL value. We take some care to guard against values of unexpected types.

```
PROCEDURE Sum(a: ARRAY OF REFANY) : REAL =
(* Sums all INTEGER and REAL references in the array *)
  VAR sum := 0.0;
  BEGIN
    FOR i := FIRST(a) TO LAST(a) DO
      IF a[i] = NIL THEN   (* Skip this value *)
      ELSIF ISTYPE(a[i], REF INTEGER) THEN
        WITH e = NARROW(a[i], REF INTEGER) DO
          sum := sum + FLOAT(e^);
        END;
      ELSIF ISTYPE(a[i], REF REAL) THEN
        WITH e = NARROW(a[i], REF REAL) DO sum := sum + e^; END;
      END (* IF *)
    END (* FOR *);
    RETURN sum;
  END Sum;
```

10.4.1 TYPECASE

The kind of type testing shown in Example 10–6 is so common when programming with open references that Modula–3 includes a special statement to simplify it: TYPECASE. In the TYPECASE statement, the control expression is a reference value and the alternative cases are type expressions. The type of the control expression is checked (as if by ISTYPE) until a match is found. Then, if an identifier follows the type expression, the identifier is bound (as if by WITH and NARROW) to the reference value. To test for a NIL value in the TYPECASE statement, use the built-in type NULL, an open reference type that contains only the value NIL.

Example 10–7

Here is the same function from Example 10–6, rewritten to take advantage of the TYPECASE statement.

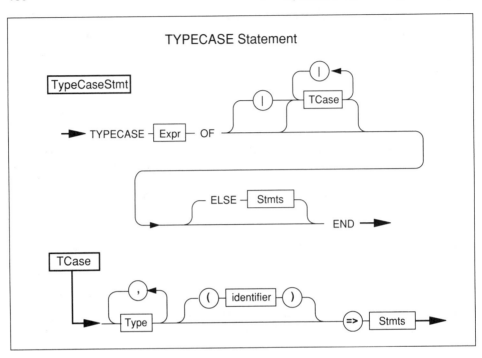

```
PROCEDURE Sum(a: ARRAY OF REFANY) : REAL =
    VAR sum := 0.0;
    BEGIN
        FOR i := FIRST(a) TO LAST(a) DO
            TYPECASE a[i] OF
            | NULL => (* skip *)
            | REF INTEGER (e) => sum := sum + FLOAT(e^);
            | REF REAL(e) => sum := sum + e^;
            ELSE (* Skip *)
            END (* TYPECASE *)
        END (* FOR *);
        RETURN sum;
    END Sum;
```

10.4.2 NULL

The built-in type NULL contains only a single value, NIL. NULL is a subtype of all reference types—traced, untraced, object, and procedure types—which allows NIL to be assigned to all those types.

The value NIL standing alone has type NULL, and therein lies a surprise for the unwary Modula–3 programmer. The effect of the declaration

```
VAR ref := NIL;
```

is to declare variable ref with type NULL. That is, the only value ref can hold is NIL. A good Modula–3 compiler would probably issue a warning on this declaration, since it appears nonsensical. (If you want a named constant for NIL, use a CONST declaration.) Be sure to specify an appropriate reference type for a variable initialized to NIL:

```
VAR
    ref1: REFANY := NIL;
    ref2: REF INTEGER := NIL
```

10.4.3   TYPECODE

There is one additional built-in function that is useful with traced reference types:

TYPECODE(ref)   returns a nonnegative integer code that uniquely identifies the allocated type of the reference ref (ref cannot be NIL)

TYPECODE(RT)   returns a nonnegative integer code that uniquely identifies the reference type RT (RT is REF T; RT cannot be REFANY)

You can use TYPECODE to obtain a token that identifies (traced) reference types. This token can be stored in data structures or printed out. A type's token is fixed for a single execution of a Modula–3 program, but may change between different executions.

Example 10–8

The function IsElementType below returns TRUE if all elements of an ARRAY OF REFANY parameter have a single, specified type. Since user-defined procedures cannot accept types as arguments, the function accepts the value returned by TYPECODE.

```
PROCEDURE IsElementType(
    a: ARRAY OF REFANY;
    typeCode: CARDINAL): BOOLEAN =
(* Returns TRUE if all elements of a have type code typeCode *)
VAR result := NUMBER(a) > 0;
BEGIN
    FOR i := FIRST(a) TO LAST(a) DO
        IF TYPECODE(a[i]) # typeCode THEN
            result := FALSE;
            EXIT;
        END;
    END;
    RETURN result;
END IsElementType;
```

To find out if all elements of array stuffList are of type REF INTEGER, the client can write

```
IF IsElementType(stuffList, TYPECODE(REF INTEGER)) THEN...
```

10.5 Introduction to Opaque Types

Reference types allow us to introduce one of Modula–3's more powerful abstraction and information-hiding facilities: the *opaque type*. The term *opaque* refers to the fact that the programmer implementing the type can hide the type's true characteristics from clients. To understand opaque types, you first have to understand subtypes.

10.5.1 Subtypes and Assignability

In Modula–3, certain types are classified as *subtypes* of other types. The subtype relationship, which was introduced on page 60, is generally used to determine type compatibility for assignment. However, subtypes become increasingly more important with reference types and (especially) object types.

When type S is a subtype of type T, we write S <: T. T is also referred to as a *supertype* of S. The subtype relationship is reflexive (i.e., T <: T) and transitive (i.e., if S <: T and T <: P, then S <: P). Here are the subtype relations for the reference types we have discussed so far. If T is any type:

        NULL <: REF T, and
        REF T <: REFANY

There is no subtype relation between different fixed reference types. That is, REF S <: REF T only if S and T are the same type. When S <: T, all elements of type S are also elements of type T. For example, all references of type REF T are also elements of the REFANY type.

We can now state the compile-time rule for assignment more precisely. A reference type R is assignable to a type L if R <: L, or if L <: R and R is not ADDRESS. When L <: R, a run-time check is needed to ensure that the value being assigned is a member of type L. (When R <: L, this is known at compile time.) The reference type compatibility rule for the = and # operators is the same: L = R is permitted as long as R is assignable to L or L is assignable to R. These rules hold for all reference types, including objects.

10.5.2 Declaring Opaque Types

An opaque type declaration for nonobject references has the form

        TYPE T <: REFANY;

This declares T to be an unspecified subtype of REFANY. That is, T is either REFANY or (more likely) REF S for some unspecified type S. The benefit of opaque types is in the ability to hide S from clients of the opaque type.

Example 10–9

The Rational interface below declares an opaque type T which will represent rational numbers. We must supply a "create" function (customarily named New) because you cannot call NEW for (nonobject) opaque reference types.

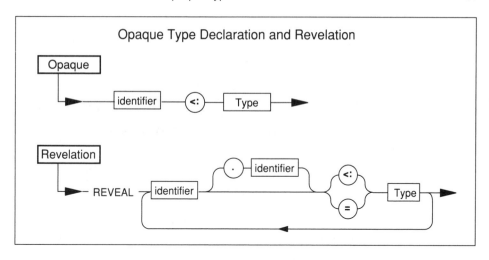

```
INTERFACE Rational;
TYPE T <: REFANY;
EXCEPTION Error;
PROCEDURE New(num: INTEGER; denom := 1): T RAISES {Error};
PROCEDURE Add(t1, t2: T): T;
...
END Rational.
```

From this interface declaration we know that Rational.T is a reference type, but we don't know its referent type.

The opaque type declaration is sufficient for use by clients, but somewhere in your Modula–3 program you must *reveal* the "real" type of each opaque type. This is done with a *revelation*, a kind of declaration which (for nonobject references) has the form

```
REVEAL T = BRANDED REF S;  or
REVEAL T = BRANDED "string" REF S;
```

The name T must be visible and defined as an opaque reference type; S can be any type. In the revelation, T can also be of the form Int.T if T is imported from interface Int. (The keyword BRANDED will be discussed on page 191.) Within the scope of the revelation, you can treat T as if it had been declared as REF S. Each opaque type must be revealed once and only once in the program.

Example 10–10

When an opaque type is declared in an interface, the revelation usually appears in the module implementing that interface. Here is an implementation of the Rational interface, which includes a revelation of Rational.T (Example 10–9) as a reference to a record containing a numerator and a denominator:

```
MODULE Rational;
REVEAL T = BRANDED REF RECORD
    n: INTEGER := 0;
    d: [1..LAST(INTEGER)] := 1;
    END;

PROCEDURE New(num: INTEGER; denom := 1): T RAISES {Error} =
    BEGIN
        IF denom = 0 OR denom = FIRST(INTEGER) THEN
            RAISE Error;
        ELSIF denom < 0 THEN
            num := −num;
            denom := −denom;
        END;
        RETURN NEW(T, n := num, d := denom);
    END New;

PROCEDURE Add(t1, t2: T): T = ...
... (* etc. *) ;
BEGIN
END Rational.
```

Notice that when the REVEAL declaration appears, the name T is already defined because it is visible from the exported interface Rational.

10.5.3 Using Opaque Types

Since opaque types are used to hide information, they almost always appear in interfaces, which are also designed to hide information. An opaque reference type is, nonetheless, a reference type and values of the type can be used where references are normally permitted. Opaque types can be used in declarations; in the TYPECASE statement; as arguments to ISTYPE, TYPECODE, and NARROW; and they can be assigned, passed to procedures as arguments, and tested for equality. Unless their revelation is visible, they cannot be dereferenced with ^ or created with NEW. (Opaque object types can be created with NEW; see page 216.)

Example 10–11

Here is a sample use of the Rational interface containing some legal and illegal uses of the opaque type Rational.T (Example 10–9 on page 188).

```
MODULE UsesRational;
IMPORT Rational;
VAR
    r: Rational.T;                       (* OK *)
    zero := Rational.New(0);             (* OK *)
    something := NEW(Rational.T);        (* Illegal! *)
    numerator := zero.n;                 (* Illegal! *)
    ...
END UsesRational.
```

The call of Rational.New(0) is the normal way of creating a new rational number. The call NEW(Rational.T) is illegal because NEW cannot be applied to opaque (nonobject) reference types. The reference to zero.n is an error because the referent type and its fields are hidden.

10.5.4 Branded Types

You will have noticed that in the revelation of an opaque reference type, the "definitive" type must be labeled with the keyword BRANDED. Branding can be applied only to reference (and object) types, and has the effect of "defeating" the structural type equivalence rules of Modula–3.

Branding a reference or object type makes that type different from all other types that would normally be the same under the structural equivalence rules. For example, if we declare types A and B as

```
TYPE
    A = BRANDED REF INTEGER;
    B = BRANDED REF INTEGER;
```

then types A and B are different, although both are still reference types with integer referents and can be used just like the REF INTEGER type. Without branding, the structural equivalence of types would allow programmers to defeat the security of opaque types, as illustrated in the following example.

Example 10–12

Without branding, if you discovered the structure of Rational.T (Example 10–10 on page 189), you could write this module :

```
MODULE KnowsTooMuch;
    IMPORTS Rational;
    TYPE IKnowWhatRationalIs = REF RECORD
        n: INTEGER := 0;
        d: [1..LAST(INTEGER)] := 1;
        END;
    VAR r := Rational.New(1);

    BEGIN
        TYPECASE r OF
        |   IKnowWhatRationalIs(r) => r.d := 0;
        END; ...
    END KnowsTooMuch;
```

The type IKnowWhatRationalIs has the same structure as the revelation of Rational.T, and therefore by structural equivalence it is the same type. Thus, the TYPECASE statement effectively grants KnowsTooMuch access to the internal representation of Rational.T. It is only because Rational.T is branded that Rational.T is not treated as the same as IKnowWhatRationalIs.

All revelations of opaque types must be branded, and therefore they are all distinct.

You can include a text string after the keyword BRANDED, in which case the string becomes the "brand." This may be useful for debugging or documentation, but you can't use the brand string to duplicate a brand. All brand strings in a program must be distinct, and this distinctness is checked when the program is assembled. Without a brand string, Modula–3 assigns a distinct brand for every occurrence of BRANDED in the program.

10.6 A Generic List Example

A simple integer list was developed in Section 10.3 on page 182. In this section we show part of a more realistic implementation that employs opaque types and makes the list element type generic. Functions Head, Tail, IsEmpty, and Empty are added to isolate the representations.

```
GENERIC INTERFACE List(Element);
(* Implements lists of Element.T *)
TYPE T <: REFANY;
PROCEDURE Empty(): T;
    (* returns an empty list *)
PROCEDURE IsEmpty(list: T): BOOLEAN;
    (* returns TRUE if list contains no elements *)
PROCEDURE Length(list: T): CARDINAL;
    (* the number of items in the list *)
PROCEDURE Head(list: T): Element.T;
    (* returns first item from a non-empty list *)
PROCEDURE Tail(list: T): T;
    (* returns the last n - 1 items from a non-empty list *)
PROCEDURE Cons(head: Element.T, tail: T): T;
    (* creates a new list *)
    ...(* Other operations not shown *)
END List.
```

The implementation of the interface is shown below. The internal structure of the list is the same as on page 183.

```
GENERIC MODULE List(Element);
REVEAL T = BRANDED REF RECORD
    head: Element.T;
    tail: T := NIL;
END;

PROCEDURE IsEmpty(list: T): BOOLEAN =
    BEGIN
        RETURN list = NIL;
END IsEmpty;

PROCEDURE Head(list: T): Element.T=
    BEGIN
        RETURN list.head;    (* Fails if IsEmpty(list) *)
    END Head;
```

```
PROCEDURE Tail(list: T): T =
  BEGIN
    RETURN list.tail; (* Fails if IsEmpty(list) *)
  END Tail;

PROCEDURE Cons(head: Element.T; tail: T): T =
  BEGIN
    RETURN NEW(T, head:= head; tail := tail);
  END Cons;
...
END List;
```

To use the generic list package, you have to instantiate the generic. To create a list of integers, for example, you first have to create an interface that exports the list element type:

```
INTERFACE Integer; TYPE T = INTEGER;... END Integer.
MODULE Integer; END Integer.
```

(A usable list package would have many more procedures in its interface and would need additional functions, such as Equal, in the element interface.) Then, you would create an IList ("integer list") interface and module:

```
INTERFACE IList = List(Integer); END IList.
MODULE IList = List(Integer); END IList.
```

Finally, here is a sample function, Iota, which uses IList to construct a list of the first N positive integers:

```
IMPORT IList;
PROCEDURE Iota(n: CARDINAL): IList.T =
  VAR list := IList.Empty();
  BEGIN
    FOR i := N TO 1 BY −1 DO
      list := IList.Cons(i, list);
    END;
  END Iota;
```

10.7 Exercises

Answers to the exercises marked "[A]" appear in Appendix D.

1. Given the declarations below, which of the following pairs of types are the same? Which are related by the subtype relation?   [A]

```
TYPE
    IntPtr = REF INTEGER;
    Int = INTEGER;
    Sub = [0..10];
```

a. REF INTEGER and IntPtr
b. IntPtr and REFANY
c. REF INTEGER and REF Int
d. REF Int and REF Sub
e. REF Sub and REF [5-5..5+5]

2. What types cannot be used as the referent of a traced reference type?

3. Which types can be branded? When must brands be used?

4. Suppose that type T were defined by

    TYPE T <: REFANY;

   Which of the following revelations of T would not be permitted?   [A]
   a. REVEAL T = BRANDED RECORD a, b: CHAR END;
   b. REVEAL T = BRANDED REF ARRAY OF INTEGER;
   c. REVEAL T = REF CHAR;
   d. REVEAL T = INTEGER;

5. This exercise refers to the integer list example in Section 10.3 on page 182.
   a. Rewrite the Insert procedure, using iteration instead of recursion.
   b. Rewrite the Length procedure, using recursion instead of iteration.
   c. Write a function Delete with the specification shown:

      PROCEDURE Delete(list: List, n: INTEGER): L;
      (* Delete the first element of list with value n, if any, and return the resulting list. If no such
      element exists, return the original list unchanged. *)

6. In a TYPECASE statement, why should any NULL type alternative be the first one?

7. Which of the following calls of NEW are illegal, and why? Assume that Opaque is an opaque,
   non-object reference type whose revelation is not visible.   [A]
   a. NEW(ARRAY OF INTEGER, 10)
   b. NEW(REF RECORD a, b: Opaque END, a:= NIL)
   c. NEW(REF INTEGER, 34)
   d. NEW(REF ARRAY OF ARRAY OF INTEGER)
   e. NEW(REFANY)
   f. NEW(Opaque)
   g. NEW(REF Opaque)

8. Add to the generic List interface and module (Section 10.6 on page 192) a function Iterate which
   takes as arguments a list and a procedure. Iterate should apply the procedure to each element of
   the list. Show how you would use this new feature in a client module to sum the elements of an
   integer list.

9. Discuss when it would be appropriate to use generics to generate different list packages, and
   when it would be appropriate to use a single list package whose element type is REFANY.

11

Objects

The surest way to improve programming productivity is so obvious that many programmers miss it. Simply write less code. Every module, procedure, and statement you can avoid means one less to design, write, debug, and maintain. But, how do you do the same work with less code? Part of the answer is to reuse existing code—either pieces of other programs you can adapt to the current problem, or pieces of code already in your program that can be made to do double duty.

We saw in Chapter 9 how generics could be used to produce modules and interfaces that could easily be adapted to different situations. Object-oriented programming (OOP) offers a different and more powerful technique for customizing existing code to new purposes. Whereas modules records let you express the "has a" relationship between program components, OOP lets you define "is a" relationships between data types. The "is a" relationship is fundamental to reuse, since it allows much of an existing body of code to be reused in a more specialized setting. Only the exceptions ("A is a B, *except...*") need to be programmed. See the examples in the following table

Using "has a" relationships	Using "is a" relationships
"A car has four wheels, an engine, and carries people. A truck has four wheels, an engine, and carries people and cargo."	"A car has four wheels, an engine, and carries people. A truck is like a car, but also carries cargo."
"To service a car, add gas, check the oil, and wash the windshield. To service a truck, fill with gas, check the oil, wash the windshield, and check that the cargo is secure."	"To service a car, add gas, check the oil, and wash the windshield. To service a truck, do the same things, but also check that the cargo is secure."
"The procedure HSpeed takes a Horse as a parameter and returns how fast the horse is moving. The procedure MSpeed takes a Mouse as a parameter and returns how fast the mouse is moving."	"Animals move. Horse and Mouse are kinds of animals. The Speed method can be applied to any Animal to determine how fast the animal is going.

11.1 Basic Concepts

Object-oriented programming (OOP) is one of the newest programming methodologies to become popular. It is both a "way of looking at the world" and a set of specific techniques that require support from programming languages. Although sometimes characterized as a "revolution," it is in fact an evolution from older techniques, building upon the ideas of abstract data types, information hiding, and modularization.

Because OOP is still new, the programming language community is still trying out different ways to implement it and use it. Some languages, such as SmallTalk and Eiffel, use objects as their central concept; these languages depend on OOP completely. Some designers have grafted object-oriented features onto more familiar languages, such as Pascal and C. Some programmers profit from adhering to the OOP philosophy even when their languages don't truly support objects.

Modula–3 supports object-oriented programming with a specific set of features that is integrated with the rest of the language. OOP is not the central concept in Modula–3, but neither is it an afterthought. In fact, the concepts of subtyping and opaque types introduced in Chapter 10 achieve their greatest power with objects.

The basic concepts underlying OOP include encapsulation, inheritance, polymorphism, and dynamic binding. We'll look at each of these concepts in the following sections.

11.1.1 Encapsulation

The programming style we have discussed so far in this book is based on traditional data abstraction. Typically, you declare a new data type (e.g., a record) and define some procedures that operate upon variables of that type. The data type and procedures are encapsulated in an interface and its associated module. The type and operations together are referred to as an abstract data type (ADT). If the new data type as opaque, clients can only operate on the data by calling the public procedures.

Objects achieve a similar kind of data abstraction. In fact, without inheritance and other OOP facilities, the differences would be minor. Like the traditional ADT, an object type (or *class*) is a kind of a record containing a set of data components. However, the procedures that operate on objects of that type are also specified as part of the object type—as a list of *methods*. Thus, an object type encapsulates both its data and its operations, instead of relying on another mechanism like the interface.

Let's look at a side-by-side comparison of a record-based ADT and an object-based ADT. (We haven't discussed the syntax of object declarations yet, but you should have no trouble following the example.) The ADT we'll define is a "person" whose only characteristics are a name and a birth date. We'll supply operations to create new people and to inquire about the age of a person in a given year. First, the interface declaration:

Record-based interface	Object-based interface

INTERFACE Person;
TYPE
    Year = [1900..2000];
    T <: REFANY;
 	
PROCEDURE Age(r: T; asOf: Year)
    : CARDINAL;
PROCEDURE New(
    name: TEXT;
    birthDate: Year): T;
END Person.
	INTERFACE Person;
	TYPE
	    Year = [1900..2000];
	    T<: Public;
	    Public = OBJECT
	    METHODS
	      age(asOf: Year)
	        : CARDINAL;
	      init(name: TEXT;
	        birthdate: Year): T
	    END;
	END Person.

In both interfaces, the exported ADT is a type named T. In the record interface, we define the type as an opaque reference type (a subtype of REFANY) and include two procedures: Age, which returns the age of the person, and New, which creates a person. In the object interface, T is defined as an opaque object type (a subtype of a type Public) which has two methods, age and init. The init method corresponds to the New procedure in a way we'll see in a moment. (The capitalization of the names is not completely random; it follows the conventions in Appendix A.) Here are how the interfaces are used:

Record-based client	Object-based client

IMPORT Person;
 	
...
 	
VAR henry := Person.New(
    "Henry", 1952);
BEGIN
    IF Person.Age(henry, 1991) > 65 THEN
      (* Henry's pretty old ... *)
	IMPORT Person;
	
	...
	
	VAR henry := NEW(Person.T).init(
	    "Henry", 1952);
	BEGIN
	    IF henry.age(1991) > 65 THEN
	      (* Henry's pretty old ...*)

Notice the conceptional difference between using an object type and using a traditional ADT. A traditional abstract type is passive; it is a collection of data that must be "given" to the appropriate procedure to be operated upon. An object, on the other hand, is active. You can think of an object as being able to operate on itself through its list of methods. To see this, compare the two operations:

```
Person.Age(henry, 1956)          (* in the record-based ADT *)
henry.age(1956)                  (* in the object-based ADT *)
```

In the first expression, the procedure seems more important; this can be called procedure-oriented programming. In the second version, the object (henry) is; this is called object-oriented programming.

In the record-based interface, a New procedure allocates and returns an object. In the object-based interface, the client simply called NEW directly, and then applies an initialization method to the result. Recall (page 190) that you cannot apply NEW to an opaque reference type; this restriction is lifted for opaque object types.

Here are the modules for each ADT implementation:

Record-based module	Object-based module

MODULE Person;
REVEAL T = BRANDED
REF RECORD
   name: TEXT;
   birth: Year;
END;
	MODULE Person;
	REVEAL T = Public BRANDED
	OBJECT
	   name: TEXT;
	   birth: Year;
	OVERRIDES
	   init := Init;
	   age := Age;
	END;

PROCEDURE New(
   name: TEXT;
   date: Year): T =
BEGIN
   RETURN NEW(T,
     name := name,
     birth := date);
END SetBirthDate;
	PROCEDURE Init(
	   self: T; name: TEXT;
	   date: Year): T =
	BEGIN
	   self.birth := date;
	   self.name := name;
	   RETURN self;
	END Init;

PROCEDURE Age
   (r: T; asOf: Year)
   : CARDINAL =
BEGIN
   RETURN asOf – r.birth;
   END Age;
BEGIN
END Person.
	PROCEDURE Age(
	   self: T; asOf: Year)
	   : CARDINAL =
	BEGIN
	   RETURN asOf - self.birth;
	   END Age;
	BEGIN
	END Person.

The modules reveal the internal structure of the ADT (a string and a Year) and provide bodies for the operations. In the object-oriented module, the methods are first initialized to procedures which are provided in the module. Notice that the procedures include an initial parameter, self, that does not appear in the method signatures in the interface. This first parameter, which is mandatory, is the object being operated upon. This parameter is needed because the method call henry.age(1991) is really implemented as the procedure call Age(henry, 1991). (Methods in Modula–3 are programmed just like ordinary procedures. This is convenient but seldom seen in other object-oriented languages.)

Implementation   It might be useful to digress for a moment and talk about how objects are implemented. You may think that objects are magic or hopelessly huge and inefficient. In fact, they are basically just dynamically allocated records. As you can see in Figure 11–1, the record henry contains only the two declared fields; the New and Age procedures are called directly and don't involve the record at all. The object henry (Figure 11–2) is simply the same record with an extra field that locates a *method suite* (another record) associated with object type Person.T. All objects of type Person.T will point to the same method suite, which contains references to the method procedures. The space overhead in each object is therefore small: only one reference per object. Method calls do involve calling procedures through two levels of references. However, this bit of extra work has great benefits, as we'll see in the next section.

Figure 11–1   Record implementation of a Person.T

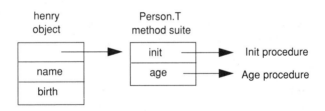

Figure 11–2   Object implementation of a Person.T.

11.1.2 Inheritance

So far, it looks as if objects are just another syntax for the encapsulation of procedures in a record type. In fact, however, we have set the stage for the mechanisms that implement the "is a" relationship among objects: *inheritance* and *polymorphism*.

Reference types have only a single hierarchical level: REFANY is the "root" supertype and all other reference types are immediate subtypes of it. (We're ignoring the NULL type since it's not very interesting.) Object types, unlike reference types, can be defined in type hierarchies that are arbitrarily deep. For example, Figure 11–3 shows an object type hierarchy. In it, object types B and C are subtypes (or *descendants*) of A, B and E are descendants of C, and F is a descendant of D. Object supertypes are also called *ancestors*, so you can say that A is the ancestor of B, D is the ancestor of F, etc. The terms *ancestor* and *descendant* are transitive, so you can say that A is an ancestor of F, or E is a descendant of A. An object type can have any number of descendants, but only one (immediate) ancestor.

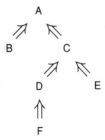

Figure 11–3   An object type derivation tree.

The important point is that descendant types *inherit* the fields and methods of all their ancestors, and the descendant can also add its own fields and methods. The descendant "is an" ancestor, with some extra (or different) abilities. For example, from the diagram in Figure 11–3, an object of type F would have all the fields and methods it declared, plus those declared by type D, plus those declared by type C, plus those declared by type A. In this way a descendant can customize its ancestors, adding new information without repeating the common declarations.

Example 11–1

A "point" has a position given by (x, y) coordinates and a method for moving that translates the point by some amount. A type representing it might be defined as

```
TYPE Point = OBJECT
    x, y: REAL := 0.0;
METHODS
    move(deltaX, deltaY: REAL) := Move;
END;

PROCEDURE Move(self: Point; deltaX, deltaY: REAL) =
    BEGIN
        self.x := self.x + deltaX;
        self.y := self.y + deltaY;
    END Move;
```

A "big point" is like a point, but it also has a size. It can be defined as a descendant of Point, like this:

```
TYPE BigPoint = Point OBJECT
    size: REAL := 1.0;
END;
```

Since BigPoint is a descendant of Point, it has the coordinates of a Point and the move method. That is, if big is a variable of type BigPoint, you could write

```
big.x := 0.0;
big.size := 100.0;
big.move(1.0, 0.0);
```

Inheritance can be used to model many real-world situations, which are characterized by layers of abstractions. Higher-level abstractions are more general with less detail. Lower-level abstractions typically supply more detail and differentiate between several instances of the general abstraction. Inheritance allows you to build new object types by extending existing ones.

Implementation   Inheritance simply adds new fields to objects and method suites. Consider the types defined in Example 11–1 on page 200. The structure of the objects and types are shown in Figure 11–2. You see that a BigPoint object is just a record with all the fields from Point plus the size field. The method suite for BigPoint has slots (fields) for all the methods of Point, plus any new ones defined in BigPoint. (There were no new methods defined in the example.)

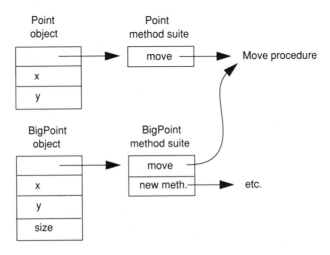

Figure 11–4   Object implementation of Point and BigPoint.

11.1.3 Polymorphism

The second important characteristic of object types is *polymorphism*. Polymorphism means the ability of an operation to do the appropriate thing depending on the type of the operand. In strongly typed programming languages without OOP facilities, this is not usually possible—the language designers go to great lengths to restrict procedure arguments to be of the same type as the formal parameters.

In Modula–3, operations defined on a type T can also be used on subtypes of T. For example, a procedure that takes an argument of type INTEGER will also accept an argument of type [1..10] (as long as the parameter does not have mode VAR), since [1..10] is a subtype of INTEGER. Likewise, value of type REF INTEGER can be assigned to a variable of type REFANY because REF INTEGER is a subtype of REFANY. Similarly, descendants of an object type can be used in place of the object type itself, because a subtype has all the characteristics of the supertype. However, this relationship doesn't work in reverse.

Supertypes (ancestors) cannot be used in place of descendants, because they do not have the additional features declared by the descendant.

Example 11–2

The Reflect procedure below operates on values of type Point. This procedure changes the (x, y) location of a point by exchanging the point's x and y coordinates. (Objects are represented by references, so when the Reflect procedure changes the contents of the point, it also changes the point the caller is referring to.)

```
PROCEDURE Reflect(point: Point) =
    VAR temp := point.y;
    BEGIN
        point.y := point.x;
        point.x := temp;
    END Reflect;
```

The reflect procedure will take an argument either of type Point or type BigPoint, since both have the characteristics of Point. However, consider the Reduce procedure below:

```
PROCEDURE Reduce(big: BigPoint) =
    BEGIN
        big.size := big.size / 2.0;
    END Reduce;
```

Reduce expects a BigPoint argument. Suppose that point and bigPoint are variables holding objects of type Point and BigPoint, respectively, The call Reduce(bigPoint) is all right, but the call Reduce(point) will cause a run-time error, since a Point object does not have all the characteristics of a BigPoint object. (In particular, it doesn't have a size.) By the way, the call Reduce(point) is legal when compiled, because the variable point might hold a value of type bigPoint. Only at run-time will the call cause an error.

Implementation   The inherited fields in an object always occupy the same relative position in the object as they did in the original ancestor. (See Figure 11–2 on page 199.) Similarly, inherited methods occupy the same relative position in the method suite as they did in the ancestor's suite. This means that a descendant's object resembles its ancestors well enough that operations on the ancestor will also work on the descendant; the extra fields and methods are simply ignored.

11.1.4 Dynamic Binding

Another concept related to polymorphism is the *dynamic binding* of methods. This means that a descendant type can *override* (replace) a method declared in an ancestor by supplying a different procedure to be invoked for the descendant. This lets you inherit most of the characteristics of the ancestor but change the behavior of some of the ancestor's methods on your new objects—even when those methods are called in other code that you cannot change directly. The static (compile-time) type of an object expression determines which methods or fields can be referenced, but it is the actual type of the expression's value that determines which implementation of the method to use.

Example 11–3

The move method of type Point (Example 11–1 on page 200) moves a point by adding the method's arguments to the point's current position. That works just fine for objects of type Point or BigPoint. However, suppose we decide that big points are subject to "erosion," and should get smaller as they are moved. Each time the move method is called on a big point, its size should be halved. To accomplish this, we change the definition of BigPoint so that it overrides the move method with another procedure:

```
TYPE BigPoint = Point OBJECT
    size: REAL := 1.0;
OVERRIDES
    move := MoveBigPoint;
END;

PROCEDURE MoveBigPoint(self: BigPoint; deltaX, deltaY: REAL) =
    BEGIN
        self.x := self.x + deltaX;
        self.y := self.y + deltaY;
        self.size := self.size / 2.0;
    END MoveBigPoint;
```

To see how dynamic binding works, let's create a variable of type Point:

```
VAR point: Point;
```

First, we assign a Point object to point and call move:

```
point := NEW(Point);
point.move(1.0, 1.0);
```

The method call is effectively translated to the procedure call Move(point, 1.0, 1.0). Now, let's set point to another value, this time one of type BigPoint.

```
point := NEW(BigPoint);
point.move(1.0, 1.0);
```

This time, the method call is translated to MoveBigPoint(point, 1.0, 1.0). In other words, the same written method call, point.move(1.0,1.0), results in different procedures being executed depending on the dynamic (run-time) value of the expression point.

Implementation   Overriding is simply replacing a pointer in the method suite of an object type. In Figure 11–4 on page 201, the method suites of Point and BigPoint both referenced the Move procedure. In Example 11–3, the move method override gives rise to the structure shown in Figure 11–5 on page 204. Notice, however, that the layout of the slots—which slots contain which method references—is determined statically, at compile time.

11.1.5 Constructors and Destructors

Several languages that support object-oriented programming include special facilities to invoke user-defined initialization code (a *constructor*) when an object is created, and to invoke user-defined cleanup code when the object is destroyed (a *destructor*). Modula–3

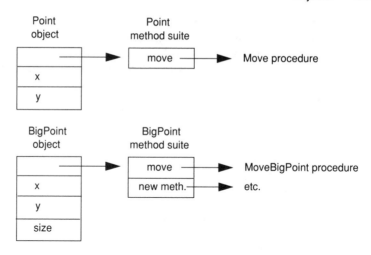

Figure 11–5   Point and BigPoint after method override.

does not include either of them for various reasons. Some programmers consider this to be a deficiency in the language, but they are needed in relatively few cases and we'll see how their absence can be mitigated.

Field declarations in object types can include constant initialization expressions. If your objects require more initialization, you must provide methods or procedures to be called by the client. We will show a convenient style for creating and using initialization methods in Example 11–10 on page 214.

In other languages, user-defined destructors often have the responsibility for releasing storage occupied by the objects. Releasing storage in Modula–3 is the responsibility of the garbage collector, so that task does not have to be programmed. The SRC Modula–3 run-time library does have an interface that allows you to register procedures to be called when your program exits.

11.2 Object Types

We'll now begin looking at Modula–3's OOP facilities in more detail, beginning with the syntax for declaring object types.

11.2.1 Declaring Object Types

As shown in "Object Type Syntax" on page 205, you build an object type from five components, each of which is optional:

1. an ancestor
2. a brand for opaque type revelations
3. a set of field declarations

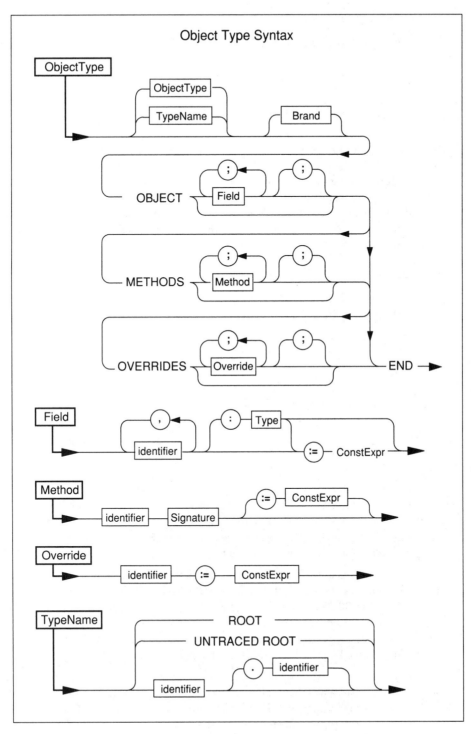

Object Type Syntax

4. a set of method declarations

5. a set of method overrides

Each of these components is described below.

11.2.2 Ancestors and Subtypes

You can derive an object type from another object type, called its ancestor. All the fields and methods from the ancestor are inherited by the new type, the descendant. You specify the ancestor by writing the name of the ancestor object type. (You could specify the ancestor by writing an equivalent object type expression, but that is cumbersome and takes no advantage of the language.) If you do not specify an ancestor in an object type declaration, the predefined type ROOT is assumed to be the ancestor. ROOT is an object type with no fields or methods.

Example 11–4

The following declarations define the object types Animal, Mammal, and Reptile, in the indicated type hierarchy:

```
TYPE
    Animal = OBJECT ... END;
    Mammal = Animal OBJECT ... END;
    Reptile = Animal OBJECT ... END;
```

Descendant object types are subtypes of their ancestors, and, therefore, also subtypes of type ROOT. Variables of type ROOT can be used to hold any object, in the same way that variables of type REFANY can hold any reference. In fact, object variables are implemented as references and ROOT is a subtype of REFANY. This means that the REFANY type includes not only all the reference types REF T, but all the object types as well.

Actually, this is a slight simplification. There is a second, parallel object type hierarchy rooted in a predefined object type called UNTRACED ROOT. All objects descended from UNTRACED ROOT are untraced (ignored by the garbage collector) but otherwise behave the same as traced objects. UNTRACED ROOT is a subtype of ADDRESS. The complete subtype tree for reference and object types is shown in Figure 11–6 on page 207. (Traced and untraced types are discussed beginning on page 258.)

As you can see, the traced and untraced reference types are disjoint. Since they are not related by the subtype relation, they cannot be mixed. Untraced objects types are provided for those programmers who—for real or imagined reasons—want to avoid the garbage collector. We don't recommend the use of untraced objects, and we don't use them in this book.

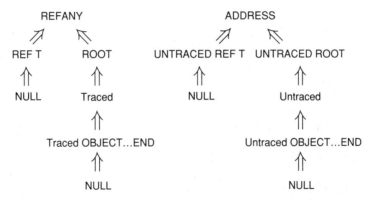

Figure 11–6 Modula–3 reference type hierarchy. T is any type, Traced is any traced object type, and Untraced is any untraced object type.

11.2.3 Brands

You must include a brand in an object type when it is used in a REVEAL declaration. It is used for the same reason that brands are used in revelations of other reference types—to prevent two structurally equivalent types from being considered the same. (See page 191.)

11.2.4 Fields

You can include data fields in an object type declaration just as in a record declaration, and the fields can have constant initialization expressions. When an object is created by NEW, all fields—including inherited ones—are initialized as specified. If no initial value is included in the declaration, the field is initialized to an arbitrary value of the declared type, as is normally done in Modula–3. If you omit a field's type in the declaration, the type is taken from the initialization expression (which must be present).

Example 11–5

The object type Box below has components size and color, and both have initial values:

```
TYPE
    Color = {black, white, blue, green, red};
    Box = OBJECT
        size: CARDINAL := 1;
        color := Color.white;
    METHODS ...
    END;
```

If you declare a field whose name happens to be the same as a field or method in one of the new type's ancestors, the new field will hide the inherited field or method in the new type and in all future types descended from it. You can still reference the hidden field or method, but you have to explicitly specify the type in which it occurs unhidden. (See Example 11–10 on page 214.)

OOP Terminology

Many terms are used for OOP concepts. Sometimes different terms mean the same thing, and sometimes their meanings are subtly different to OOP purists. Modula–3 often ignores traditional OOP terms in favor of terms drawn from traditional programming languages.

What is called *class* in traditional OOP terminology is called an object type in Modula–3 to emphasize its integration with other data types. Similarly, the terms *supertype/subtype* are used in place of the traditional *superclass/subclass* (or *ancestor/descendant, parent/child*). In this book, we tend to mix the terms for variety.

An *instance* is traditionally an object of some class. In Modula–3 it is simply called a variable or value of an object type.

An *instance variable* is a variable local to each class instance. In Modula–3, instance variables are the fields of the object types. A *class variable* is a variable shared among all instances of a class. Modula–3 does not have class variables *per se*, but you can get their effect by defining variables at the top level of the module that implements the object type. (Some recent writers use the term *class variable* to mean simply an instance, a variable of some class.) Class and instance variables are also sometimes called *slots*, from their implementation as fields with particular offsets in object records.

11.2.5 Methods

You declare methods when you want to provide operations on objects of the new type. You specify the method name and signature after the keyword METHODS in the object type declaration.

Simply declaring a method does not actually create a procedure to perform the operation; to do that, you set the method to the value of some procedure. You can do that either by initializing the method to a compatible procedure, or by overriding the method in a descendant type. To initialize the method, simply specify a constant procedure value in the declaration. The following code declares method penUp and initializes it to procedure PenUp:

```
TYPE
    PenPosition = {Down, Up};
    Turtle = OBJECT
        penPosition := PenPosition.Down; ...
    METHODS
        penUp() := PenUp; ...
    END;
```

```
PROCEDURE PenUp(self: Turtle) =
  BEGIN
    self.penPosition := PenPosition.Up;
  END PenUp;
```

If you don't initialize a method when it is declared, the method is instead set to the value NIL. Since it is a checked run-time error to call a method that has the value NIL, the expectation is that the method will be overridden in a descendant type. Overriding will be discussed in the next section.

Procedures used as methods   A method must be implemented by a matching procedure. Every method has an implicit first parameter for the object used to invoke the method. This extra parameter, which has mode VALUE, does not appear in the method signature but has to appear in the signature of a procedure that implement or override the method. (Some people make a habit of calling this parameter self, but you can give it any name you wish.) For example, in the Turtle object above, the method signature appears to be PROCEDURE(), but the corresponding procedure signature is PROCEDURE(self: Turtle). If barney is a variable of type Turtle, the method call barney.penUp() is translated to the procedure call PenUp(barney).

A method's procedure must have a signature that *satisfies* the method. This means that the procedure's first parameter must have mode VALUE and a type that is either the same as the type of the object being declared or is an ancestor of that type. Also, disregarding this first parameter, the procedure's signature must be covered by the method's signature. (Covering signatures were discussed on page 126.) In brief, this means that the method and procedure must have the same number of arguments with the same type and return type, and the procedure can raise any exception in the method's raises set.

Example 11–6

In the following declaration, the object type SizedThing has a method setSize initialized to procedure SetSize.

```
TYPE SizedThing = OBJECT (* whatever fields are needed *)
  METHODS
    setSize(size: CARDINAL) := SetSize;
END;
```

The procedure SetSize must be visible in the same scope containing the object declaration. Here are some possible declarations of SetSize; can you determine which of the declarations satisfies the method?

(a) PROCEDURE SetSize(size: CARDINAL);
(b) PROCEDURE SetSize(self: SizedThing; x: CARDINAL);
(c) PROCEDURE SetSize(self: UNTRACED ROOT; x: CARDINAL);
(d) PROCEDURE SetSize(VAR self: SizedThing; x: CARDINAL);
(e) PROCEDURE SetSize(x: SizedThing; self: CARDINAL);
(f) PROCEDURE SetSize(self: SizedThing; x: CARDINAL) RAISES ANY;
(g) PROCEDURE SetSize(self: SizedThing; x: [0..10]);

Solution (a) does not satisfy setSize because it is missing the required first parameter. (b) satisfies setSize; the parameter names do not have to be identical. (c) does not because UN-

TRACED ROOT is not an ancestor of SizedThing; types ROOT or REFANY would have been legal alternatives to SizedThing in this declaration of SetSize. (d) does not have mode VALUE for the first parameter. (e) satisfies setSize—the names of the parameters don't matter. (f) does not satisfy setSize because it can raise exceptions, whereas the method declaration specifies no exceptions. (g) does not satisfy setSize because the type of parameter x in SetSize is not the same as the parameter in the setSize method.

Just as with fields, you can declare a method whose name is the same as a field or method in an ancestor type. If you do, the ancestral name is hidden in this type and in descendants of the type. Section 11.3.3 on page 213 discusses how you can reference these hidden components.

11.2.6 Overrides

You can change the value of an inherited method by assigning a new procedure value to the method in the OVERRIDES clause of the object type declaration. If you do that, any invocation of the method on an object of the new type—or of any descendant type—will cause the new procedure to be executed. The new procedure's signature must satisfy the method signature, except that the first parameter can have any type that includes the *new* object type. That is, you can use a procedure that is more specialized than any inherited method procedure.

Overrides are used for several distinct purposes. We've already mentioned the case in which you want to replace an existing procedure for a method. That use was demonstrated in Example 11–3 on page 203. You may also wish to use overrides to supply a procedure for a method that has none; that is, for a method that was not initialized. When declaring an opaque object type, for example, you ordinarily don't initialize the methods until the REVEAL declaration. (See the examples on page 196 and the discussion on page 216.)

The visible ancestor of an opaque object type declaration is actually an example of a more general kind of object type called an *abstract class*. An abstract class is never intended to be used for real objects. Instead, it simply defines some common characteristics that will be shared by descendant types created by clients. The abstract class hardly ever specifies method procedures; clients are expected to override the methods with appropriate procedures.

Example 11–7

If you were writing a graphics program, you might want to manipulate objects of various sorts. A common approach is to declare an abstract class that captures the operations to be implemented across all types of objects. For example, a GeometricShape might have methods draw, move, and area:

```
TYPE GeometricShape = OBJECT
METHODS
    draw();                          (* draw the shape *)
    move(deltaX, deltaY: REAL);      (* move the shape *)
    area(): REAL;                    (* return the area of the shape *)
END;
```

There would be no point in creating an object of type GeometricShape. Instead, you would create descendants with their own fields and method overrides:

```
TYPE Square = GeometricShape OBJECT
    x, y: REAL;   (* position of top-left corder *)
    side: REAL;   (* length of sides *)
OVERRIDES
    draw := DrawSquare;
    move := MoveSquare;
    area := AreaOfSquare;
END;

PROCEDURE DrawSquare(self: Square) = ...;
PROCEDURE MoveSquare(self: Square) = ...;
PROCEDURE AreaOfSquare(self: Square) = ...;
```

11.3 Operations on Objects

Now that you know how to declare object types, we'll look at the operations you can perform on objects, including creation, assignment, and accessing fields and methods.

11.3.1 Creation

You create new objects by calling NEW, just as for reference types. The object type itself should be the first parameter to NEW. Thus, if Square is an object type, you can create a new object of type Square and store (a reference to) it in a new variable a by writing

```
VAR square := NEW(Square);
```

The fields and methods of the newly created object are initialized according to the object type declaration. If the object has an ancestor, the ancestor's fields and methods are likewise initialized.

It is so common to create an object and immediately set some of its fields that Modula–3 provides a shortcut, allowing you to give the fields values when the object is created. The call

```
NEW(Square, x := 0.0, y := FLOAT(Math.Sqrt(2.0D0)));
    (* Example 11–7 on page 210 *)
```

allocates a new object of type Square and sets fields x and y to zero and the square root of 2, respectively. In addition to setting fields, it is possible to override methods when calling NEW. The call

```
NEW(Square, move := MoveDifferently)
```

allocates a new object of type Square and changes method move to be procedure MoveDifferently. Although this looks just like a field assignment, it is quite different. This call to NEW is actually considered shorthand for

NEW(Square OBJECT OVERRIDES move := MoveDifferently; END)

That is, the created object is a member of a new object type descended from Square with the specified method override. This new descendant is an *anonymous type*, since it is given no name. The procedure values used to override methods in calls to NEW must be constant, as they must be in ordinary type declarations.

Field and method initializations can be mixed within a single call to NEW.

Example 11–8

Here are some declarations of objects descended from GeometricShape (Example 11–7 on page 210):

```
VAR
    bigSquare := NEW(Square, side := 1000.0);
    smallSquare := NEW(Square, size := 10.0, area := AreaOfSmallSquare);
    tinySquare := NEW(Square, size := 0.001, move := MoveTinySquare);
```

Each of these variables has a different type, with bigSquare having type Square and the other variables having types descended from Square. As a consequence, the assignment bigSquare := tinySquare would be legal, but the assignment smallSquare := tinySquare would not, since no subtype relation exists between them.

As with reference types, when a variable of an object type is not initialized it will have an arbitrary value of that type. The value will probably be NIL, but the language does not require it to be so. You should only depend on it being NIL if you explicitly initialize it to NIL.

11.3.2 Assignment

The assignment rules for object types are an extension and generalization of those for reference types. Recall that a variable of reference type T can hold any value whose type is a subtype of T. If designator L has reference type T_L and expression R has reference type T_R, then the following table shows when you can write the assignment L := R.

If...	then...
$T_R = T_L$	the assignment is legal and cannot cause a run-time error
$T_R <: T_L$	the assignment is legal and cannot cause a run-time error
$T_L <: T_R$	the assignment is legal, but a run-time check will be made to ensure that the value of R is a member of T_L
otherwise	the assignment is illegal

Example 11–9

Suppose the object types A, B, C, and D are related as shown at the right. We have C <: B, B <: A, and D <: A, but no subtype relation exists between B and D or between C and D. Suppose that variables a, b, c, and d have types A, B, C, and D, respectively, and consider the following sequences of assignments. [Ellipses (…) indicate intervening statements that do not alter the variables being discussed.]

```
A
B   D
C
```

(1) c := NEW(C); … a := c;

The assignments in (1) are both legal and will not require a run-time check.

(2) a := NEW(C); … c := a;

The assignments in (2) are likewise legal because in each case the type of the value being assigned is a subtype of the variable receiving the value. However, the assignment c := a will require a run-time check to ensure this.

(3) a := NEW(A); … b := a;

The assignments in (3) are legal at compile time but b := a will result in a run-time error because the value of type A doesn't contain all the characteristics of type B.

(4) b := d;

The assignment in (4) will be rejected at compile time because there is no subtype relation between the types B and D.

11.3.3 Component and Method Access

The fields and methods of an object are referenced using the . (period) operator. If obj is an object with data field field and method method, then

    obj.field   refers to field in object obj
    obj.method(a,b)   calls the method in object obj with arguments a and b

It does not matter if field and method were declared directly in obj's object type or were inherited from an ancestor. If the method's value is NIL, then invoking method will cause a run-time error.

You can change the value stored in an object's fields any time you wish, just as with record variables. However, you cannot change a method after an object has been allocated. That is, you cannot attempt to override a method by writing a statement like

    obj.method := AnotherMethodProc;   (* Illegal! *)

We mentioned earlier that you can hide a field or method in an ancestor type by declaring a new field or method with the same name. You can access such a hidden field or method by temporarily considering the object to be of an ancestor type using NARROW. This is illustrated in the following example.

Example 11–10

A convention in object types is for each type to provide a method, init, which initializes the object according to the values of the arguments to init. When a descendant type is declared, it should provide its own init method, hiding the ancestor's method. The descendant's init should take whatever arguments are necessary, first to call the ancestor's init and then to initialize the descendant's own fields. It is convenient if the init function also returns the initialized object.

Suppose we define Point, PositionedObject, and Rectangle types as below:

```
TYPE
    Point = RECORD x, y: REAL; END;
    PositionedObject = OBJECT
        location: Point;
    METHODS
        init(location: Point): PositionedObject := InitPosition;  (* Set the position *)
    END;
    Rectangle = PositionedObject OBJECT
        height, width: REAL;
    METHODS
        init(topLeft: Point; height, width: REAL): Rectangle := InitRectangle;
    END;
```

The PositionedObject.init method is straightforward:

```
PROCEDURE InitPosition(self: PositionedObject; location: Point)
    : PositionedObject =
BEGIN
    self.location := location; RETURN self;
END InitPosition;
```

The Rectangle.init method is slightly more complicated because it must first access the hidden PositionedObject.init method. It does this by narrowing self to its parent type, PositionedObject, which exposes the hidden init method:

```
PROCEDURE InitRectangle(self: Rectangle; topLeft: Point; height, width: REAL)
    : Rectangle =
BEGIN
    EVAL NARROW(self, PositionedObject).init(location := topLeft);
    self.height := height; self.width := width;
    RETURN self;
END InitRectangle;
```

A client of the Rectangle object type might write the following declaration to create a rectangle two units on a side with the top left at location (10, 10):

```
VAR
    r := NEW(Rectangle).init(
        topLeft := Point{x := 10.0, y := 10.0},
        height := 2.0,
        width := 2.0);
```

An alternative to the use of NARROW for accessing hidden methods (not fields) is to use the object type name. If OT is an object type and m is one of its methods, then OT.m refers to the procedure for the m method for objects of type OT. This procedure is always the one that appears in the declaration (or revelation) of type OT.

Example 11–11

Suppose we declare an object type Citation and a derived type ArticleCitation. ArticleCitation overrides the method titleString:

```
TYPE
    Citation = OBJECT
        title: TEXT;
    METHODS
        titleString(): TEXT := NormalTitle;   (* just returns title *)
    END;
    ArticleCitation = Citation OBJECT
    OVERRIDES
        titleString := ArticleTitle;   (* returns title enclosed in quotation marks *)
    END;
```

If citation is a variable of type Citation, what are the values of these two expressions:

```
citation.titleString()
Citation.titleString(citation)  ?
```

Solution The expression Citation.titleString(citation) is always the same as the expression NormalTitle(citation), because the procedure activated depends only on the type Citation. (It is not dynamically bound.) However, the value of citation.titleString() depends on the type of the value stored in citation. If it has type ArticleCitation, the result is the same as the expression ArticleTitle(citation); if it has type Citation, the result is the same as the expression Normal-Title(citation).

11.3.4 Other Operations

Equality operators = and # are defined for objects, but they merely test that two object references are the same. You cannot write obj1^ = obj2^, as you can with non-object references. (The dereference operator cannot be applied to objects.) To test if two objects are field-by-field equal, you must write a function that compares the fields individually.

The TYPECODE function and TYPECASE statement (page 183) can be used with object types:

TYPECODE(T)   returns a CARDINAL value that represents the reference (object) type T

TYPECODE(o)   returns TYPECODE(AT), where AT is the allocated type of object o

TYPECASE is particularly useful in discriminating among several descendant types from a common ancestor.

The NARROW function can be used to change the type of any reference expression:

NARROW(e, T)   returns e as a value of type T. The value of e must be a member of T, and e must be assignable to T; that is, T and the type of e must be related by the subtype relation.

11.4 Opaque Object Types

Now that you know basically how to use objects, you are ready to learn how to create well-structured abstractions with them. In particular, you will want to package object types inside interfaces and modules, and you will want to hide from clients all "nonessential information" about the objects. This nonessential information typically includes the object type's fields and the procedures used to implement the methods; all the client should see are the methods. The way to accomplish this hiding is to use opaque object types. In order to provide a complete abstraction, the opaque types will be declared in an interface, possibly with other types and procedures to be used by clients. While opaque types and interfaces are separate facilities in Modula–3, they are often used together.

11.4.1   Defining the Opaque Object Type

When we declared opaque reference types in Section 10.5 on page 188, the declarations were of the form

```
TYPE OpaqueRef <: REFANY;
```

That is, we declared the new type (OpaqueRef) to be a subtype of REFANY. REFANY is the only reasonable supertype for (nonobject) opaque reference types. For object types, however, we are free to choose any ancestor to use in the opaque type declaration:

```
TYPE OpaqueObj <: SomeAncestorType;
```

Our plan will be to invent an ancestor that defines just the "public" information of the opaque type—typically, just the public methods. This type is defined publicly. The eventual revelation of the opaque type—which will not be made accessible to clients—will add in the data fields, the method implementations, overrides, and any additional, private methods. Here's how to create the public ancestor: Assume that we start with a type, Real-Object, whose immediate ancestor is Ancestor:

```
TYPE RealObject = Ancestor OBJECT
    (* fields *)
METHODS
    (* public methods, with initializers *)
OVERRIDES
    (* overrides of Ancestor methods, if desired *)
END;
```

We first declare an intermediate type, PublicObject, which is a descendant of Ancestor and contains the "public" parts of RealObject. Start by creating PublicObject as a new descendant of Ancestor, containing only the public methods for RealObject. Don't initialize the methods in PublicObject or include any overrides. This gives us the following declaration:

```
TYPE PublicObject = Ancestor OBJECT
METHODS
    (* public methods, no initializers *)
END;
```

Now, change the declaration of RealObject to be an opaque descendant of PublicObject:

```
TYPE RealObject <: PublicObject.
```

This allows clients to create objects of type RealObject and to invoke their methods, but clients cannot access any fields from RealObject. (Clients could access fields in Ancestor, if those field declarations were visible.) Finally, you must include a revelation of RealObject in the program:

```
REVEAL RealObject = PublicObject BRANDED OBJECT
    (* fields *)
METHODS
    (* additional private methods *)
OVERRIDES
    (* implementations of public methods and other overrides *)
END;
```

The keyword BRANDED is required to ensure that the revelation is unique. An opaque object type can be used just like any other object type. You can invoke its methods, use it as an ancestor, etc. You just can't access any fields or methods that aren't visible (revealed).

11.4.2 Packaging Objects in Interfaces

Opaque object type declarations are usually placed in interfaces, where they can be accessed by clients. The revelation is placed in the exporting module, where it can be used to implement the interface but is not available to clients. This is illustrated in the following example.

Example 11–12

Here is a rewritten version of "positioned object" code from Example 11–10 on page 214, using interfaces and opaque types. We've decided to name the interface PositionedObject, to name the primary type T (see Appendix A), and to keep the name Rectangle. This choice will make it easier to add new "positioned objects" to the interface, such as Ellipse, Polygon, etc.

```
INTERFACE PositionedObject;
TYPE
    Point = RECORD x, y: REAL; END;
    T <: Public;
    Public = OBJECT
    METHODS
        init(location: Point): Public;
    END;
```

```
Rectangle <: PublicRectangle;
PublicRectangle = T OBJECT
 METHODS
     init(topLeft: Point; height, width: REAL): PublicRectangle;
 END;
END PositionedObject.
```

Notice that the interface now includes only the essential information about the object types (in this case, the init methods; a realistic program would presumably include others). The revelations of these types are placed in the implementing module:

```
MODULE PositionedObject;
REVEAL
   T =  Public BRANDED OBJECT
       location := Point{x:=0.0, y:=0.0};
   OVERRIDES
       init := InitPosition;
   END;
   Rectangle = PublicRectangle BRANDED OBJECT
       height, width := 1.0;
   OVERRIDES
       init := InitRectangle;
   END;

PROCEDURE InitPosition(self: T; location: Point): Public =
   BEGIN
       self.location := location; RETURN self;
   END InitPosition;

PROCEDURE InitRectangle(self: Rectangle; topLeft:Point; height,width: REAL)
   : PublicRectangle =
   BEGIN
       EVAL NARROW(self, T).init(location := topLeft);
       self.height := height; self.width := width;
       RETURN self;
   END InitRectangle;

BEGIN
END PositionedObject.
```

A client of the PositionedObject interface might write the following declaration to create a rectangle two units on a side with the top left at (10, 10):

```
IMPORT PositionedObject;
...
VAR r := NEW(PositionedObject.Rectangle).init(
   topLeft := PositionedObject.Point{x := 10.0, y := 10.0},
   height := 2.0,
   width := 2.0);
```

11.4.3 Extending Object Types

The preceding section showed an example of two opaque types in the same interface. In fact, you can easily extend an opaque type from another interface.

Example 11–13

Given the interface PositionedObjects from Example 11–12 on page 217, here is how you could create a new interface to extend the set of positioned objects to include a circle.

```
INTERFACE Circle;
IMPORT PositionedObject;
FROM PositionedObject IMPORT Point;
TYPE
    T <: Public;
    Public = PositionedObject.T OBJECT
    METHODS
        init(center: Point; radius: REAL): Public;
    END;
END Circle.

MODULE Circle;
IMPORT PositionedObjects;
FROM PositionedObjects IMPORT Point;
REVEAL
    T = Public BRANDED OBJECT
        radius := 1.0;
        OVERRIDES
        init := InitCircle;
    END;

PROCEDURE InitCircle(self: T; location: Point; radius: REAL): Public =
    BEGIN
        EVAL NARROW(self, PositionedObject.T).init(location);
        self.radius := radius;
        RETURN self;
    END InitCircle;

BEGIN
END Circle.
```

11.4.4 Allocating Opaque Types

When an object type is exported from an interface as an opaque type, clients cannot access fields directly. However, they can allocate new objects, and do not have to call your Init methods. Therefore, it is important that you guard against any problems caused by a failure to call Init. In the examples above, we've supplied default values for the fields in the types PositionedObjects.T, PositionedObjects.Rectangle, and Circle.T. This ensures that a newly allocated object has "reasonable" characteristics. In more complicated types—for which such simple default initializations might not be sufficient—you could include a special Boolean field, Initialized, that would be set to FALSE by default and would be set to

TRUE when your Init method was called. This would let you detect objects that were not initialized by Init and take appropriate action.

11.5 Example: Symbol Tables

Let's look at a larger example. The Symbol interface in this section provides a symbol table facility, which is a way to associate an *entry* with a *name*. Names are simply text strings. Entries are abstract objects; clients must create derived entry types to hold the information they want in the table. We'll show the Symbol interface, the Symbol module, and a test program that exercises the facility.

11.5.1 Symbol Interface

The Symbol interface exports two opaque object types: Table and Entry. This violates the general principle that each interface should export only one type, but in this case creating two interfaces seems cumbersome. Table is a symbol table that associates names with Entry's. Symbol names, which are text strings, must be non-NIL. Entry is an abstract class; clients should derive their own entry types from Entry. Each distinct Entry object must be entered in a table at most once. Operations defined on symbol tables include:

init   Initialize a symbol table, specifying approximately how many entries the table is to hold. Calling the init method is optional.

add   Add an entry to the symbol table. It must not already exist.

find   Retrieve an entry corresponding to a given name.

print   Print the table using the user-specified Entry print method

The Entry type has only two methods:

name   Return the name under which this entry is filed in the symbol table. This method is provided by the Symbol facility.

print   Print the entry. This method must be provided by clients.

Exceptions are raised when errors occur, such as attempting to add an entry that is already in the table.

```
INTERFACE Symbol;
IMPORT Wr;
CONST
    ProbableNumberOfSymbols = 100;  (* See init method *)
EXCEPTION
    Duplicate;   (* name already in table, or Entry already in some table *)
    NotFound;    (* name not in table *)
TYPE
    Table <: PublicTable;   (* a symbol table *)
    Entry <: PublicEntry;   (* an entry in the table *)
```

```
PublicEntry = OBJECT
METHODS
    name(): TEXT;
    print(wr: Wr.T) := NIL;
END;


PublicTable = OBJECT
    METHODS
        init(size: CARDINAL := ProbableNumberOfSymbols): Table;
        add(name: TEXT; entry: Entry) RAISES {Duplicate};
        find(name: TEXT): Entry RAISES {NotFound};
        print(wr: Wr.T);
    END;
END Symbol.
```

11.5.2 Test Program

The main program Test imports Symbol and runs some modest tests. In particular, it de-
rives a type IndexEntry from Symbol.Entry, which holds a single integer. It then reads successive lines from the standard input stream, each of which is assumed to contain a name.
Each name plus an IndexEntry indicating on which line the name occurred are entered into
the table. Finally, the table's print method is called to dump the symbol table to the standard output.

```
MODULE Test EXPORTS Main;
IMPORT Symbol, Rd, Wr, Stdio, Fmt;
CONST
    NumberOfSymbols = 32;
TYPE
    IndexEntry = Symbol.Entry OBJECT
        index: CARDINAL := 0;
    OVERRIDES
        print := PrintIndexEntry;   (* provide our own print method *)
    END;
VAR
    table := NEW(Symbol.Table).init(NumberOfSymbols);
    linesRead: CARDINAL := 0;


PROCEDURE PrintIndexEntry(self: IndexEntry; wr: Wr.T) =
    BEGIN
        Wr.PutText(Stdio.stdout, Fmt.Int(self.index));
        Wr.PutText(Stdio.stdout, ": \"");
        Wr.PutText(Stdio.stdout, self.name());
        Wr.PutText(Stdio.stdout, "\"\n");
    END PrintIndexEntry;
```

```
BEGIN
    (* Read names from input; store in table with sequence number. *)
    Wr.PutText(Stdio.stdout,"Type one name per line; end with ctrl-D\n");
    TRY
        LOOP
            table.add(
                name := Rd.GetLine(Stdio.stdin),
                entry := NEW(IndexEntry, index:=linesRead+1));
            INC(linesRead);
        END;
    EXCEPT
        Rd.EndOfFile => (* ignore *)
    END;


    Wr.PutText(Stdio.stdout, Fmt.Int(linesRead));
    Wr.PutText(Stdio.stdout, " lines read.\n");
    Wr.PutText(Stdio.stdout, "\nSymbol.Table.print...\n");
    table.print(Stdio.stdout);
END Test.
```

11.5.3 Symbol Module

The Symbol module reveals the structure of the Table and Entry types and provides procedures to implement the methods. A Table contains a reference to an array of Entry which
serves as a hash table. When multiple names hash to the same array index, the entries are
linked together. The names for the entries are stored in the entries. The hash function is
implemented as a nonpublic method in type Table.

```
MODULE Symbol;
IMPORT Text, Wr, Fmt, Word, Stdio;
CONST
    SymbolsPerHashBucket = 4;  (* what will give adequate performance *)
    MinimumHashBuckets = 2;


REVEAL
    Entry = PublicEntry BRANDED OBJECT
        myName: TEXT := NIL;  (* the name under which this entry is entered *)
        next: Entry := NIL;   (* overflow entries in the hash table *)
    OVERRIDES
        name := Name;
        print := PrintEntry;
        (* Clients should override print, but we provide a default in case they do not. *)
    END;
```

```
Table = PublicTable BRANDED OBJECT
    buckets: REF ARRAY OF Entry := NIL;   (* hash table *)
METHODS
    hash(name: TEXT): CARDINAL := Hash;
        (* Computes bucket index from name. *)
OVERRIDES
    add := Add;
    find := Find;
    init := Init;
    print := PrintTable;
END;
```

```
PROCEDURE Hash(self: Table; name: TEXT): CARDINAL =
(* Returns the bucket index where 'name' should be stored. *)
VAR hash: Word.T := 0;   (* uses Word.T to ignore overflow *)
BEGIN
    FOR i := 0 TO Text.Length(name) − 1 DO
        hash := Word.Plus(hash, ORD(Text.GetChar(name, i)));
    END;
    IF hash < 0 THEN hash := −hash; END;
    hash := hash MOD NUMBER(self.buckets^);
    RETURN hash;
END Hash;
```

```
PROCEDURE Init(
    self: Table;
    size: CARDINAL := ProbableNumberOfSymbols): Table =
(* Allocate and initialize the bucket array. *)
BEGIN
    (* Ignore all but first call to init for this table. *)
    IF self.buckets = NIL THEN
        WITH NumberOfBuckets =
            MAX(MinimumHashBuckets,
                size DIV SymbolsPerHashBucket)
        DO
            self.buckets := NEW(REF ARRAY OF Entry,
                                                NumberOfBuckets);
            FOR i := 0 TO LAST(self.buckets^) DO
                self.buckets[i] := NIL;
            END;
        END;
    END;
    RETURN self;
END Init;
```

```
PROCEDURE Find(self: Table; name: TEXT): Entry RAISES {NotFound} =
    (* Find the named symbol and return it. Raises NotFound
      if the name is not in the table. *)
    VAR
        sym: Entry;
    BEGIN
        IF self.buckets = NIL THEN EVAL self.init(); END;   (* initialize if necessary *)
        (* Look down chain of symbols on the bucket for a match. *)
        sym := self.buckets[self.hash(name)];
        WHILE sym # NIL AND NOT Text.Equal(sym.myName, name) DO
            sym := sym.next;
        END;
        IF sym = NIL THEN RAISE NotFound; END;
        RETURN sym;
    END Find;




PROCEDURE Add(self: Table; name: TEXT; newSym: Entry)
        RAISES{Duplicate} =
    (* Add the symbol to the table. Raises Duplicate if 'name' is already in this table
      or if 'newSym' is already in this or some other table. *)
    VAR
        sym: Entry;
    BEGIN
        IF newSym.myName # NIL THEN
            (* Someone already called Add with this Entry. *)
            RAISE Duplicate;
        END;
        (* Store name in Entry; initialize table if necessary *)
        newSym.myName := name;
        IF self.buckets = NIL THEN EVAL self.init(); END;
        WITH bucket = self.buckets[self.hash(newSym.myName)] DO
            sym := bucket;   (* Walk down the bucket chain looking for duplicates. *)
            WHILE sym # NIL DO
                IF Text.Equal(sym.myName, name) THEN
                    RAISE Duplicate;
                END;
                sym := sym.next;
            END;
            (* No duplicates, so add to front of chain. *)
            newSym.next := bucket;
            bucket := newSym;
        END (*WITH*);
    END Add;
```

```
PROCEDURE PrintTable(self: Table; wr: Wr.T) =
(* Print the contents of the symbol table. *)
VAR sym: Entry;
BEGIN
    IF self.buckets = NIL THEN
        Wr.PutText(wr, "Table is empty\n");
    ELSE
        FOR slot := 0 TO LAST(self.buckets^) DO
            Wr.PutText(wr, "Bucket ");
            Wr.PutText(wr, Fmt.Int(slot));
            Wr.PutText(wr, ": \n");
            sym := self.buckets[slot];
            WHILE sym # NIL DO
                sym.print(wr);
                sym := sym.next;
            END;
        END (*FOR*);
    END;
END PrintTable;


PROCEDURE Name(self: Entry): TEXT =
BEGIN
    RETURN self.myName;
END Name;


PROCEDURE PrintEntry(self: Entry; wr: Wr.T) =
(* This method is usually overriden in classes derived from T. *)
BEGIN
    Wr.PutText(wr, "\t");
    Wr.PutText(wr, Fmt.Ref(self));
    Wr.PutText(wr, ": ");
    Wr.PutText(wr, self.myName);
    Wr.PutText(wr, "\n");
END PrintEntry;


BEGIN
END Symbol.
```

11.6 Exercises

Answers to the exercises marked "[A]" appear in Appendix D.

1. Which one of the following features of OOP will cause you the most grief as you try to read and understand a program using objects? Why? Which one (if used well) will be most beneficial to you?

   a. encapsulation

   b. polymorphism

   c. dynamic binding

   d. inheritance

2. If A is a subtype of B, is A a descendant of B? If C is an object type derived from D, is D a super-type of C?   [A]

3. Given the delcarations

        TYPE Obj = OBJECT METHODS m() := M; END;
        VAR obj: Obj;

   If obj contains a value of type Obj, must Obj.m(obj) and obj.m() give have the same effect?   [A]

4. Which of the following pairs of terms or phrases mean the same thing? For those that are different, explain the difference.

   a. object type; class

   b. "A is descended from B"; "A is derived from B"

   c. traced objects; untraced objects

   d. override a method; hide a method

5. What is the type of the variable declared below, assuming that Class is an object type?   [A]

        VAR class := NEW(Class, x := X);

6. Assume that Class is an object type containing method m, and obj is a variable of type Class. If you see the method invocation obj.m(...), how would you go about determining which procedure was activated by the method call?

7. When must an object type be branded?   [A]

8. Write a series of object type declarations that duplicate the inheritance diagram of Figure 11–3 on page 200. Leave the fields and methods of the object types empty.

9. Suppose we have defined the object types A, B, C, D, E, and F, and that they are related as shown in Figure 11–3 on page 200. Suppose further that we define some variables:

        VAR a:A; b: B; c: C; d: D; e: E; f: F;

   For each of the following assignment statements, indicate whether or not the statement is legal (at compile time). For those that are legal, list the values of the right-hand-side expressions that will cause a run-time error.

   a. a := b; [A]

   b. b := a;

   c. b := c;

   d. d := c; [A]

   e. f := e;

10. Suppose type Child is defined as follows:

        TYPE
            Child = Parent OBJECT
        METHODS
            m() := P;
        END;
        Grandchild = Child OBJECT ... END;

Which of the following declarations of P would make the method declaration in Child legal?

a. PROCEDURE P();

b. PROCEDURE P(x: Parent);

c. PROCEDURE P(self: Child);

d. PROCEDURE P(VAR Self: ROOT);

e. PROCEDURE P(parent: REFANY);

f. PROCEDURE P(self: Grandchild);

11. Which of the following can you do with untraced objects? (Untraced objects and references are discussed beginning in Section 13.2 on page 258.)

a. apply the TYPECODE function to them   [A]

b. apply the NARROW function to them

c. assign them to variables of type REFANY   [A]

d. store them as fields in traced objects

e. eliminate all references to them   [A]

f. assign them to variables of type ADDRESS

g. include in them fields whose types are traced

12. A compiler must maintain internal data structures and operations to describe the various data types defined in a program. The type data structure and operations are naturally implemented with object types and methods. Assume a simplified type model with only three kinds of types: INTEGER, integer subranges [a..b], and reference types REF T where T is any type (including another reference). The INTEGER and subrange types are known as ordinal types. Two operations are defined on types: Equal(A,B) is true if and only if: A and B are both INTEGER; A and B are subranges with equal bounds; or A and B are reference types whose referent types are equal. The operation Compatible(A,B) is true if and only if: A and B are equal, or if A and B are both ordinal types.

   Write a Modula–3 program that implements the type data structures and operations Equal and Compatible. There should be an interface, Type, that exports a generic "data type" type T plus specific types for the three kinds of data types Integer, Subrange, and Reference. Type T should also have methods Equal and Compatible. Also include initialization methods for each kind of data type. The Type module should implement the methods. Also write a test program that creates at least the data types listed below and checks each against all the others for equality and compatibility. The types to create are INTEGER, [1..10], [5..10], REF INTEGER, REF [1..10], REF [5..10], REF REF INTEGER.

13. In the Symbol facility in Section 11.5 on page 220, type Entry holds the entry name and the hash bucket links, which means that an Entry cannot be in a table more than once. Remove this restriction by separating out the name and link information, keeping them private to the Symbol module. You will have to give up the name method on type Entry. (Why?)   [A]

14. The Symbol facility in Section 11.5 on page 220 uses an abstract class, Entry, to store in the table. There are two other plausible ways to implement entries: as REFANY types and as generic types. Write a Symbol interface that uses each implementation, and also write the implementation of the Add procedure. Before you start, you may wish to change the implementation of the symbol table in the way described in Exercise 13.

12

Threads

In a *sequential program*, there is a single flow of control. That is, at any one time, the computer is executing at a single point in the program—a statement inside a procedure or inside the top-level block in a module. A *concurrent program* is one in which there are multiple points of execution—multiple *threads*, each of which is an individual sequential program. All the Modula–3 programs we have discussed so far have been sequential programs, but Modula–3 can also support concurrent programs by allowing the creation and control of any number of additional threads.

Concurrent programming offers its own set of benefits and liabilities. On the positive side, it can improve the structure of certain kinds of applications—particularly, ones that interact with unpredictable and asynchronous devices, such as storage devices, laboratory equipment, and human beings. It also provides a way to take advantage of certain new multiprocessor computers—computers that can execute more than one program at a time. On the minus side, concurrent programs must pay some execution time penalties in setting up and synchronizing threads. They are also subject to a number of new kinds of bugs—race conditions and deadlocks—that must be anticipated and avoided.

The concurrent facilities of Modula–3 are designed to be "lightweight," that is, there is relatively little overhead in using them. All the threads in a Modula–3 program live in the same address space, which means they all share the same code and global (top-level) variables. There are other types of concurrency, principally those designed around *processes*, in which each flow of control has its own address space and does not share variables with other processes. Processes tend to have a higher overhead than threads, but processes are also better protected from interference by other processes.

This chapter discusses some basic concepts of concurrent programming and describes the Modula–3 facilities that support it. However, this chapter is not a complete course in concurrent programming.

12.1 Implementing Threads

It may help if you understand something of how threads are implemented. Every sequential program residing on a computer typically comes in four parts (Figure 12–1):

code	the procedures, statements, and expressions of the program, translated into machine language by a compiler or assembler
global data	the top-level (static) variables of the program
heap data	a pool of storage used by the NEW function when allocating new dynamic variables
stack	a storage area used to hold all local variables, procedure parameters, and bookkeeping information during execution

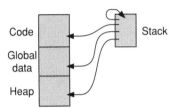

Figure 12–1   A sequential program in the computer.

Code is often kept in read-only memory, because it is never changed during execution. The size of the static data area is determined when the program is linked by adding up the sizes of the top-level variables in each module and interface. The contents of the static data area will change as the program modifies the top-level variables during execution. The heap starts as an area of unused storage; each time NEW is called, a piece is carved out and given to the program. When the garbage collector is run (or when the unsafe DISPOSE function is called), some storage may be returned to the pool for future use. The stack also starts out unused, but every time a procedure is called a chunk of storage at the top of the stack is reserved to hold the procedure's parameters and local variables. Every time a procedure returns, the storage it used on the stack is released.

When multiple threads are present in a concurrent program, each must have its own stack because each could call a different set of procedures in a different order. However, all the threads use the same code, global data, and heap areas (Figure 12–2). This means that any changes a thread makes to its local variables cannot affect other threads, because those variables are on the thread's own stack. However, changes made to global or heap data can affect other threads, in the sense that the other threads could be referring to the same global or dynamic variables at the same time.

When your program has more than one thread, it is the duty of the Modula–3 runtime system—in particular, the part known as the *thread scheduler*—to see that all the threads get a share of the available computing resources. On some multiprocessor computers, it may be possible to execute some or all of the threads simultaneously. However, it is more common to have many more threads than processors, and so the scheduler makes the threads take turns using the computer. In general, you cannot predict when one thread may be suspended and another may begin executing. For example, the scheduler may interrupt the running thread every 50 milliseconds and switch to a different thread. Only when all

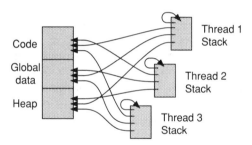

Figure 12–2   A multithreaded program in the computer.

the threads have had their 50-millisecond *time slice* will the first thread get another chance to run.

A thread may not be able to execute, even if the computer is not busy. A thread becomes *blocked* when it requests some resource that is temporarily unavailable. For instance, attempting to read a character from a keyboard can cause the current thread to block if no character has been typed. When a thread blocks, it is put aside temporarily and another thread is selected for execution. If a blocked thread later becomes *runnable*—if a character becomes available to be read, for example—then the blocked thread rejoins the other threads being scheduled for execution. A thread can also *complete*, in which case it stops permanently.

Finally, exceptions are always confined to a single thread in Modula–3. Exceptions propagate upward towards the top-level procedure in a thread, and it is a checked run-time error if the exception is not handled in some procedure in the thread. (Such an error usually halts the entire program.) Exceptions never "cross" from one thread to another.

12.1.1 Benefits

Let's look at a small example of how threads might be useful in a Modula–3 program. Suppose you want to read a line of text—a command, say—from the user's terminal. The SRC Modula–3 run-time library interface Rd provides a function GetLine that returns a line from the input stream. However, if you call Rd.GetLine and a full line is not available, the call will block until the line is complete. This is OK if your program doesn't have anything better to do than wait for input, but it's a nuisance if the program wants to perform some background tasks, like animating a graphics display, monitoring a real-time device, or processing the database transactions that accumulated overnight.

The solution to the problem is to place the call to Rd.GetLine in a separate thread, allowing it to block if necessary until a line is available. Meanwhile, your program can continue getting work done in the main thread. We introduce a top-level variable to hold the new text line, and a procedure, GetALine, which will be executed in a new thread:

```
IMPORT Rd, Stdio;
VAR theLine: TEXT := NIL;

PROCEDURE GetALine() =
    BEGIN
        theLine := Rd.GetLine(Stdio.stdin);
    END GetALine;
```

If Rd.GetLine finds that a line is not available, the thread will block until the line is available, but other threads will continue running.

The main program will start the new thread and then perform its background tasks, occasionally checking to see if a line has been read. (This is signaled by the variable theLine becoming nonnil.) When a line is available, you process it and then start another thread to read the next line, and so forth.We'll assume that the procedure StartAThread handles the creation and starting of a thread and that the procedure DiscardTheThread removes it when it has completed.The final code might look like this:

```
LOOP
    theLine := NIL;
    StartAThread(GetALine);
    WHILE theLine = NIL DO
        HandleBackgroundEvents();
    END;
    DiscardTheThread();
    ProcessCommand(theLine);
END;
```

Either ProcessCommand or HandleBackgroundEvents could raise an exception in order to terminate the processing loop.

12.1.2 Pitfalls

We mentioned that concurrent programs are subject to problems that do not affect sequential programs. One such problem is a *race*, in which a program's behavior depends upon the order in which different threads execute. Races are caused by threads accessing shared data in an uncontrolled fashion.

Let's look at an example. Many computer applications require the generation of a stream of distinct numbers. The numbers—sometimes in conjunction with other identification, like a process number or host name—can be used to give unique tags to messages or generate unique variable names in a computer-generated program. A simple generator is shown below: it is an object with a single method, next(), that returns an integer. Successive calls to next() return the integers 1, 2, 3, ….

```
TYPE Counter = OBJECT
        nextValue: INTEGER := 1;
    METHODS
        next() : INTEGER := Next;
    END;

PROCEDURE Next(self: Counter): INTEGER =
    VAR result: INTEGER;
    BEGIN
        result := self.nextValue;
        INC(self.nextValue);
        RETURN result;
    END Next;
```

The nextValue component of the Counter type is private, but to keep this example small we haven't made Counter an opaque type to hide it. We'll just assume that clients don't access nextValue.

The code below calls the next() method in a loop and prints the result:

```
IMPORT Fmt;
VAR counter: Counter;
...
LOOP
    Wr.PutText(Stdio.stdout, "I got " & Fmt.Int(counter.next()) & "\n");
END;
```

The output of the loop looks like this:

```
I got 1
I got 2
I got 3
...
```

Now, suppose that a Counter object was used in a multithreaded program, and that two threads called next() on the same object:

```
VAR counter: Counter;
PROCEDURE ThreadA() =
    BEGIN
        LOOP
            Wr.PutText(Stdio.stdout,"Thread A got " & Fmt.Int(counter.next()));
        END;
    END Thread1;
PROCEDURE ThreadB() =
    BEGIN
        LOOP
            Wr.PutText(Stdio.stdout,"Thread B got " & Fmt.Int(counter.next()));
        END;
    END Thread1;
```

Executing the program containing these threads, you would probably see output like this, as each thread has its turn to execute and calls counter.next():

```
...
Thread B got 21
Thread A got 22
Thread A got 23
Thread B got 24
Thread B got 25
Thread B got 26
...
```

However, if you let this program run for a long time and study the output, you might find lines like this:

```
...
Thread B got 94861
Thread A got 94861
Thread A got 94863
Thread B got 94864
...
```

Apparently, both calls on counter.next() returned 94861, and neither thread received number 94862! How did this happen?

In a multithreaded environment, the Modula–3 scheduler is free to stop one thread at any time and begin executing another thread. In this example, the switch occurred in the middle of the next() method. The table below shows how the various statements within next() might have been interleaved. The sequence starts with self.nextValue having the value 94861.

Time	Thread A	Thread B
t_0	result := self.nextValue;	
t_1	(suspend execution)	(resume execution)
t_2		result := self.nextValue;
t_3		INC(self.nextValue);
t_4		RETURN result;
t_5	(resume execution)	(suspend execution)
t_6	INC(self.nextValue);	
t_7	RETURN result;	

Both RETURN statements return the value 94861, because both threads read the value of self.nextValue before either could increment the value.

Race conditions are caused by multiple threads accessing shared data. The data can be declared globally to the threads or, as in this case, shared by means of references. Since each thread has its own stack, procedures that use only parameters and local variables are not subject to races.

Example 12–1

The Increment procedure below is not subject to races because it does not share any data with other threads:

```
PROCEDURE Increment(n: INTEGER): INTEGER =
  BEGIN
    INC(n);
    RETURN n;
  END Increment.
```

You can correct a race condition by temporarily forcing the threads to synchronize their execution, preventing them from accessing shared data at the same time. You do this by introducing a *critical section*, in which only one thread can execute at a time. Critical sections will be discussed in Section 12.3 on page 239.

12.2 Using Threads

Modula–3 provides several built-in types and operations to support concurrent programming. All the facilities are provided in the built-in interface Thread, which is shown in Listing 12–1 on page 236. The types and operations are summarized in the box below. This section will discuss how you create a thread, start it running, and wait for it to stop. Later sections will discuss how to synchronize and control threads.

Types for Concurrent Programming

Threads

Type:	Thread.T
Built-in functions:	Thread.Fork, Thread.Join, Thread.AlertJoin, Thread.Alert, Thread.TestAlert, Thread.Self

Mutual Exclusion Semaphores

Type:	Thread.Mutex (or MUTEX)
Built-in functions:	Thread.Wait, Thread.AlertWait, Thread.Acquire, Thread.Release
Statements:	LOCK

Condition Variables

Type:	Thread.Condition
Built-in functions:	Thread.Wait, Thread.AlertWait, Thread.Broadcast, Thread.Signal

---

12.2.1 Starting Threads

A thread is represented by a reference of type Thread.T, called the thread's *handle*. There are only two ways of getting a thread handle: calling the function Thread.Self, which returns a handle for "your" thread (i.e., the thread currently executing); or calling Thread.-Fork to create a new thread, start it running, and return its handle. (You cannot use NEW to create a Thread.T, since it is an opaque, nonobject reference.)

Let's look at what Fork will do before we examine its precise signature. We have to tell Fork what code to execute in the new thread; basically, we will do this by specifying

```
INTERFACE Thread;
TYPE
    T <: REFANY;
    Mutex = MUTEX;
    Condition <: ROOT;
    Closure = OBJECT  METHODS apply (): REFANY; END;
EXCEPTION Alerted;
PROCEDURE Fork (cl: Closure): T;
PROCEDURE Join (t: T): REFANY;
PROCEDURE Wait (m: Mutex; c: Condition);
PROCEDURE Acquire (m: Mutex);
PROCEDURE Release (m: Mutex);
PROCEDURE Broadcast (c: Condition);
PROCEDURE Signal (c: Condition);
PROCEDURE Self (): T;
PROCEDURE Alert (t: T);
PROCEDURE TestAlert (): BOOLEAN;
PROCEDURE AlertWait (m: Mutex; c: Condition) RAISES {Alerted};
PROCEDURE AlertJoin (t: T): REFANY RAISES {Alerted};
CONST AtomicSize = ... (* bits in memory-coherent block *);
END Thread.
```

Listing 12–1   The Modula–3 Thread interface.

some top-level procedure, P. Space for a new stack will be allocated, and the thread will be created so that when it begins executing, the first thing it will do is call procedure P. Fork will then return the thread's handle, and eventually—the precise moment depends on how threads are scheduled—the new thread will start executing in P. In fact, the thread could even start before Fork returns. If and when P returns, the thread halts. Once halted, a thread cannot be restarted; you have to discard the old thread and create a new one. (Threads are reclaimed by the garbage collector when no more references to them exist.) The signature of Fork is

```
PROCEDURE Fork(cl: Thread.Closure): Thread.T;
```

Instead of passing a procedure P to Fork directly, a slightly more general mechanism is used. The argument to Fork will be a *closure*, an object descended from Thread.Closure, which has this structure:

```
TYPE Closure = OBJECT METHODS apply(): REFANY END;
```

What Fork actually does is call the apply method of its argument inside the new thread. You must create a suitable subtype of Thread.Closure which at least overrides the NIL value for apply with a suitable procedure. Your closure object can also include fields to hold any arguments needed by the procedure. When your apply method returns, it can return a REFANY argument.

Example 12–2

On page 231 we outlined a program that used a separate thread to wait for a line of input. We presumed that the statement StartAThread(ReadTheLine) would call ReadTheLine in the context of a new thread. We can now implement StartAThread using Thread.Fork. The signatures of ReadTheLine and StartAThread must be changed to make them compatible with thread mechanism: ReadTheLine must become the apply method of a closure, and StartAThread must take the closure as a parameter, rather than taking the procedure directly:

```
VAR theThread: Thread.T;    (* Save the new thread, so it can be removed later. *)

PROCEDURE ReadTheLine(self: Thread.Closure): REFANY =
    BEGIN
        theLine := Rd.GetLine(Stdio.stdin);
        RETURN NIL;    (* We don't use the result or the parameter. *)
    END ReadTheLine;

PROCEDURE StartAThread(cl: Thread.Closure) =
    BEGIN
        theThread := Thread.Fork(cl);
    END StartAThread;
```

Now, the "logical" call StartAThread(ReadLine) is actually written like this:

```
StartAThread(NEW(Thread.Closure, apply := ReadTheLine));
```

You can't move the NEW call inside StartAThread and pass ReadTheLine as a parameter because the apply method override must use a procedure constant (Section 11.3.1 on page 211).

12.2.2 Thread Completion

A thread is normally created to do its work concurrently with other processing. Some threads do their work continually, never stopping. Other threads complete their work and stop (like the one in Example 12–2). If you want to wait for a thread to complete, you must use the Thread.Join procedure:

```
PROCEDURE Join(t: Thread.T): REFANY;
```

The Thread.Join procedure waits if necessary for thread t to complete (i.e., for the original closure's apply method to return). The REFANY return value from the apply method of the closure is then returned by Join. It's all right if the thread completes before Join is called; in that case, the thread just hangs around and Join returns the proper result immediately.

Example 12–3

In Example 12–2, the StartAThread procedure creates a thread and stores it in a global variable, theThread. The procedure DiscardTheThread, below, can be used to remove the thread from the run-time environment. If the thread's apply method has not already completed (i.e., if Rd.GetLine has not yet returned), then the call to Thread.Join will block until it does.

```
PROCEDURE DiscardTheThread() =
BEGIN
    EVAL Thread.Join(theThread);   (* ignore result of apply *)
    theThread := NIL;
END DiscardTheThread;
```

The EVAL statement is used because we don't care about the return value from Thread.Join.
Setting theThread to NIL ensures that the thread will be reclaimed by the garbage collector.

Example 12–4

Suppose we have a function F given by the declaration

```
PROCEDURE F(x, y: REAL): REAL;
```

The problem is that F takes a very long time to complete—minutes, let's say—and we'd like
to do some other things while F grinds away. Create two functions, StartF and WaitForF, to
start the computation of F and to fetch the result, respectively. The signatures are to be

```
PROCEDURE StartF(x, y: REAL): FHandle;
PROCEDURE WaitForF(FHandle): REAL;
```

where FHandle identifies the particular call of F. We want to be able to start several calls of F
simultaneously, for example,

```
FirstF := StartF(1.0, -3.4);
SecondF := StartF(2.456, 7.9);
… (* do something else *) …
FirstResult := WaitForF(FirstF);
SecondResult := WaitForF(SecondF);
```

Solution   StartF and WaitForF will be short interfaces to Fork and Join. The FHandle type
can be Thread.T:

```
IMPORT Thread;
TYPE
    FHandle = Thread.T;
    FClosure = Thread.Closure OBJECT
        x, y: REAL;   (* Arguments to F *)
    OVERRIDES
        apply := ApplyF;
    END;

PROCEDURE StartF(x, y: REAL): Thread.T=
    VAR closure := NEW(FClosure, x := x, y := y);
    BEGIN
        RETURN Thread.Fork(closure);
    END StartF;

PROCEDURE ApplyF(cl: FClosure): REFANY =
    VAR ResultHolder := NEW(REF REAL);
    BEGIN
        ResultHolder ^ := F(cl.x, cl.y);
        RETURN ResultHolder;
    END ApplyF;
```

```
PROCEDURE WaitForF(handle: Thread.T): REAL =
  BEGIN
    RETURN NARROW(Thread.Join(handle), REF REAL) ^ ;
  END WaitForF;
```

12.3 Synchronizing Threads

On page 232 we showed how multiple threads can interfere with each other by engaging in races. In this section we'll see how to prevent these races.

Whenever several threads access the same data, their access must be synchronized to avoid race conditions. That is, you must arrange for one of the threads to perform all of its operations on the shared data before allowing any other thread to access the data. In the example on page 233, the problem was that we couldn't guarantee that each thread would have the opportunity to perform *both* statements

```
result := self.nextValue;
INC(self.nextValue);
```

before another thread entered the same code. Another way of saying this is that we want the pair of statements to be an *atomic action*.

To synchronize access to shared data, you designate the group of statements that access the shared data as a *critical section*. Critical sections are introduced with the LOCK statement shown below.

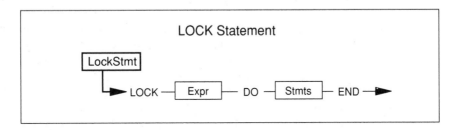

The statements between DO and END are in the critical section. The value of the expression must have type MUTEX; this is a *mutual exclusion semaphore* (mutex, for short) which identifies the critical section. At most one thread will be able to execute in any LOCK statement using a particular mutex. The thread executing in the critical section is said to *hold* the mutex. Any other thread wishing to enter the critical section *blocks* until the first thread releases the mutex. You create a mutex by calling NEW(MUTEX).

Because MUTEX is an object type, the easiest way to associate a mutex with a new object is to make the new object type a descendant of MUTEX.Then, the mutex is automatically created when the object is, and LOCK may be applied to the new object itself. For example, here is how to fix the Counter object example on page 232 by associating a mutex with the object and placing a critical section around the references nextValue:

```
TYPE Counter = MUTEX OBJECT
    nextValue: INTEGER := 1;
METHODS
    next(): INTEGER := Next;
END;

PROCEDURE Next(self: Counter): INTEGER =
VAR result: INTEGER;
BEGIN
    LOCK self DO
        result := self.nextValue; INC(self.nextValue);
    END;
    RETURN result;
END Next;
```

By forcing the two statements

```
result := self.nextValue; INC(self.nextValue);
```

to be executed together, this critical section prevents two threads from receiving the same value from a call on next(). The LOCK statement does not prevent two threads from executing inside the critical section at the same time if they are operating on different counters, because then each thread would be holding a different mutex. Also, the LOCK statement does not prevent the scheduler from suspending the thread that is executing inside the critical section; it just prevents any other thread from holding the same mutex.

12.3.1 A Buffer Example

A buffer is a data structure often used to facilitate communication between threads. The buffer can hold a list of elements. One thread, the *producer*, adds items to the buffer as those items are created. A second thread, the *consumer*, removes items from the buffer and processes them. Using a buffer allows the producers and consumers to operate at their own rates. Only if the producer completely fills the buffer, or if the consumer completely empties it, will one thread have to wait for the other.

An interface to a simple fixed-size, circular buffer is shown below. The buffer holds items of type REFANY and provides Add and Remove methods:

```
INTERFACE Buffer;
EXCEPTION Full; Empty;
TYPE
    T <: Public;
    Public = MUTEX OBJECT
        METHODS
        add(item: REFANY) RAISES {Full};
        remove(): REFANY RAISES {Empty};
        init(size:  [1 .. LAST(INTEGER)]): T;
    END;
END Buffer.
```

A new buffer that can hold N elements is created like this:

```
IMPORT Buffer;
VAR buffer := NEW(Buffer.T).init(N);
```

The producer adds items by calling buffer.add(item), and the consumer removes them by executing item := buffer.remove(). Exceptions are used to signal an empty or full buffer. The Buffer.T type needs a mutex to prevent races among the producers and consumers; in this case, we just make Buffer.T a descendant of MUTEX. The complete implementation of the Buffer module is shown below:

```
MODULE Buffer;
IMPORT Thread;

REVEAL
    T = Public BRANDED OBJECT
            data: REF ARRAY OF REFANY := NIL;
            itemsInBuffer: CARDINAL := 0;   (* How many items in buffer? *)
            nextRemove: CARDINAL := 0;   (* Slot with item to next remove *)
        OVERRIDES
            add := Add; remove := Remove; init := Init;
    END;

PROCEDURE Add(self: T; item: REFANY) RAISES {Full} =
    BEGIN
        LOCK self DO
            IF self.itemsInBuffer= NUMBER(self.data^) THEN RAISE Full; END;
            WITH nextFreeSlot =
                (self.nextRemove + self.itemsInBuffer) MOD
                 NUMBER(self.data^) DO
                self.data[nextFreeSlot] := item
            END;
            INC(self.itemsInBuffer);
        END (*LOCK*);
        RETURN;
    END Add;

PROCEDURE Remove(self: T): REFANY RAISES {Empty} =
    VAR item: REFANY;
    BEGIN
        LOCK self DO
            IF self.itemsInBuffer = 0 THEN RAISE Empty; END;
            item := self.data[self.nextRemove];
            self.nextRemove := (self.nextRemove + 1) MOD NUMBER(self.data^);
            DEC(self.itemsInBuffer);
        END (*LOCK*);
        RETURN item;
    END Remove;
```

```
PROCEDURE Init(self: T; size: [1 .. LAST(INTEGER)]): T =
  BEGIN
    self.data := NEW(REF ARRAY OF REFANY, size);
    RETURN self;
  END Init;


BEGIN
END Buffer.
```

12.3.2 Locks and Exceptions

The Buffer example uses exceptions to signal empty and full buffers. In particular, there are RAISE statements inside LOCK statements in the code for procedures Add and Remove. You might wonder if the buffer's mutex is unlocked when an exception causes the lock statement to terminate prematurely. The answer is yes. If an exception is propagated out of a LOCK statement, the mutex is released. That is, the statement

```
LOCK mu DO stmts END
```

is the same as

```
WITH m = mu DO
  Thread.Acquire(m);
  TRY
    stmts
  FINALLY
    Thread.Release(m);
  END ;
END;
```

where Thread.Acquire and Thread.Release are the operations that lock and unlock a mutex, and m is some identifier not used inside stmts. This rewriting implies that RETURN and EXIT from within a LOCK statement also correctly release the mutex. (See page 140.)

12.3.3 Monitors

Although it is generally best to associate mutexes with data structures, it is possible to associate them with modules and procedures. Some concurrent programs are synchronized by placing a single critical section around all procedures in, say, a module. While this may eliminate race conditions, it generally oversynchronizes clients. That is, thread A can be forced to wait for thread B to exit a critical section, even though A and B are operating on different data structures and no interference between them is possible.

For example, in the Buffer module, a mutex is associated with each buffer. We can rewrite the module to use a single mutex that allows no more than one thread to execute in the module at any time. Instead of making Buffer.T a descendant of MUTEX, we create a single mutex at the top level of the module, and then place a critical section around the body of each procedure. The term for this kind of module is a *monitor*. Here is a sketch of the changes:

```
MODULE Buffer;
  ...

VAR moduleMutex := NEW(Thread.Mutex);
  ...


PROCEDURE Add(self: T; item: REFANY) RAISES {Full} =
  BEGIN
    LOCK moduleMutex DO ... END;
    RETURN;
  END Add;


PROCEDURE Remove(self: T): REFANY RAISES {Empty} =
  VAR item: REFANY;
  BEGIN
    LOCK moduleMutex DO ... END;
    RETURN item;
  END Remove;

BEGIN
END Buffer.
```

The module's mutex is created by an initialization expression on the variable moduleMutex. This initialization is performed when the module is initialized, before any procedures are called.

12.3.4 Mutexes as Components of Data Structures

Sometimes you want to associate a mutex with a data structure, but that data structure is not an object that can be made a descendant of type MUTEX. Perhaps the data is not an object at all, or perhaps it is already a descendant of some supertype that you cannot modify. In that case, you have to include a mutex as a component of the data structure, and allocate it explicitly when the data structure is allocated. This allocation, if not done properly, can lead to race conditions.

To illustrate some of the subtleties, let's rewrite the Counter example (page 232) to associate a mutex as a component of each Counter object. First we'll sketch the code without thinking about allocation:

```
TYPE Counter = OBJECT
    nextValue: INTEGER := 1;
    mutex: MUTEX;
  METHODS
    next(): INTEGER := Next;
  END;
```

```
PROCEDURE Next(self: Counter): INTEGER =
    VAR result: INTEGER;
    BEGIN
        LOCK self.mutex DO
            result := self.nextValue;
            INC(self.nextValue);
        END;
        RETURN result;
    END Next;
```

A mutex is associated with each Counter as a component, and the Next procedure correctly locks the object's mutex. However, where do we create the mutex? We can't write an initialization expression in the type declaration, because the call on NEW is not a constant expression. Therefore, we'll have to create an initialization method that does the work:

```
TYPE Counter = ...OBJECT
        mutex: MUTEX := NIL;

        ...
    METHODS
        init(): Counter := Init; ...
    END;


PROCEDURE Init(self: Counter): Counter =
    BEGIN
        IF self.mutex = NIL THEN self.mutex := NEW(MUTEX); END;
        RETURN self;
    END Init;
```

By initializing Counter.mutex to NIL in the type declaration, we ensure that the LOCK statement will fail and halt the program if the client fails to call the init method. Similarly, the test inside Init guards against clients calling Init multiple times. When creating a counter, the client should call init when NEW is called:

```
VAR counter := NEW(Counter).init();
```

However, we can't force the client to call init() in the proper way. Failing to call init() is all right—in the sense that the Modula–3 run-time system will detect the error when an attempt is made to lock the mutex. However, what if two threads try to call init() on the same object simultaneously? In fact, this can allow two threads be in the critical section at the same time. A sequence of actions that produces this race is shown in Table 12–1 on page 245. To prevent this race, use a separate, module-level mutex to protect the code inside the Init procedure. (See Exercise 6.)

12.4 Deadlocks

When entering a critical section, a thread may have to wait until a second thread releases the critical section's mutex. When a thread blocks and there is no possibility of it ever con-

Table 12–1   Race Caused by Simultaneous Initializations

Time	Thread A	Thread B
t_0	Init: IF self.mutex = NIL THEN	
t_1		Init: IF self.mutex = NIL THEN
t_2		self.mutex := NEW(MUTEX); END(*IF*)
t_3		Next: LOCK self.mutex DO
t_4		result := self.nextValue;
t_5	self.mutex := NEW(MUTEX); END(*IF*)	
t_6	Next: LOCK self.mutex DO	
t_7	result := self.nextValue;	
t_8	INC(self.nextValue);	
t_9	END(*LOCK*)	
t_{10}	RETURN result;	
t_{11}		INC(self.nextValue);
t_{12}		END(*LOCK*)
t_{13}		RETURN result;

tinuing, a *deadlock* occurs. The simplest deadlock arises when a thread tries to acquire a mutex it already holds:

```
LOCK Mutex1 DO
   LOCK Mutex1 DO
       ...
   END;
END;
```

The thread executing this code will block forever trying to enter the inner critical section. Real programs can deadlock in more subtle ways. In more complicated programs, for example, it may be necessary to lock more than a single data structure at one time. That is, a thread may have to be in two *different* critical sections simultaneously—one critical section nested inside another. The following example demonstrates how deadlocks can occur in these programs.

Example 12–5

Threads A and B are part of a banking transaction program. Thread A is processing requests on behalf of account A and thread B is handling account B. Let's assume it is important that all accounts balance at all times, that is, the sum of the amounts over all accounts must be a constant value. This means that both accounts in a transaction must be locked while the transaction is made. Suppose that thread A gets a request to pay $100 into account B. Therefore, it executes this code:

```
LOCK AccountA DO
    LOCK AccountB DO
        Transfer(from := AccountA, to := AccountB, amt := 100.0);
    END;
END;
```

Meanwhile, thread B gets a request to pay $200 into account A, so it executes this code:

```
LOCK AccountB DO
    LOCK AccountA DO
        Transfer(from := AccountB, to := AccountA, amt := 200.0);
    END;
END;
```

Suppose that thread A successfully locks AccountA and enters the outer critical section. However, before A can proceed further, B successfully locks AccountB and enters its outer critical section. Now, A holds AccountA and cannot release it until A acquires AccountB. But, B holds AccountB and will not release it until B acquires AccountA. The threads are deadlocked; they cannot proceed.

You can design your programs to avoid deadlocks of this sort. Any time you must hold two or more mutexes, be sure you always lock them in the same order. In the situation in Example 12–5, one strategy might be always to lock the account with the lower account number first.

12.5 Condition Variables

We've seen three ways a thread may block indefinitely and then restart:

1. When making calls to I/O services, a thread may block if an input operation cannot be completed. The thread is unblocked when input is available.

2. When attempting to enter a critical section, a thread will block if another thread currently holds the critical section's mutex. The thread is unblocked when the mutex is released.

3. The Thread.Join procedure blocks until the thread's top-level procedure completes.

These are specific instances in which a thread must be suspended until it is able to make useful progress. When you write multithreaded applications, you may find many other circumstances in which you would like to suspend threads until they can make progress. Condition variables are provided in Modula–3 to let you do this. A condition variable is a kind of parking lot for threads. You can have any number of condition variables and you can suspend any number of threads on each condition variable. A thread remains suspended on a condition variable until another thread *signals* the condition variable, which allows the blocked threads to continue.

Before using a condition variable, you must also identify the shared variables that will determine whether or not to suspend a thread, and the mutex that protects those shared variables. Condition variable, shared data, and the mutex are used together to control threads.

A new condition variable is created by calling

```
NEW(Thread.Condition)
```

Then, there are three main procedures in the Thread interface for condition variables:

Wait(mu, cv)   blocks the current thread on condition variable cv; the thread must already hold mutex mu

Signal(cv)   unblocks one (and sometimes more than one) of the threads blocked on condition variable cv

Broadcast(cv)   unblocks all the threads blocked on cv

Let's see how these facilities are used. First, create the condition variable and mutex:

```
IMPORT Thread;
VAR
    cv := NEW(Thread.Condition);
    mu := NEW(Thread.Mutex);
```

The code to suspend a thread typically looks like this:

```
LOCK mu DO
    WHILE ICantMakeProgress DO Thread.Wait(mu, cv); END;
    MakeProgress;
END;
```

The identifier *ICantMakeProgress* represents some test that determines whether the thread should suspend or continue. *MakeProgress* represents the statements that make up the thread's useful work. The mutex mu is used to protect any shared data used in the *ICantMakeProgress* test and the *MakeProgress* code. The call to Thread.Wait suspends the thread on a queue associated with cv, and unlocks the mutex mu. When the suspended thread is awoken—we'll get to that in a minute—the Thread.Wait procedure will relock the mutex before returning. It's important that the awakened thread retest the *ICantMakeProgress* condition, because some other thread X might acquire the mutex after the suspended thread is released but before the suspended thread can acquire the mutex. Thread X might change the data so that the *ICantMakeProgress* test is TRUE, requiring the newly released thread to suspend itself again.

The code that awakens a suspended thread typically looks like this:

```
LOCK mu DO
    PerformActions;
    IF OughtToWakeUpSomeone THEN Thread.Signal(cv); END;
END
```

The thread executing this code does some work (*PerformActions*) and then decides whether any threads suspended on cv ought to be allowed to try to continue. If so, the Thread.-Signal call unblocks a thread on cv—if there are any there. For implementation reasons, Thread.Signal might release more than a single thread blocked on cv; this is another reason the loop on *ICantMakeProgress* in the suspension code is beneficial.

12.5.1 A Buffer Example Using Condition Variables

An interface to a simple fixed-size, circular buffer was shown on page 240. In that example, the Add method raised an exception if the buffer was full, and the Remove method raised an exception if the buffer was empty. If we assume that some threads are adding to the buffer and other threads are removing from it, another design option would be to have a thread calling Add simply suspend itself until there was room to add an item, and have a thread calling Remove suspend itself until a new item was available. To do this, we must add two condition variables to each buffer: one for producers waiting for space in a full buffer, and one for consumers waiting for items to be added to an empty buffer. The new interface is unchanged except for the removal of the exceptions:

```
INTERFACE Buffer;
  IMPORT Thread;
  TYPE
    T <: Public;
    Public = Thread.Mutex OBJECT
      METHODS
        add(item: REFANY);          (* Blocks if buffer full *)
        remove(): REFANY;           (* Blocks if buffer empty *)
        init(size: [1..LAST(INTEGER)]): T;
    END;
END Buffer.
```

In the Add procedure in the new implementation, the loop

```
WHILE self.itemsInBuffer= self.size DO Thread.Wait(self, self.NotFull); END;
```

suspends the thread if the buffer is full. The thread resumes when the consumer executes

```
Thread.Signal(self.NotFull)
```

in the Remove procedure. The consumer always signals this condition variable, because it is not possible to tell if any producers are waiting to be awoken. There is a similar wait and signal with the NotEmpty condition variable. Here is the complete code:

```
MODULE Buffer; (* with condition variables *)
IMPORT Thread;
```

```
REVEAL
    T = Public BRANDED OBJECT
        data: REF ARRAY OF REFANY := NIL;
        notFull, notEmpty: Thread.Condition;
        itemsInBuffer: CARDINAL := 0;        (* How many items in buffer? *)
        nextRemove: CARDINAL := 0;           (* Slot of item to next be removed *)
    OVERRIDES
        add := Add; remove := Remove; init := Init;
    END;


PROCEDURE Init(self: T; size: [1..LAST(INTEGER)]): T =
    BEGIN
        self.data := NEW(REF ARRAY OF REFANY, size);
        self.notFull := NEW(Thread.Condition);
        self.notEmpty := NEW(Thread.Condition);
        RETURN self;
    END Init;


PROCEDURE Add(self: T; item: REFANY) =
    BEGIN
        LOCK self DO
            WHILE self.itemsInBuffer= NUMBER(self.data^) DO
                Thread.Wait(self, self.notFull);
            END;
            WITH nextFreeSlot =
                (self.nextRemove + self.itemsInBuffer) MOD NUMBER(self.data^) DO
                self.data[nextFreeSlot] := item
            END;
            INC(self.itemsInBuffer);
            Thread.Signal(self.notEmpty);
        END (*LOCK*);
        RETURN;
    END Add;


PROCEDURE Remove(self: T): REFANY =
    VAR item: REFANY;
    BEGIN
        LOCK self DO
            WHILE self.itemsInBuffer= 0 DO
                Thread.Wait(self, self.notEmpty);
            END;
            item := self.data[self.nextRemove];
            self.nextRemove := (self.nextRemove + 1) MOD NUMBER(self.data^);
            DEC(self.itemsInBuffer);
            Thread.Signal(self.notFull);
        END (*LOCK*);
        RETURN item;
    END Remove;
BEGIN
END Buffer.
```

12.6 Alerts

An *alert* is an indication to a thread that it should cease what it is doing. Alerts are typically used to terminate long-running computations or to force a thread to stop waiting for I/O or a condition variable. Alerts are often initiated by user interaction: a user might get tired of waiting for a long computation, and push a "cancel" button, which in turn is translated to one or more alerts on busy threads.

To alert a thread th, you call the procedure Thread.Alert(th). This sets an "alert flag" in thread th. If thread th is embarked on a long computation, it can test the alert flag by periodically calling the function Thread.TestAlert(). If the alert flag is set, this function returns TRUE and clears the flag. If the alert flag is not set, the function returns FALSE. Notice that threads must explicitly test the alert flag at appropriate intervals; Modula–3 does not force them to stop. This gives a thread the opportunity to pick a convenient time for stopping.

Example 12–6

The Repeat procedure below calls the parameter procedure p many times. After each iteration, it checks the alert flag, and stops if it is set. This gives an outside agent the opportunity to stop Repeat after each iteration of p, although there is no way the caller of Repeat can tell if Repeat completed normally or because of an alert.

```
PROCEDURE Repeat(n: CARDINAL; p: PROCEDURE()) =
  BEGIN
    FOR i := 1 TO n DO
      p();
      IF Thread.TestAlert() THEN RETURN; END;
    END;
  END Repeat;
```

If a thread is blocked on a condition variable, it certainly cannot test the alert flag. Therefore, Modula–3 provides procedures in the Thread interface that raise the exception Thread.Alerted when the blocked thread is alerted:

AlertWait(mu, cv) like Thread.Wait, but raises the Alerted exception (with mu locked) if the thread is alerted during the wait

AlertJoin(t) like Thread.Join, but raises the Alerted exception if the current thread (not the thread t) is alerted during the wait

Again, you must anticipate the alert by using the alertable form of the Wait and Join procedures. Many I/O procedures check the alert flag and include the Thread.Alerted exception in their raises set, to allow a thread to be forced off an I/O wait. However, notice that you cannot use alerts to unblock a thread that is waiting for a mutex.

Example 12–7

The buffer interface on page 248 can be made alertable. First, add the Alerted exception to the method interfaces:

```
INTERFACE Buffer;
  IMPORT Thread;
  TYPE
    T <: Public;
    Public = Thread.Mutex OBJECT
      METHODS
        add(item: REFANY) RAISES {Thread.Alerted}; (* Blocks if buffer full *)
        remove(): REFANY RAISES {Thread.Alerted}; (* Blocks if buffer empty *)
        init(size: [1..LAST(INTEGER)]): T;
      END;
END Buffer.
```

Next, in the Buffer module change the calls on Thread.Wait to Thread.AlertWait. Inspection shows that raising an exception at that point leaves the buffer in a stable state. As the exception propagates out of the LOCK statement, the mutex will be released.

When you write an interface, you should always anticipate that clients may be in a multithreaded environment, and should handle alerts gracefully.

12.7 Other Facilities

The Thread interface also provides low-level procedures for locking and unlocking mutexes.

> Acquire(mu)   blocks until mu is free, and then locks it
> Release(mu)   unlocks mu

You should avoid using these calls whenever possible, choosing the LOCK statement instead. It is more difficult to ensure that Acquire and Release are properly paired and called at the right times, especially in the presence of exceptions.

Acquire and Release are occasionally useful when you want to briefly release a mutex inside a lock statement. For example, the following code unlocks mutex mu while statements S2 are executed:

```
LOCK mu DO
  S1;
  Thread.Release(mu);
  S2;
  Thread.Acquire(mu);
  S3;
END
```

The intent here is to allow other threads to acquire mu during the (perhaps lengthy) execution of S2. The programmer writing this would have to ensure that:

1. S2 does not use or modify the shared data protected by mu.
2. S1 has left the shared data in a consistent state.

3. S3 anticipates that the shared data may have changed between the calls to Release and Acquire.

4. S2 does not raise any exceptions.

(See Exercise 10.)

12.8 Exercises

Answers to the exercises marked "[A]" appear in Appendix D.

1. What is the difference between:

    a. a process and a thread?

    b. a sequential program and a concurrent program?

    c. a mutex and a condition variable?

2. Describe each of the following. Which can occur in sequential as well as concurrent programs?

    a. race condition

    b. deadlock

    c. critical section

3. Does executing the RETURN statement in the following code leave mu locked? Why?   [A]

    ```
    LOCK mu DO
        IF b THEN RETURN; END;
    END;
    ```

4. When does a call to Thread.Alert cause an exception to be raised and when does it simply cause a flag to be set?

5. Rewrite the Counter type as an opaque object type with its own interface and module. Include the required synchronization for multiple threads. Make Counter a descendant of MUTEX, but do not reveal that fact in the interface.

6. In Table 12–1 on page 245, at time t_{12}, thread B unlocks self.mutex. Will that be the mutex Thread B created, or the one more recently created by Thread A? Explain why there might be an ambiguity. (Hint: Consider the rewriting of LOCK on page 242, which a Modula–3 implementor might or might not follow exactly.)

7. In the Buffer implementation in Section 12.3.1 on page 240, a mutex was associated with each buffer. If no synchronization was provided (i.e., if the LOCK statements were removed), what specific problems might arise? Demonstrate (in the manner of Table 12–1 on page 245) how two nearly simultaneous calls to Add by different threads could result in items being lost.

8. Example 12–5 on page 245 demonstrated a deadlocking problem in a banking application. The purpose of this exercise is to eliminate the deadlock. Here is a definition of type Account and a function Pay that transfers money between two accounts, without any synchronization: [A]

```
TYPE Account = Thread.Mutex OBJECT
    acctNumber: INTEGER;
    amount: EXTENDED;
END;
```

```
PROCEDURE Pay(from, to: Account; amt: EXTENDED) =
BEGIN
    from.Amount := from.Amount – amt;
    to.Amount := to.Amount + amt
END Pay;
```

Change the Pay procedure to properly lock both accounts during the transaction, without any possibility of deadlock. Assume that every account has a unique account number held in the AcctNumber field.

9. Refer to the Repeat procedure of Example 12–6 on page 250. Suppose that the parameter procedure p called Thread.TestAlert and returned immediately if the alert flag was set. How would that affect the alertability of Repeat? What does this suggest about a good way for low-level procedures to handle alert signals?   [A]

10. In the text (item 4 on page 252) we hinted that the following code would not have the intended effect if statement S2 raised an exception. Why not? (Hint: Translate the LOCK statement into the equivalent TRY-FINALLY statement.) Change the code so that it will tolerate exceptions from S2:   [A]

```
LOCK mu DO
    S1;
    Thread.Release(mu);
    S2;
    Thread.Acquire(mu);
    S3;
END
```

13

Low-Level Programming

A cleanly designed and elegant programming language can be unusable in practice if it does not contain the "nitty-gritty" features that allow a programmer to get the job done. Some of these features help improve the space/time performance of the program; others allow you to combine parts of a program written in Modula–3 with other parts written in other languages; still others are "loopholes" in the type safety of the language. These features should be used very carefully.

13.1 Packed Types

If T is a type and n is an integer-valued constant expression, then a type P declared as

    BITS n FOR T

is a *packed type*. Variables of type P can contain any of the values that are members of type T, but variables of type P that occur as elements of records, objects, or arrays will occupy exactly n bits at run time and will be placed immediately adjacent to the preceding element. The values allowed for n are implementation-dependent and may depend on alignment constraints and where the packed type appears in a record or object. The number of bits specified must be sufficient to hold all the elements of T. The most common choices for T are subranges of CARDINAL and enumerated types and subranges. Integer subranges that include negative values may not be able to be packed into bit fields.

Example 13–1

The legality of packed types is implementation-dependent, but we can make some general comments and anticipate some problems. Consider these declarations:

255

```
TYPE
    P1 = BITS 5 FOR [0..31];
    P2 = BITS 8 FOR [0..31];
    P3 = BITS 3 FOR [0..31];          (* ?! *)
    A1 = ARRAY [1..60] OF P1;         (* ?! *)
    A2 = ARRAY [1..60] OF P2;

VAR
    V1: P1;
    V2: A1;
```

The type [0..31] requires at least 5 bits to represent all its values, so the type P3 must be illegal. Types P1 and P2 are (probably) legal. If we are compiling for a computer that has 32-bit words, it is possible that our Modula–3 implementation will reject the declaration of A1, because a tight packing of array elements, at 5 bits per element, would result in some elements of the array crossing 32-bit word boundaries. This is difficult to handle on many computers. The declaration of A2 is likely to be accepted, because the 8-bit elements pack four to a word. Finally, the variable V1 may very well occupy more than 5 bits of storage, because packed types are treated specially only when they occur in arrays, records, or objects. You could expect that variable V2 would occupy a total of 15 words. (60*8 = 480 bits; 480/32 = 15 words.)

There are typically two reasons for using packed types: to reduce the storage consumed by a data structure, or to match the layout of an externally defined data structure.

13.1.1 Compatibility of Packed Types

If P is the type BITS n for T, then P <: T and T <: P. This is reasonable, because P and T contain the same set of values and can be mixed in most contexts. However, P and T are *not* the same type.

Example 13–2

Suppose we have the declarations

```
TYPE P = BITS n FOR T;
VAR
    p: P;   t: T;
    pRef: REF P;   tRef: REF T;
PROCEDURE ProcP(x: P) = ... END ProcP;
PROCEDURE ProcT(VAR x: T) = ... END ProcT;
```

Which of the following four statements are legal?

```
p := t;
tRef := pRef;
ProcP(t);
ProcT(p);
```

Solution   The statements p := t and ProcP(t) are legal because P and T are assignable, which follows from the subtype relation. However, tRef := pRef is not legal because the types REF P and REF T are not related by the subtype relation and are not assignable. Similarly, ProcT(p) is not legal, because the argument to ProcT must have the same type as the VAR-mode formal parameter, but P and T are not the same type.

13.1.2 Packed Types and Byte Ordering

When you use packed types to achieve a specific data layout, you may find that your types work properly on one computer but not on another. The packed fields in a record are allocated in order of increasing addresses, but computers differ in "which way" addresses increase within words. In what follows, let's assume that the computers have 32-bit words which are divided into four 8-bit bytes. We'll also assume that each byte is addressable.

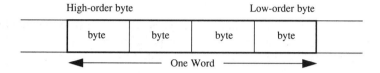

The low-order byte of the word is on the right, and the high-order byte is on the left. That means that if the word contains the integer 16_11223344, then the leftmost, high-order byte will contain 16_11 and the rightmost, low-order byte will contain 16_44.

On a "big endian" or "left-to-right" computer, a word's address is also the address of the high-order byte. Addresses increase left to right, so that if the high-order byte has address A, then the low-order byte will have address A+3. Packed fields are also laid out left to right.

On a "little endian" or "right-to-left" computer, a word's address is also the address of the low-order byte. Addresses increase right to left, so that if the high-order byte has address A, then the low-order byte will have address A−3. Packed fields are also laid out right to left.

Now suppose you are trying to duplicate the format of an international standard for floating-point numbers, which occupies two words and is specified in terms of words as follows:

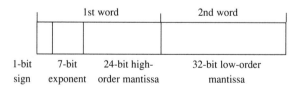

On a big endian computer, you could define the structure in Modula–3 as

```
TYPE FloatingPointFmt = RECORD          (* Big endian version *)
    sign: BITS 1 FOR BOOLEAN;
    exponent: BITS 7 FOR [0..127];
    highMantissa: BITS 24 FOR [0..16_FFFFFF];
    lowMantissa: INTEGER;
END;
```

However, on a little endian computer, you have to change the definition to reflect the different packing within each word:

```
TYPE FloatingPointFmt = RECORD          (* Little endian version *)
    highMantissa: BITS 24 FOR [0..16_FFFFFF];
    exponent: BITS 7 FOR [0..127];
    sign: BITS 1 FOR BOOLEAN;
    lowMantissa: INTEGER;
END;
```

Of course, if you are using packed types just to save space and not to match an external format, the different packing order is probably irrelevant to you and a single declaration will probably work on all computers with the same word size.

13.1.3 Type Sizes

The functions ADRSIZE, BYTESIZE, and BITSIZE can be used to determine the size of a type or variable. Each takes a single argument, which can be a variable designator or a type other than an open array type. The argument is not evaluated unless it is a designator for an open array. Each function returns an integer value of type CARDINAL.

BITSIZE(x)   returns the size of x in bits
BYTESIZE(x)   returns the size of x in 8-bit bytes
ADRSIZE(x)   returns the size of x in addressable locations

The majority of modern computers are byte-addressable, and BYTESIZE and ADRSIZE should return the same value on these computers. On word-addressable computers, and computers whose natural "character" size is not 8, the value of BYTESIZE is more problematic. BYTESIZE and ADRSIZE applied to packed types that do not occupy an integral number of bytes or addressable locations will probably round up to the next integral value.

Example 13–3

Given the declarations

```
TYPE P = BITS 5 FOR [0..31];
VAR
    p: P;
    r: RECORD f: P; END;
```

the value of BITSIZE(P) and BITSIZE(r.f) would be 5, but the value of BITSIZE(p) could very well be the same as BITSIZE(INTEGER), since packed types need only be packed in records, objects, and arrays. The value of BYTESIZE(P) and ADRSIZE(P) will (probably) be 1.

13.2 Untraced References

Suppose you are writing a low-level systems program and want to reference a control block maintained by the computer hardware. The operating system documentation describes the layout of the control block, which you decide you can mimic with Modula–3 packed type like this:

```
TYPE
    ControlBlock = RECORD
        Status: BITS 4 FOR [0..15];
        Device: BITS 12 FOR [0..4095];
        Unused: BITS 16 FOR [0..65535];
    END;
```

You also learn that there is a built-in function that returns the address of the control block. How will you declare that function? It will return a reference to a type ControlBlock, but you can't use a normal Modula–3 traced reference because the control block lacks the type tag and other bookkeeping information Modula–3 expects in a traced referent. Therefore, you must declare an "untraced" reference:

```
TYPE
    RefControlBlock = UNTRACED REF ControlBlock;
```

This declaration allows you to reference the control block, but does not confuse the garbage collector.

The rules for using untraced references are described in the following sections. However, keep in mind that untraced references are almost never needed in normal programs. Traced types and automatic garbage collection are major features of Modula–3. Don't throw away their benefits by using untraced types needlessly.

13.2.1 Traced and Untraced Types

The Modula–3 garbage collector must be able to find all traced references in a program to determine when dynamic variables may be reclaimed. A type is *traced* if the Modula–3 garbage collector must examine values of the type in order to locate traced references. The following types are traced:

1. traced reference types
2. traced object types
3. record types that contain at least one field that has a traced type
4. array types whose element type is traced
5. packed types whose underlying type is traced

All other types are untraced. No traced type can be the referent of an untraced reference, and no untraced object type can contain any field whose type is traced. (Otherwise, a traced reference could "hide" where the garbage collector might not find it.) These two restrictions are lifted only in UNSAFE modules and interfaces (page 261).

Type ADDRESS is a built-in untraced reference type. ADDRESS <: UNTRACED REF T for each type T. It corresponds to the REFANY type for traced references, but there is no subtype relation between REFANY and ADDRESS.

13.2.2 Operations on Untraced, Nonobject References

Untraced references are created with NEW just like traced references. That is, to create an untraced reference to an integer, you can write

```
VAR
    refInt := NEW(UNTRACED REF INTEGER);
```

An object of type UNTRACED REF T can also be dereferenced:

```
refInt^ := 5;
```

However, certain other operations permitted on traced references are not permitted on untraced (nonobject) references. While traced references designate variables that contain special run-time type information, untraced references designate variables that may not have this information. Therefore, the ISTYPE, TYPECODE, TYPECASE, and NARROW functions (page 183) are not permitted on untraced reference types.

Assignment is also restricted. If variables a and u have types ADDRESS and UNTRACED REF T, respectively, then you can perform the assignment a := u, but you *cannot* perform the assignment u := a. That assignment is unsafe because the run-time system cannot check that a in fact points to a value of type T. (This restriction is lifted in UNSAFE modules; see page 261.)

13.2.3 Untraced Objects

The type UNTRACED ROOT is the ancestor of all untraced objects. To declare an untraced object type, you specify its ancestor to be either UNTRACED ROOT or some descendant of UNTRACED ROOT. UNTRACED ROOT is a subtype of ADDRESS, just as ROOT is a subtype of REFANY. There is no subtype relation between ROOT and UNTRACED ROOT. Untraced objects are allocated by NEW exactly as traced objects.

Whereas the referents of untraced, nonobject references lack run-time type information, untraced objects retain that information. (Otherwise, fundamental OOP operations such as dynamic binding and polymorphism would be impossible.) Therefore, all operations permitted on traced objects are also permitted on untraced objects, including the ISTYPE, TYPECODE, TYPECASE, and NARROW functions, and assignment between untraced ancestors and descendants. The only difference between traced and untraced objects is that untraced objects are not subject to garbage collection.

13.2.4 Deallocating Untraced Dynamic Variables

The storage allocated for untraced variables by NEW can only be reclaimed by the DISPOSE function, which is legal only in unsafe programs (page 263). You must be sure that no active references remain to such variables when you free them.

13.3 Unsafe Programming

A language feature is *safe* if it cannot be (mis)used to cause an unchecked run-time error or otherwise violate the language semantics. Otherwise, it is *unsafe*.

Example 13–4

> In the Ada language, if a variable of type [1..10] is declared without an explicit initializer, its initial value is undefined, and it may be outside the range [1..10]. Using this variable before assigning a value to it is an unchecked run-time error.

Example 13–5

> The C language treats each separate source file in a program independently. One file may declare an external function F as taking an integer parameter, while the file actually defining F specifies a floating-point parameter. This mismatch permits the function to be called with a value that is not a member of the parameter type.

Almost all programming languages have unsafe features. In some cases, the language designers simply emphasized other goals (e.g., efficiency) more than safety. However, unsafe features can't be eliminated entirely from a strongly typed systems programming language without crippling it. Certain low-level systems applications, such as storage allocators, have to break the rules, at least occasionally.

13.3.1 UNSAFE Interfaces and Modules

Modula–3 also provides unsafe features, but it differs from many other languages in isolating those features. The unsafe language features are accessible only in interfaces and modules that are labeled by the keyword UNSAFE. (Refer to the syntax diagrams on page 149 and page 151.) Interfaces and modules so labeled are termed *unsafe*; others are *safe*. When all modules and interfaces are safe, Modula-3 guarantees that there will be no unchecked run-time errors. By introducing UNSAFE, the programmer assumes part of that burden.

A safe interface or module cannot import an unsafe interface. A safe module cannot export an unsafe interface. If you must use unsafe features of the language, you should create a safe interface for clients, and then implement that interface with an unsafe module that uses the unsafe features. You are responsible for using the unsafe features safely.

It is difficult to make general statements about how an unsafe feature may be used safely, because unsafe features tend to be very system-dependent and nonportable. It is a benefit of Modula-3 that you can find these system dependencies simply by looking for the keyword UNSAFE in your modules and interfaces. Some Modula-3 compilers may even flag the uses of unsafe features with warning messages.

13.3.2 Mixing Traced and Untraced Types

In an unsafe module or interface:

1. The type UNTRACED REF T is allowed even when T is a traced type.

2. The fields of an untraced object can be traced types.

By creating an untraced reference to a traced variable, you are creating a situation in which the traced variable could be reclaimed by the garbage collector even though the variable was still accessible through the untraced reference. If this happens, the result is unpredictable. An untraced reference to a traced variable could be safe if:

1. you knew that some traced reference to the variable remained, so it wouldn't be reclaimed, or
2. you could detect (somehow) whether the variable still existed before using the untraced reference.

The problem becomes even more difficult if the run-time system uses a compacting garbage collector. If it does, traced references might be relocated at arbitrary times during program execution, but untraced references to relocated storage won't be updated. (SRC Modula–3 has such a collector.)

13.3.3 Address Arithmetic

In safe modules, references always point to variables allocated dynamically. In unsafe modules, the ADR function can be used to obtain the address of any variable. The expression ADR(x) returns the address (of type ADDRESS) of the variable designated by x. The designator x need not be writable. The ADR function can lead to dangling references. If used to obtain the address of a local variable, for instance, the address will be invalid after the enclosing procedure returns.

In an unsafe module, the + and – operators can be applied to addresses. That is, if a1 and a2 are untraced references (type ADDRESS or type UNTRACED REF T), and if k is an integer, then

a1 + k	has type ADDRESS and is obtained by adding k to a1
a1 – k	has type ADDRESS and is obtained by subtracting k from a1
a1 – a2	has type INTEGER and is obtained by subtracting a2 from a1

These operations treat addresses as integers. The validity of the addresses obtained by these operations is highly implementation-dependent. You can also use INC and DEC on designators of type ADDRESS.

13.3.4 Type Conversions

In an unsafe module, you can assign a value of type ADDRESS to a variable of type UNTRACED REF T. You must ensure that the value assigned actually designates a variable of type T; otherwise, the result is unpredictable.

More generally, you can use the built-in function LOOPHOLE in an unsafe module. The result of the expression

    LOOPHOLE(e, T)

is the expression e's bit pattern interpreted as a value of type T. e cannot be an open array. The result is a designator if e is, and is writable if e is. In general, e and T must have the same size (i.e., BITSIZE(e) = BITSIZE(T)). However, if T has the open array type ARRAY OF S, then BITSIZE(e) must be N * BITSIZE(S) for some integer N, and e is interpreted as a sequence of N elements of type S.

LOOPHOLE may cause an unchecked run-time error in two circumstances: if it is used in a value context and e's bit pattern is not a member of type T, or if it is used as a designator and a bit pattern that is a member of type T but not a member of e's type is stored in the designated variable.

Example 13–6

Suppose that R has type REF T for some type T, W has type INTEGER, and both INTEGER and REF T occupy one word of storage. Then, the statement

    W := LOOPHOLE(R, INTEGER);

will not cause a problem because every word-sized bit pattern is a member of INTEGER. On the other hand, the statement

    LOOPHOLE(R, INTEGER) := W;

could result in R pointing to nonexistent memory, which could cause an unchecked error later when R is used. Although it seems the same as the first statement, the statement

    LOOPHOLE(W, REF T) := R;

could cause problems, since it is an assignment of a traced reference value. Some implementations might perform hidden bookkeeping activities with such assignments, such as updating a reference count. These activities might not be compatible with variable W.

13.3.5 Dispose

Storage may be explicitly freed in unsafe modules. If v is a writable designator of some reference type other than ADDRESS, then the statement

    DISPOSE(v)

frees the storage associated with the referent of v. If v is traced, the effect of the statement is just to set v to NIL. However, if v is untraced, the statement frees the storage occupied by the referent of v and then sets v to NIL. It is an unchecked run-time error if any active references remain to this storage.

13.4 Pragmas

A pragma is a special directive to the Modula–3 system. It consists of an arbitrary string of characters bracketed by <* and *>. Like comments, pragmas can nest and can extend over more than one line. Only two pragmas are "recommended" in the definition of Modula–3, INLINE and EXTERNAL, but implementations are free to define others and SRC Modula–3 has done so.

13.4.1 INLINE

The pragma <*INLINE*> can precede a procedure declaration to indicate that calls to the procedure should be expanded in-line, eliminating the overhead of an actual call. Inlined procedures can be local to a module or can be exported from an interface (in which case the INLINE pragma should appear in the interface).

Some Modula–3 implementations may ignore the INLINE pragma completely. Others may be unable to in-line procedures imported from interfaces, because that is difficult to implement. Methods probably cannot be inlined, since inlining is not compatible with dynamic binding.

13.4.2 EXTERNAL

The pragma <*EXTERNAL N:L*> should precede an interface or a declaration in an interface to indicate that the following entity has name N and is implemented by language L. If :L is omitted, a default external language is assumed (probably C). If N is omitted, the Modula–3 system is free to create a name for the entity as it normally does when the pragma does not appear.

The EXTERNAL pragma can be used to give special link-time names to Modula–3 procedures or variables. The renamed items are assumed to be provided by code written in another language, and they will not be expected to appear in any module exporting the interface.

13.4.3 ASSERT

In SRC Modula–3, the pragma <*ASSERT exp*>, where exp is an arbitrary Boolean expression, may appear anywhere that a statement can appear. It is a checked run-time error if the expression's value is FALSE when the pragma is encountered. A compiler option can be used to turn off all assertions to speed up the program.

13.4.4 NOWARN, UNUSED

In SRC Modula–3, the pragma <*NOWARN*> suppresses warning messages concerning the line of code where the pragma appears.

The pragma <*UNUSED*> can precede the keyword VAR in a variable declaration. It has the effect of suppressing "unused variable" warnings on any variable declared in that section.

13.4.5 OBSOLETE

In SRC Modula–3, the pragma <*OBSOLETE*> can appear before any declaration in an interface. Any attempt by a client to use the tagged declaration will result in a warning message. This pragma is used to warn clients of evolving interfaces.

13.4.6 LINE

In SRC Modula–3, the pragma <*LINE n "f" *> is used to inform the compiler that the line on which it appears originally came from line n (an integer literal) in file "f". This may be useful in generating error messages in Modula–3 code that was generated by an automated tool from a specification in another file. If "f" is omitted, it remains the same from the last LINE pragma.

13.5 Exercises

Answers to the exercises marked "[A]" appear in Appendix D.

1. Which of the following types are likely to be illegal, and why? You should assume that BITSIZE(INTEGER) is 32.   [A]

   a. BITS 13 FOR INTEGER

   b. BITS 13 FOR BOOLEAN

   c. BITS 2 FOR [–2..1]

   d. BITS 2 FOR [0..3]

   e. ARRAY [1..2] OF BITS 13 FOR [0..15]

   f. ARRAY [1..10] OF BITS 13 FOR [0..15]

2. If BITSIZE(INTEGER) is 32, what subtype relation exists between INTEGER and BITS 32 FOR INTEGER? Give an example in which a program becomes illegal by changing a use of INTEGER to a use of BITS 32 FOR INTEGER.

3. If type T were defined by

       TYPE T <: REFANY;

   would the revelation REVEAL T = UNTRACED BRANDED "Huh?" REF INTEGER be legal? Why?

4. Sketch how the following type would be laid out in memory on big endian and little endian computers. Assume that BITSIZE(INTEGER) is 32.

       TYPE Thing = RECORD
           a: INTEGER;
           b, c: BITS 3 FOR [0..7];
           d: BITS 1 FOR BOOLEAN;
           e: BITS 12 FOR [0..0];
           f: BITS 13 FOR [0..63];
       END;

5. Given the declaration for a record type, how would you tell if the type were traced or untraced?

6. Given the declarations below, which of the following type expressions would be legal in a safe module or interface? Which ones would be legal in an unsafe module or interface?   [A]

TYPE
    Traced = REF INTEGER;
    Untraced = UNTRACED REF INTEGER;

a. REF Traced
b. REF Untraced
c. UNTRACED REF Traced
d. REF RECORD ptr: Untraced END
e. UNTRACED REF RECORD ptr: Traced; END
f. UNTRACED REF RECORD proc: PROCEDURE (): Traced; END
g. REF ARRAY OF Untraced
h. UNTRACED REF ARRAY OF UNTRACED REF Traced
i. UNTRACED REF RECORD int := BYTESIZE(Traced); END

7. Explain the difference between NARROW (page 178) and LOOPHOLE.

8. If u is a variable of type UNTRACED REF INTEGER, what is the type of the expression u + 4 in an unsafe module? If t has type REFANY, what is the type of the expression t + 4?   [A]

9. Why would it be nonsensical to place an EXTERNAL pragma before a procedure declaration in a module?

10. In the figure below, unsafe units are marked UNSAFE. Which of the configurations are illegal, and why?

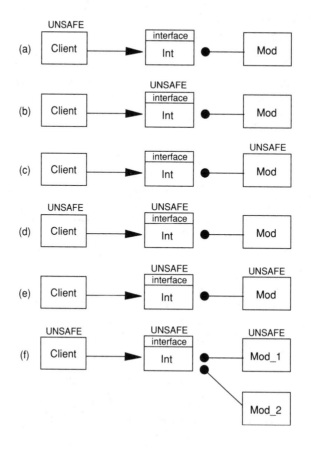

A

Programming Conventions

This appendix presents some conventions that may help you make your Modula–3 programs more consistent and understandable. Although there is no single "correct" programming style, the conventions discussed here have been used successfully by many programmers. If you already follow a set of conventions or a "style guide" for programming in another language, you may wish to adapt those conventions for Modula–3. If you don't currently follow a consistent set of guidelines, you might as well try these.

A.1 Interfaces and Modules

A.1.1 Unit Names

When an interface is exported by only one module, and that module exports only one interface, give both the interface and the module the same name.

File name conventions may be dictated by your Modula–3 system. It is customary for interfaces to be kept in files with the suffix .i3. Modules should be kept in files with the suffix .m3. The root of the file name should be the same as the enclosed interface or module, including capitalization (on systems that support case-sensitive file names). That is, an interface named DrawingTools is usually kept in a file named DrawingTools.i3; the corresponding module would be kept in DrawingTools.m3.

A.1.2 Qualified Names

Clients should generally use qualified notation when referencing names defined in interfaces. Avoid using the FROM–IMPORT style of importing names. That is, write

```
IMPORT Math; ... x := Math.Sqrt(y);
```

rather than

```
FROM Math IMPORT Sqrt; ... x := Sqrt(y)
```

A reader immediately associates a qualified name with the abstract interface to which it belongs. This provides a richer "context" for the name. Choose interface and procedure names with this convention in mind. Using qualified names also avoids problems when several interfaces define a common name, such as Init.

When an imported name is heavily used, you may find that using the qualified notation results in more clutter than clarity. In this case, you may make an exception and import the name directly. For example, the stdin and stdout variables from interface Stdio can be heavily used in I/O-intensive applications, and it may make sense to import these names directly:

```
IMPORT Wr;
FROM Stdio IMPORT stdout;
...
Wr.PutText(stdout, "Thank you, come again.\n");
```

A.1.3 The .T Convention

Ideally, an interface defines a single abstract type and procedures or methods that operate on that type. Choose an interface name that describes the type, and then simply name the primary type T. This convention makes client code that uses qualified names concise and clear.

For example, the required Thread interface exports a type which represents threads. The type is named T, which clients refer to as Thread.T. Operations are Thread.Alert, Thread.Join, etc. Compare this with cumbersome alternatives such as TextFunctions.Text-Type, TextFunction.Equal, etc.

A.1.4 Opaque Types

The visible ancestor of an opaque object type T is usually named Public:

```
TYPE
    T <: Public;
    Public = OBJECT ... END;
```

Methods that are not initialized are automatically initialized to NIL. However, omitting the initialization of an method in an opaque type usually means that the implementor of the opaque type will supply the method, whereas an explicit initialization to NIL means that the client must override the method:

```
TYPE Public = OBJECT METHODS
    print();                        (* an opaque method; defined in revelation *)
    draw() := NIL;                  (* an abstract method; clients must override *)
    END;
```

A.1.5 Variables in Interfaces

It is often dangerous to declare a variable in an interface where clients can access it directly. You cannot prevent a client from writing to the variable, and you cannot synchronize the use of the variable with actions taken by interface procedures. (This is particularly dangerous in multithreaded applications.) It is better to keep the variable in the implementation of the interface and to put in the interface procedures for reading and/or modifying the variable.

A.2 Spelling and Capitalization

Identifiers that are not reserved should be written entirely in lowercase except:

1. The initial letter of each embedded word except the first should be capitalized (e.g., thisLongName). Acronyms are considered to be a sequence of one-letter words (e.g., CPUType, or thisCPU). (However, cpuTime is probably better than cPUTime.)

2. Identifiers that name modules, procedures, exceptions, types, and constants (including elements of an enumeration type) should start with an uppercase letter. Other identifiers should begin with a lowercase letter. This includes variables, parameters, record and object components, methods, and identifiers bound by WITH.

Notice that when these rules are followed, all compile-time constant names begin with an uppercase letter and all other names begin with a lowercase letter.

Do not use multiple-character identifiers consisting entirely of uppercase letters, as they may conflict with reserved words. You can use other capitalizations of reserved words as identifiers. That is, you could use begin or real as variable names. Don't be afraid to use two identifiers that differ only in capitalization if the two identifiers are related in an obvious fashion:

```
TYPE Class = Ancestor OBJECT
    OVERRIDES
        add := Add;
    END;
VAR class: Class;
```

This convention—after you get used to it—is probably more readable than artificially inventing identifiers such as AddMethod to avoid Add, or theClass to avoid class.

An alternative to capitalizing the embedded words in an identifier is to use underscore characters to separate the embedded words. This results in this_long_name instead of thisLongName, cpu_time rather than cpuTime, etc.

A.3 Formatting Conventions

The way your program is laid out on the page (or screen) can significantly affect its readability. It is important to be consistent, so the reader is not distracted.

A.3.1 Punctuation

A single space usually appears before and after all binary operators, including := and = used in assignments and declarations. In very short statements and expressions, the space is sometimes omitted (e.g., x:=x+1). If a long statement or declaration must be spread over multiple lines, a newline character can replace the space following an operator.

A single space or a newline appears after colon, comma, and semicolon, but none before. Unless required by adjacent tokens, no spaces appear before or after left and right parentheses, square brackets, or curly braces, or the up-arrow (^), period(.), or double period (..). Thus

```
x := (a + b) * c + F(x);
rec.field[n] := 10;                        (* not  rec .field [n] *)
TYPE Enum = {One, Two, Three}; Subrange = [1..10];
PROCEDURE P(x, y: REAL; int: INTEGER);
```

Sequences   Statements in a sequence are separated by semicolons. For consistency, also place a semicolon after the last statement in a sequence (i.e., just before the END that terminates the sequence).

The TRY–EXCEPT, CASE, and TYPECASE statements each contain sequences of alternatives separated by vertical bars. A vertical bar should precede the first alternative.

A semicolon should follow the last field in a field list in a record or object.

A.3.2 Indentation

Statements and declarations should be indented to show their structure. The "unit" of indentation should be the same for all statements in a program—two to four spaces seem to be good values. A recommended indentation scheme is shown in Figure A–1 on page 271. Statements not shown on the chart should be indented like similar statements. For example, CASE statements are indented like TYPECASE statements, and WHILE like REPEAT.

There is some value to compactness, since it lets you see more of the program on a single page or screen window. If a structured statement or declaration can be placed entirely on one line without appearing cramped, consider doing so. It is probably better to write

```
WHILE array[index] # 0 DO INC(index); END;
```

rather than

```
WHILE array[index] # 0 DO
    INC(index);
END;
```

```
declarations                          TRY
BEGIN                                     stmts
   stmts                              EXCEPT
END                                   | e1, e2 =>
                                         stmts
CONST                                 | e3(v3) =>
   Ident = expr;                         stmts
                                      ELSE
FOR i := a TO b BY c DO                   stmts
   stmts                              END
END
                                      TRY
IF expr THEN                              stmts
   stmts                              FINALLY
ELSEIF expr THEN                          stmts
   stmts                              END
ELSE
   stmts                              TYPE
END                                       Class = Ancestor OBJECT
                                             fields
INTERFACE Ident;                          METHODS
imports                                      methods
declarations                              OVERRIDES
END Ident.                                   overrides
                                          END;
LOCK mu DO                                Subrange = [1..10];
   stmts
END                                   TYPECASE expr OF
                                      | T1, T2 =>
MODULE Ident EXPORTS Ident;              stmts
imports                               | T3(v3) =>
declarations                             stmts
BEGIN                                 ELSE
   stmts                                 stmts
END Ident.                            END

PROCEDURE Ident signature =           VAR
   declarations                          x, y, z: Type := expr;
   BEGIN                                 a: [1..10];
      stmts
   END Ident                          WHILE expr DO
                                         stmts
REPEAT                                END
   stmts
UNITL expr                            WITH id = expr DO
                                         stmts
                                      END
```

Figure A–1   Indentation conventions.

Also, single declarations can be placed on one line. Write

```
VAR this: That;
CONST One = 1;
```

rather than

```
VAR
    this: That;
CONST
    One = 1;
```

On the other hand, WITH statements that bind several identifiers should have the bindings placed one per line. For example:

```
WITH
    this = that,
    these = those
DO
    stmts
END
```

Statements or declarations needing more than one line should have subsequent lines indented one level. Long procedure declarations should be written putting each parameter on its own line:

```
PROCEDURE ManyArgs(
    x, y, z: INTEGER;
    READONLY vector: ARRAY OF REAL)
    : ReturnType RAISES {Exception} =
    BEGIN
        stmts
    END ManyArgs;
```

Procedure declarations should be separated by a blank line. Nested procedures are indented under their enclosing procedure:

```
PROCEDURE Outer =
    VAR size: INTEGER;

    PROCEDURE Inner =
        VAR temp: INTEGER;
        BEGIN
            stmts
        END Inner;

    BEGIN
        stmts
    END Outer;
```

A.3.3 Comments

A space appears after the (* beginning a comment and before the *) ending a comment. If a comment extends over more than one line, it should begin on the same line as the initial (*. Subsequent lines should be indented to the same level as the (*. Text within comments that form complete sentences should be capitalized and punctuated accordingly:

```
(* a short comment on one line *)

(* This comment extends over two lines. The second line
   is not indented. *)
```

A comment that applies to a single statement or declaration should appear immediately afterwards, indented to the same level. A comment that applies to a group of declarations or statements should appear before the group and be preceded by a blank line. Major sections of code may be introduced by comments in boxes:

```
(* * * * * * * * * * * * * * *)
(*  Section Name  *)
(* * * * * * * * * * * * * * *)
```

(However, sections of code much longer than a page should probably be abstracted into several procedures.)

The comment that describes an interface or module should be placed beginning on a new line following any import clauses in the interface or module. The comment that describes a procedure should follow the procedure heading on a new line. In an interface, the comment follows the semicolon that terminates the procedure declaration. In a module, the comment follows the equals sign that separates the heading from the body. In both cases the comment is typically indented one level in from the PROCEDURE keyword.

When (* and *) are used to comment out a section of code, the opening (* should be indented less than the code. The terminating *) appears on a line by itself, lined up vertically with the opening (*:

```
(* Omit this code until Log interface is completed.
    IF error THEN Log.Message("Whoops!"); END;
*)
```

B

SRC Modula–3

SRC Modula–3 is a portable implementation of the Modula–3 language. It was written at the Systems Research Center (SRC) of Digital Equipment Corporation by members of the group that designed the Modula–3 language. SRC Modula–3 serves as both a test of the language concepts and a production system that lets programmers use Modula–3 for real programs. SRC Modula–3 includes a Modula–3-to-C compiler, a driver program, a loader, run-time libraries, a test suite, demonstration programs, a pretty-printer, a coverage analyzer, and a dependency tool. Standard UNIX debuggers can be used to debug Modula–3 programs.

To promote the widespread use of Modula–3, Digital has made SRC Modula–3 available for general use. Noncommercial use does not require signing a license agreement. If you choose to sign and return the commercial license included with the software, you will be able to use the SRC Modula–3 run-time libraries in programs that you sell to others. There is no fee. SRC Modula–3 is not a Digital Equipment Corporation product. It is a research work which is provided "as is."[1]

Version 1.6 of SRC Modula–3, released in April 1991, ran on the UNIX workstations listed in Table B–1. More computers will be added to the list in future releases. You can also port the software yourself, since it is distributed in source form.

B.1 Getting SRC Modula–3

You can obtain SRC Modula–3 on the Internet, the electronic data network that links thousands of educational, government, and commercial groups around the world. It is located on several Internet hosts, including gatekeeper.dec.com (host address [16.1.0.2]), which supports anonymous FTP. (If this statement does not make any sense to you, seek out

[1] The information in this appendix was adapted from the SRC Modula–3 user manual and run-time libraries, copyright 1989-1991 Digital Equipment Corporation. Used with permission.

275

Table B–1 Computers Compatible with SRC Modula–3 Version 1.6

Computer	Operating System
DEC VAX	Ultrix 4.2
DECstation 3100 & 5100	Ultrix 4.2
SPARCstation	SunOS 4.0.3
Apollo DN4500	Domain/OS
IBM PS/2	AIX PS2 1.2 (*not* DOS)
IBM RT	IBM/4.3
IBM RISC System/6000	AIX 3.1
HP 9000/300	HP-UX 8.0
Encore Multimax	UMAX 4.3 (R4.1.1)
Acorn R260	RISC iX 1.2.1

someone who is familiar with Internet procedures.) On that host, the directory /pub/DEC/ Modula–3 contains a file named README which provides detailed information on how to download the software. After downloading and unpacking the software, you will find more instructions on how to build and install the system. Other documentation describes the extensions to the language provided by SRC Modula–3.

SRC Modula–3 is written almost entirely in Modula–3. The distribution includes both the Modula–3 sources and the C code generated by the Modula–3 compiler, to make porting easier. You must have a C compiler to use the system. Building and installing release 1.6 required about 35 megabytes of disk storage. Installed, the system required 5–7 megabytes, depending on the host computer.

You will also want to look at the Modula–3 news group on Usenet: comp.lang.modula3. There you will find many discussions of the Modula–3 language, the SRC Modula–3 compilation system, and other Modula–3 developments. Bugs and comments on SRC Modula–3 may be reported to m3-request@src.dec.com.

B.2 Using SRC Modula–3

To compile a Modula–3 program, invoke m3(1). This driver operates in the style of cc(1), which is familiar to most UNIX programmers. The output is an object file or an executable program, according to the options.

m3 parses the command line and invokes the compiler and linker as required. m3 tells the compiler where to seek imported interfaces and where to find the Modula–3 runtime library. Arguments ending in .m3 or .i3 are assumed to name Modula–3 source files to be compiled. Arguments ending in .mo, .io, or .o are assumed to name object files, possibly created by other language processors, that are to be linked with the object files created by m3. Arguments ending in .mc, .ic, or .c are assumed to name C source files to be compiled. Arguments ending in .ms, .is, or .s are assumed to name assembly language files to be translated into object files by the assembler. Arguments starting with a hyphen (-) specify compiler options. Other arguments are assumed to name library files, and are simply passed along to the linker.

The source for a module named Mod is normally in a file named Mod.m3. The source for an interface named Int *must* be in a file named Int.i3. The main program is the module that implements the interface Main.

There are options to compile without linking, stop compiling after producing C, emit debugger symbols, generate profiling hooks, retain intermediate files, override search paths, select nonstandard programs for the various passes, and pass arguments to individual phases. For the full details, see the m3(1) man page.

In a source file, an occurrence of IMPORT Mumble causes the compiler to seek an interface named Mumble. The compiler will step through a sequence of directories looking for the file Mumble.i3. It will parse the first such file that it finds, which is expected to contain an interface named Mumble. If no file Mumble.i3 exists, or if the parse fails, the compiler will generate an error. The particular sequence of directories to be searched is determined by the options passed to m3. See the m3(1) manual page for full details.

Example B-1

Here's a simple program composed of a main module, an imported interface, and its implementation. In the file Main.m3:

```
MODULE Main;
   IMPORT A;
BEGIN
      A.Dolt ();
END Main.
```

In the file A.i3:

```
INTERFACE A;
   PROCEDURE Dolt ();
END A.
```

In the file A.m3:

```
MODULE A;
   IMPORT Wr, Stdio;
   PROCEDURE Dolt () =
      BEGIN
         Wr.PutText (Stdio.stdout, "Hello world.\n");
         Wr.Close (Stdio.stdout);
      END Dolt;
BEGIN
END A.
```

And finally, in Makefile:

```
OBJECTS = Main.mo A.io A.mo
M3FLAGS = –g

program: $(OBJECTS)
    m3 –o program $(OBJECTS)

A.mo:        A.m3 A.io
Main.mo:     Main.m3 A.io

.SUFFIXES: .m3 .mo .i3 .io
.m3.mo: ; m3 –c $(M3FLAGS) $*.m3
.i3.io: ; m3 –c $(M3FLAGS) $*.i3
```

If SRC Modula–3 is installed properly, running make will compile the three compilation units and link them with the standard libraries. The result will be left in the executable file named program.

B.3 Library Support

SRC Modula–3 includes a large number of run-time interfaces that you can use in your programs to save development time and make your programs more portable. The rest of this appendix discusses the library contents as of release 1.6. As more people develop Modula–3 software, the library will grow. For easier presentation, we've divided the library into sections:

Input/output	Interfaces Rd, Wr, Stdio, FileStream, and Filename provide facilities for reading and writing information from external storage.
Conversions	Interfaces Fmt and Scan provide facilities to convert numeric data to text form, and vice versa.
Math	Interfaces Math, Stat, Random, and RandomPerm provide mathematical and statistical functions.
Pkl	The Pkl interface provides type-safe storage of linked data structures.
C and UNIX	Many interfaces are included to give you access facilities in C and UNIX libraries and to parse UNIX-style command lines.
Other	Also included are interfaces to the X Window System, interfaces to lists and tables, and interfaces for other useful facilities.

B.4 Input/Output Interfaces

SRC Modula–3 includes several simple IO interfaces modeled on "character steams" similar to those in the C programming language. The interfaces and their uses are listed below:

Rd	This interface provides basic procedures for reading characters from input streams and returning them as values of type CHAR, TEXT, or ARRAY OF CHAR.
Wr	This interface provides basic procedures for writing values of type CHAR, TEXT, and ARRAY OF CHAR to output streams.
Stdio	This interface exports predefined streams—a standard input stream and two standard output streams. These streams are usually directed to the user's keyboard and display.
FileStream	This interface provides procedures for opening text files and associating them with input or output streams.
Filename	This interface provides procedures for parsing file names and using directory search paths.

The interfaces are discussed in the following sections.

B.4.1 The Rd Interface

An Rd.T (or reader) is a character input stream. The basic operation on a reader is Get-Char, which returns the source character at the current position and advances the current position by one. Some readers are *seekable*, which means that they also allow setting the current position anywhere in the source. For example, readers from random access files are seekable; readers from terminals and sequential files are not.

Some readers are *intermittent*, which means that the source of the reader trickles in rather than being available to the implementation all at once. For example, the input stream from an interactive terminal is intermittent. An intermittent reader is never seekable.

Several kinds of errors can be encountered during reading. Illegal operations cause the exception Rd.Error to be raised with an appropriate parameter; these problems are independent of the kind of reader. Other problems depend on the class of reader; these problems cause the Rd.Failure exception to be raised, which has a REFANY parameter defined by the reader class. The EndOfFile exception is raised if no more data is available from the reader.

Every reader is a *monitor*; that is, it contains an internal lock that is acquired and held for each operation in this interface, so that concurrent operations will appear atomic. For faster, unmonitored access, the UnsafeRd interface is provided, but it is not discussed here.

Many operations on a reader can wait indefinitely. For example, GetChar can wait if the user is not typing. In general these waits are alertable, so each procedure that might wait includes Thread.Alerted in its RAISES clause.

The individual procedures are described briefly below. In many cases, more detailed information is given in the comments inside the actual interfaces distributed with SRC Modula–3.

GetChar	returns the next character
EOF	returns TRUE iff the reader is at end-of-file

```
INTERFACE Rd;
FROM Thread IMPORT Alerted;
TYPE
    T <: ROOT;
    Code = {Closed, Unseekable, Intermittent, CantUnget};
EXCEPTION
    EndOfFile;
    Failure(REFANY);
    Error(Code);
PROCEDURE GetChar(rd: T): CHAR RAISES {EndOfFile, Failure, Alerted, Error};
PROCEDURE EOF(rd: T): BOOLEAN RAISES {Failure, Alerted, Error};
PROCEDURE UnGetChar(rd: T; c: CHAR) RAISES {Error};
PROCEDURE CharsReady(rd: T): CARDINAL RAISES {Failure, Error};
PROCEDURE GetSub(rd: T; VAR (*out*) str: ARRAY OF CHAR): CARDINAL
        RAISES {Failure, Alerted, Error};
PROCEDURE GetSubLine(rd: T; VAR (*out*) str: ARRAY OF CHAR): CARDINAL
        RAISES {Failure, Alerted, Error};
PROCEDURE GetText(rd: T; length: INTEGER): TEXT
RAISES {Failure, Alerted, Error};
PROCEDURE GetLine(rd: T): TEXT RAISES {EndOfFile, Failure, Alerted, Error};
PROCEDURE Index(rd: T): CARDINAL RAISES {Error};
PROCEDURE Length(rd: T): CARDINAL RAISES {Failure, Alerted, Error};
PROCEDURE Seek(rd: T; n: CARDINAL) RAISES {Failure, Alerted, Error};
PROCEDURE Close(rd: T) RAISES {Failure, Alerted};
PROCEDURE Intermittent(rd: T): BOOLEAN;
PROCEDURE Seekable(rd: T): BOOLEAN;
PROCEDURE Closed(rd: T): BOOLEAN;
END Rd.
```

Listing B–1   The Rd interface.

UnGetChar	"pushes back" the last character read, so that the next call to Get-Char will read it again
CharsReady	returns a number of characters that can be read without indefinite waiting
GetSub	reads characters into an array of characters until the array is filled
GetSubLine	reads characters into an array of characters until a newline is read or the array is filled
GetText	reads a specified number of characters
GetLine	reads a line; the terminating newline is discarded
Index	returns the current position of the input stream
Length	returns the number of characters in the input stream
Seek	places the input stream at a designated position (e.g., as is returned by Index)
Close	closes the reader (and underlying file, if any)
Intermittent	returns TRUE if the reader is intermittent
Seekable	returns TRUE if the reader is seekable
Closed	returns TRUE if the reader is closed

Example B–2

There may be more characters available than the number returned by CharsReady, because more characters might trickle in just as CharsReady returns. For example, the code to flush buffered input without blocking requires a loop:

```
PROCEDURE FlushPendingInput(rd: Rd.T)
    RAISES {Rd.EndOfFile, Rd.Error, Rd.Failure } =
    VAR n: INTEGER;
    BEGIN
        LOOP
            n := Rd.CharsReady(rd);
            IF n = 0 THEN EXIT; END;
            FOR i := 1 TO n DO
                EVAL Rd.GetChar(rd);
            END;
        END;
    END FlushPendingInput;
```

B.4.2 The Wr Interface

A Wr.T (or "writer") is a character output stream. The basic operation on a writer is Put-Char, which extends a writer's character sequence by one character. Some writers (called "seekable writers") also allow overwriting in the middle of the sequence. For example, writers to random access files are seekable, but writers to terminals and sequential files are not.

Writers can be (and usually are) *buffered*. This means that operations on the writer don't immediately affect the underlying target of the writer, but are saved up and performed later. For example, a writer to a disk file is not likely to update the disk after each character.

Several kinds of errors can be encountered during writing. Illegal operations cause the exception Error to be raised; these problems are independent of the kind of writer. Other problems depend on the class of writer; these problems cause the Failure exception to be raised, which has a REFANY parameter defined by the writer class.

Every writer is a monitor; that is, it contains an internal lock that is acquired and held for each operation in this interface, so that concurrent operations will appear atomic. For faster, unmonitored access, there is an UnsafeWr interface.

Many operations on a writer can wait indefinitely. For example, PutChar can wait if the user has suspended output to his terminal. These waits can be alertable, so each procedure that might wait includes Thread.Alerted in its raises clause.

The individual interface components are discussed briefly below. The interface is shown in Listing B–2.

PutChar	output a single character
PutText	output all the characters in a TEXT value
PutString	output the characters in an array
Seek	position the writer to a specific location
Flush	flush any buffered characters

```
INTERFACE Wr;
FROM Thread IMPORT Alerted;
TYPE
    T <: ROOT;
    Code = {Closed, Unseekable};
EXCEPTION
    Failure(REFANY);
    Error(Code);
PROCEDURE PutChar(wr: T; ch: CHAR) RAISES {Failure, Alerted, Error};
PROCEDURE PutText(wr: T; t: TEXT) RAISES {Failure, Alerted, Error};
PROCEDURE PutString(wr: T; a: ARRAY OF CHAR)
    RAISES {Failure, Alerted, Error};
PROCEDURE Seek(wr: T; n: CARDINAL) RAISES {Failure, Alerted, Error};
PROCEDURE Flush(wr: T) RAISES {Failure, Alerted, Error};
PROCEDURE Close(wr: T) RAISES {Failure, Alerted, Error};
PROCEDURE Length(wr: T): CARDINAL RAISES {Failure, Alerted, Error};
PROCEDURE Index(wr: T): CARDINAL RAISES {Error};
PROCEDURE Seekable(wr: T): BOOLEAN;
PROCEDURE Closed(wr: T): BOOLEAN;
PROCEDURE Buffered(wr: T): BOOLEAN;
END Wr.
```

Listing B–2   The Wr interface.

Close	flush and close the writer (and the underlying file, if any)
Length	returns the length of the writer
Index	returns the current position of the writer
Seekable	returns TRUE if the writer is seekable
Closed	returns TRUE if the writer is closed
Buffered	returns TRUE if the writer is buffered

B.4.3 The FileStream Interface

The FileStream interface (Listing B–3) provides procedures to associate files with readers and writers. The interface doesn't specify whether the readers and writers are seekable or buffered. Readers and writers to disk files are probably seekable and buffered, but this depends on the system. Closing a file reader or writer (i.e., calling Rd.Close or Wr.Close) closes the underlying file. You must close your output files before your program terminates to ensure that all your data is correctly written to the files.

The failures returned by file readers and writers are errors occurring during calls to the operating system. Rd.Failure and Wr.Failure exceptions raised by these procedures will include an argument of type FileStream.Failure, which gives more information about which error occurred. The main operations are:

OpenRead	returns a reader whose source is the contents of the named file
OpenWrite	returns a writer whose target is the contents of the named file; the file is created or reset to empty

```
INTERFACE FileStream;
IMPORT Rd, Wr;
TYPE
      FailureKind = {open, close, fcntl, read, write, lseek, fstat};
      Failure = REF FailureKind;
PROCEDURE OpenRead (n: TEXT): Rd.T RAISES {Rd.Failure};
PROCEDURE OpenWrite(n: TEXT): Wr.T RAISES {Wr.Failure};
PROCEDURE OpenAppend(n: TEXT): Wr.T RAISES {Wr.Failure};
END FileStream.
```

Listing B–3   The FileStream interface.

OpenAppend   returns a writer whose target is the contents of the named file; if
                  the file exists the writer will be positioned to append to the exist-
                  ing contents of the file

B.4.4 The Stdio Interface

The Stdio interface (Listing B–4) provides streams for standard input (stdin), standard output (stdout), and standard error (stderr). These streams may be used in a Modula–3 program without taking any steps to open or initialize them. Two additional streams,
bufferedStdout and bufferedStderr, are provided as alternatives to stdout and stderr for
those systems that do not buffer stdout and stderr.

```
INTERFACE Stdio;
IMPORT Rd, Wr;
VAR
 stdin: Rd.T;
 stdout: Wr.T;
 stderr: Wr.T;
 bufferedStdout: Wr.T;      (* always buffered *)
 bufferedStderr: Wr.T;      (* always buffered *)
END Stdio.
```

Listing B–4   The StdIO interface.

B.4.5 The Filename Interface

The Filename interface (Listing B–5) provides procedures to parse file names and process
file search lists. The interface includes these procedures:

```
INTERFACE Filename;
IMPORT Text, Rd;
TYPE FilePredicate = PROCEDURE (filename: Text.T): BOOLEAN;
PROCEDURE FileIsReadable (filename: Text.T): BOOLEAN;
PROCEDURE Root (filename: Text.T): Text.T;
PROCEDURE Extension (filename: Text.T): Text.T;
PROCEDURE Head (filename: Text.T): Text.T;
PROCEDURE Tail (filename: Text.T): Text.T;
PROCEDURE DefaultExtension (filename, ext: Text.T): Text.T;
PROCEDURE ExpandTilde (filename: Text.T): Text.T;
PROCEDURE SearchPath (
    path, filename: Text.T;
    pred: FilePredicate := FileIsReadable): Text.T;
PROCEDURE RdFromPath (path, filename: Text.T): Rd.T;
END Filename.
```

Listing B–5   The Filename interface.

FileIsReadable	tests for the existence of a file
Root	returns the file name minus the extension
Extension	returns the extension part of the file name
Head	returns the directory prefix of the file name
Tail	returns the file name minus the directory prefix
DefaultExtension	adds an extension to a filename if none already exists; can also replace an existing extension
ExpandTilde	expands the ~ character at the beginning of a file name to be the appropriate "home" directory path
SearchPath	finds the first file that exists along a search path; can be customized by supplying a predicate procedure

B.5 Conversion Libraries

SRC Modula–3 provides two interfaces, Fmt and Scan, for converting integers, Booleans, etc., to TEXT objects, and vice versa. These interfaces are often used in conjunction with the input/output interfaces for reading and writing numbers.

B.5.1 The Fmt Interface

The Fmt interface (Listing B–6) provides procedures for converting integers, booleans, floating-point numbers, etc., to TEXT values. The interface components are briefly described below. More detailed information is given in the comments with the actual interface in the SRC Modula–3 distribution.

Style	Values of this enumeration type determine the style of floating-point formatting. The Sci and AltSci formats include an explicit

```
INTERFACE Fmt;
IMPORT Text;
TYPE
    Align = {Left, Right};
    Base = [2..16];
    Style = {Flo, AltFlo, Sci, AltSci, Mix};
PROCEDURE Int(n: INTEGER; base : Base := 10): Text.T;
PROCEDURE Unsigned(n: INTEGER; base : Base := 16): Text.T;
PROCEDURE Addr(n: ADDRESS; base : Base := 16): Text.T;
PROCEDURE Ref(r: REFANY; base : Base := 16): Text.T;
PROCEDURE Real(
    x: REAL; precision: CARDINAL:= 6; style := Style.Mix): Text.T;
PROCEDURE LongReal(
    x: LONGREAL; precision: CARDINAL:= 6; style := Style.Mix): Text.T;
PROCEDURE Extended(
    x: EXTENDED; precision: CARDINAL:= 6; style := Style.Mix): Text.T;
PROCEDURE Char(c: CHAR): Text.T;
PROCEDURE Pad(
    text: Text.T;
    length: CARDINAL;
    padChar: CHAR := ' ';
    align: Align := Align.Right): Text.T;
PROCEDURE F(fmt: Text.T; t1, t2, t3, t4, t5: Text.T := NIL): Text.T RAISES {};
PROCEDURE FN
    (fmt: Text.T; READONLY texts: ARRAY OF Text.T): Text.T RAISES {};
END Fmt.
```

Listing B–6   The Fmt interface.

exponent field; the Flo and AltFlo formats do not. In the Alt formats, trailing zeros are suppressed. The Mix format is AltFlo unless AltSci is shorter, and the decimal point is suppressed if the value is integral.

Bool	formats a boolean value as "TRUE" or "FALSE"
Int	format an integer
Unsigned	formats a Word.T value
Addr	formats an address
Ref	formats a reference; NIL is formatted as "NIL"
Real	formats a floating-point value, allowing the number of fractional digits to be specified
LongReal	like Real, but for type LONGREAL
Extended	like Real, but for type EXTENDED
Char	returns a character value as a one-character TEXT value
Pad	places a given text string in the left, center, or right of a longer string
F	merges up to five "argument" strings into a format string according to special codes ("format specifiers") in the format string; the codes resemble those used by the printf function in the C program-

ming language. More details are given below. It is a checked run-time error if the number of arguments does not match the number of codes in the format string.

FN   like F, but the argument strings are provided as an array

Format Codes   The F and FN functions require a format string and some number of argument strings. The result is a copy of the format string in which all format specifiers have been replaced, in order, by the text arguments. A format specifier has the form shown below.

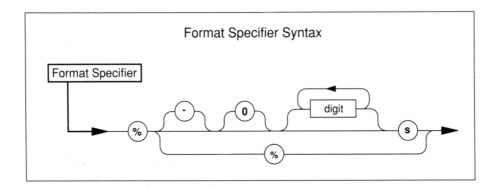

If the optional hyphen (–) is present, the argument is left-aligned in the formatted field; otherwise, it is right-aligned. If the digit 0 is present, the padding character is '0'; otherwise, it is a space. If a number is present, it specifies the field width. If the number is omitted, it defaults to zero. If two consecutive % characters appear in the format string, they are replaced by a single % in the output. Some example calls on Fmt.F are shown in Table B–2 on page 287.

B.5.2 The Scan Interface

The Scan interface (Listing B–7) performs the opposite conversions from the Fmt interface (i.e., it converts TEXT values to integers and other data values). If the input TEXT value does not have the right format, the exception Scan.BadFormat is raised. The conversion procedures are:

Bool   converts "TRUE" or "FALSE" to the appropriate boolean value

Int   returns an INTEGER value

Unsigned   returns a Word.T value

Real   returns a REAL value

LongReal   returns a LONGREAL value

Extended   returns an EXTENDED value

Char   returns the first character from the input TEXT value

```
INTERFACE Scan;
IMPORT Text, Word;
EXCEPTION BadFormat;
PROCEDURE Bool (t: Text.T): BOOLEAN RAISES {BadFormat};
PROCEDURE Int (t: Text.T): INTEGER RAISES {BadFormat};
PROCEDURE Unsigned (t: Text.T): Word.T RAISES {BadFormat};
PROCEDURE Real (t: Text.T): REAL RAISES {BadFormat};
PROCEDURE LongReal (t: Text.T): LONGREAL RAISES {BadFormat};
PROCEDURE Char (t: Text.T): CHAR RAISES {BadFormat};
END Scan.
```

Listing B–7   The Scan interface.

Table B–2 Sample Calls on Fmt.F

Call	Result
F("%s %s\n", "Hello", "World")	"Hello World\n"
F("%s", Int(3))	"3"
F("%2s", Int(3))	" 3"
F("%–2s", Int(3))	"3 "
F("%02s", Int(3))	"03"
F("%–02s", Int(3))	"30"
F("%s", "%s")	"%s"
F("%s% tax", Int(3))	"3% tax"

FN("%s %s %s %s %s %s %s",
    ARRAY OF TEXT{"Too", "many",
    "arguments", "for", "F", "to",
    "handle"})
	"Too many arguments for F to han-
	dle"

F("%–s", Int(3))	"3"
F("%0s", Int(3))	"3"
F("%–0s", Int(3))	"3"
FN("3",Text.Array{})	"3"

B.6 Math and Statistics Libraries

Interfaces Random and RandomPerm provide access to random number and permutation generators.

The statistics interface Stat (Listing B–8) is a simple set of statistical analysis routines for data of type REAL. A data structure of type Stat.T holds the characteristics of the data as it is accumulated, and other procedures can extract other statistics after all the data is entered.

```
INTERFACE Stat;
IMPORT Wr;
TYPE
    T = RECORD
          num: LONGREAL;
          mean: LONGREAL;
          variance : LONGREAL;
          maximum: REAL;
          minimum: REAL;
       END;

PROCEDURE Init (VAR s: T);(* resets s *)
PROCEDURE Accum (VAR s: T; x: REAL);
PROCEDURE Combine (READONLY r, s: T): T;

PROCEDURE Num (READONLY s: T): REAL;
PROCEDURE Max (READONLY s: T): REAL;
PROCEDURE Min (READONLY s: T): REAL;
PROCEDURE Mean (READONLY s: T): REAL;
PROCEDURE Var (READONLY s: T): REAL;
PROCEDURE SDev (READONLY s: T): REAL;
PROCEDURE RMS (READONLY s: T): REAL;

PROCEDURE Print (wr: Wr.T; READONLY s: T);
(* Prints the text string "num: %d min: %g max: %g mean: %g dev: %g". *)
END Stat.
```

Listing B–8   The Stat interface.

Example B–3

Following is a typical client of the interface.

```
MODULE UseStat;
IMPORT Stat;
VAR
   st: Stat.T;
   nPoints: INTEGER;
   datum, stdDev: REAL;
BEGIN
   Stat.Init(st);
   LOOP
      datum := ... ;
      Stat.Accum(st, datum); ...
   END (*LOOP*);
   nPoints := st.num;
   stdDev := Stat.SDev(st);
   (* Write out nPoints and stdDev. *)
END UseStat.
```

The Math interface (Listing B–9 on page 290) allows Modula–3 clients to use the C math library. Programs that call these routines must be linked with the math library by adding the switch "–lm" to the link command. Detailed specifications for these functions will be given by the C library documentation on your system.

B.7 The PKL Facility

The Pkl interface (pronounced "pickle") provides type-safe binary storage for linked data structures. A brief description of its function is given here; more details are provided in the comments to the actual Pkl interface in SRC Modula–3. The interface is shown in Listing B–10 below.

The Pkl.Write procedure takes as arguments a reference of type REFANY and a seekable writer. It traces the data structure reachable from the reference argument, converts it to a sequence of bytes (the "pickle"), and writes it to the writer. Shared and circular substructures are preserved. Only traced references are followed; untraced references are pickled as NIL. Procedures and methods in the data structure are preserved.

The Pkl.Read procedure takes a reader as an argument and reads in a pickle, rebuilding and returning the structure as a correctly typed value. Procedure and method values are correctly restored as long as those procedures and methods are present in the reading program. (The procedures themselves are not pickled; only their identities are recorded.)

It is possible to customize the action of Write and Read by registering conversion functions that will be called during the tracing and/or the byte-packing of individual types. If problems are encountered, the procedures raise exception Pkl.Error with an argument that details the cause of the error.

```
INTERFACE Pkl;
IMPORT Rd, Wr, Thread;
EXCEPTION Error(Code);
TYPE
      Code = {BadVersion, UnknownType, UnknownProc,
            NoReadBytesProc, WrongType, Unseekable};
            ConvertProc = PROCEDURE(r: REFANY);
      WriteBytesProc = PROCEDURE(r: REFANY): TEXT;
      ReadBytesProc =
            PROCEDURE(READONLY bytes: ARRAY OF CHAR): REFANY;
PROCEDURE Write(r: REFANY; wr: Wr.T; lg2maxobjs := 14)
      RAISES {Wr.Failure, Thread.Alerted, Error};
PROCEDURE Read(rd: Rd.T): REFANY RAISES {Error};
PROCEDURE RegisterConvertProcs(
      tc: INTEGER; wrproc: ConvertProc; rdproc: ConvertProc);
PROCEDURE RegisterBytesProcs(
      tc: INTEGER; wrproc: WriteBytesProc; rdproc: ReadBytesProc);
END Pkl.
```

Listing B–10   The Pkl interface.

```
INTERFACE Math;
CONST
    Pi = 3.14159265358979323846264338  33;
    LogPi = 1.144729885849400174143427  3514;
    SqrtPi = 1.772453850905516027298167  4833;
    E = 2.7182818284590452353602874  714;
    Degree = 0.0174532925199432957692369  07684;         (* One degree in radians *)
PROCEDURE exp (x: LONGREAL): LONGREAL;                    (* e^x *)

PROCEDURE expm1 (x: LONGREAL): LONGREAL;                  (* (e^x – 1, for small x *)
PROCEDURE log (x: LONGREAL): LONGREAL;
PROCEDURE log10 (x: LONGREAL): LONGREAL;
PROCEDURE log1p (x: LONGREAL): LONGREAL;                  (* log(1 + x), for small x. *)
PROCEDURE pow (x, y: LONGREAL): LONGREAL;                 (* x^y *)
PROCEDURE sqrt (x: LONGREAL): LONGREAL;
PROCEDURE cos (x: LONGREAL): LONGREAL;
PROCEDURE sin (x: LONGREAL): LONGREAL;
PROCEDURE tan (x: LONGREAL): LONGREAL;
PROCEDURE acos (x: LONGREAL): LONGREAL;
PROCEDURE asin (x: LONGREAL): LONGREAL;
PROCEDURE atan (x: LONGREAL): LONGREAL;
PROCEDURE atan2 (x, y: LONGREAL): LONGREAL;               (* arctan(x / y) *)
PROCEDURE sinh (x: LONGREAL): LONGREAL;
PROCEDURE cosh (x: LONGREAL): LONGREAL;
PROCEDURE tanh (x: LONGREAL): LONGREAL;
PROCEDURE asinh (x: LONGREAL): LONGREAL;
PROCEDURE acosh (x: LONGREAL): LONGREAL;
PROCEDURE atanh (x: LONGREAL): LONGREAL;

PROCEDURE hypot (x, y: LONGREAL): LONGREAL;               (* sqrt(x^2 + y^2) *)
TYPE Complex = RECORD x, y: LONGREAL END;
PROCEDURE cabs (z: Complex): LONGREAL;                    (* sqrt (z.x^2 + z.y^2) *)

PROCEDURE frexp (x: LONGREAL; VAR exp: INTEGER): LONGREAL;
PROCEDURE ldexp (x: LONGREAL; exp: INTEGER): LONGREAL;    (* x * 2^{exp} *)
PROCEDURE modf (x: LONGREAL; VAR exp: INTEGER): LONGREAL;

PROCEDURE erf (x: LONGREAL): LONGREAL;
PROCEDURE erfc (x: LONGREAL): LONGREAL;                   (* 1.0 – erf(x), for large x *)
PROCEDURE gamma (x: LONGREAL): LONGREAL;
PROCEDURE j0 (x: LONGREAL): LONGREAL;
PROCEDURE j1 (x: LONGREAL): LONGREAL;
PROCEDURE jn (n: INTEGER; x: LONGREAL): LONGREAL;
PROCEDURE y0 (x: LONGREAL): LONGREAL;
PROCEDURE y1 (x: LONGREAL): LONGREAL;
PROCEDURE yn (n, x: LONGREAL): LONGREAL;
END Math.
```

Listing B–9 The Math interface.

B.8 C and UNIX Compatibility

Recognizing that much existing software is written in the C language, SRC Modula–3 also includes interfaces that allow you to access common C and UNIX functions:

Cerrno	facilities from errno.h
Csetjmp	facilities from setjmp.h
Cstdarg	facilities from stdarg.h
Cstddef	facilities from stddef.h
Cstdio	facilities from stdio.h
Cstdlib	facilities from stdlib.h
Cstring	facilities from string.h
Ctypes	C types expressed in Modula–3
M3toC	functions to convert TEXT objects to C-style strings, etc.

The UNIX interfaces differ slightly depending on the variant of UNIX that is present: DEC's Ultrix, IBM's AIX, Sun's SunOS, POSIX, etc. Some of the Ultrix interfaces are listed below with their equivalent C header file as typical of what is provided. It is also easy to create your own interfaces to your own C functions.

Udir	facilities from C header file dir.h
Uerror	facilities from C header file errno.h
Uexec	facilities for process control (execl, etc.)
Unix	standard UNIX flags and functions (unistd.h: chdir, etc.)
Upwd	facilities from C header file pwd.h
Usignal	facilities from C header file signal.h

There are also two interfaces that help in parsing UNIX-style arguments:

ParseParams	parses UNIX-style keyword command line arguments
ParseShell	parses shell-style arguments, including the more extensive quoting conventions

B.9 Other Interfaces

Many other interfaces are provided with SRC Modula–3. Some of them are mentioned briefly below.

X*	interfaces to the X window system (X11R4)
Formatter	facilities for constructing pretty-printers
UID	unique identifiers, for version stamping
STextTable	sorted tables implemented as balanced trees. There are also versions for tables with integer keys, etc.
List	Lisp-like lists
Time	calendar and process timing

C

Modula–3 Syntax

This appendix reproduces the syntax of Modula–3 in a textual, BNF-like format.[1] The notation used is shown in the following table:

Notation	Means
x y	x followed by y
x | y	x or y
[x]	x or empty
{ x }	A possibly empty sequence of x's
(x)	x (used for grouping)
x & y	x or y or x y
"abc"	the characters abc
KEY	the keyword KEY

For example, the notation's grammar can be (almost) expressed in itself as follows:

Production	= Name "=" P1 { "|" P1 } "." .
P1	= P2 { "&" P2}.
P2	= P3 { P3 }.
P3	= "[" Production "]" | "{" Production "}" | Keyword | Name | Literal .
Keyword	= *identifier entirely in uppercase.*
Name	= *identifier that is not a keyword.*
Literal	= *character(s) enclosed in double quotes.*

[1] This grammar is taken from G. Nelson (ed.), *Systems Programming in Modula–3*, Prentice Hall, New York, 1991. It is used here with permission.

C.1 Compilation Unit Productions

Compilation	= Interface | Module | GInterface | GModule | IInterface | IModule.
Interface	= [UNSAFE] INTERFACE Ident ";" { Import } { Declaration } END Ident "." .
Module	= [UNSAFE] MODULE Ident [EXPORTS IDList] ";" { Import } Block Ident "." .
GInterface	= GENERIC INTERFACE Ident GFmls ";" { Import } { Declaration } END Ident "." .
GModule	= GENERIC MODULE Ident GFmls ";" { Import } Block Ident "." .
IInterface	= [UNSAFE] INTERFACE Ident "=" Ident GActls END Ident "." .
IModule	= [UNSAFE] MODULE Ident [EXPORTS IDList] "=" Ident GActls END Ident "." .
GFmls	= "(" IDList ")".
GActls	= "(" IDList ")".
Import	= FROM Ident IMPORT IDList ";"
	| IMPORT ImportItem { "," ImportItem } ";".
ImportItem	= Ident [AS Ident].
Block	= { Declaration } BEGIN Stmts END.
Declaration	= CONST { ConstDecl ";" }
	| TYPE { TypeDecl ";" }
	| EXCEPTION { ExceptionDecl ";" }
	| VAR { VariableDecl ";" }
	| ProcedureHead ["=" Block Ident] ";".
	| REVEAL { Type ID ("=" | "<:") Type.
ConstDecl	= Ident [":" Type] "=" ConstExpr.
TypeDecl	= Ident ("=" | "<:") Type.
ExceptionDecl	= Ident ["(" Type ")"].
VariableDecl	= IDList (":" Type & ":=" Expr).
ProcedureHead	= PROCEDURE Ident Signature.
Signature	= "(" Formals ")" [":" Type] [RAISES Raises].
Formals	= [Formal { ";" Formal } [";"]].
Formal	= [VALUE | VAR | READONLY] IDList (":" Type & ":=" ConstExpr).
Raises	= "{" [QualID { "," QualID }] "}".

C.2 Statement Productions

Stmts	= [Stmt { ";" Stmt } [";"]].
Stmt	= AssignStmt | Block | CallStmt | CaseStmt | ExitStmt | EvalStmt
	| ForStmt | IfStmt | LockStmt | LoopStmt | RaiseStmt | RepeatStmt
	| ReturnStmt | TryFinStmt | TryXptStmt | TCaseStmt | WhileStmt
	| WithStmt.
AssignStmt	= Expr ":=" Expr.
CallStmt	= Expr "(" [Actual { "," Actual }] ")".
CaseStmt	= CASE Expr OF [Case] { "|" Case } [ELSE Stmts] END.

ExitStmt	= EXIT.
EvalStmt	= EVAL Expr.
ForStmt	= FOR Ident ":=" Expr TO Expr [BY Expr] DO Stmts END.
IfStmt	= IF Expr THEN Stmts { ELSIF Expr THEN Stmts } [ELSE Stmts] END.
LockStmt	= LOCK Expr DO Stmts END.
LoopStmt	= LOOP Stmts END.
RaiseStmt	= RAISE QualID ["(" Expr ")"].
RepeatStmt	= REPEAT Stmts UNTIL Expr.
ReturnStmt	= RETURN [Expr].
TCaseStmt	= TYPECASE Expr OF [Tcase] { "|" Tcase} [ELSE Stmts] END.
TryXptStmt	= TRY Stmts EXCEPT [Handler] { "|" Handler } [ELSE Stmts] END.
TryFinStmt	= TRY Stmts FINALLY Stmts END.
WhileStmt	= WHILE Expr DO Stmts END.
WithStmt	= WITH Binding { "," Binding } DO Stmts END.
Case	= Labels { "," Labels } "=>" Stmts.
Labels	= ConstExpr [".." ConstExpr].
Handler	= QualID { "," QualID } ["(" Ident ")"] "=>" Stmts.
Tcase	= Type { "," Type } ["(" Ident ")"] "=>" Stmts.
Binding	= Ident "=" Expr.
Actual	= [Ident ":="] Expr | Type.

C.3 Type Productions

Type	= TypeName | ArrayType | PackedType | EnumType | ObjectType | ProcedureType | RecordType | RefType | SetType | SubrangeType | "(" Type ")".
ArrayType	= ARRAY [Type { "," Type }] OF Type.
PackedType	= BITS ConstExpr FOR Type.
EnumType	= "{" [IDList] "}".
ObjectType	= [TypeName | ObjectType] [Brand] OBJECT Fields [METHODS Methods] [OVERRIDES Overrides] END.
ProcedureType	= PROCEDURE Signature.
RecordType	= RECORD Fields END.
RefType	= [UNTRACED] [Brand] REF Type.
SetType	= SET OF Type.
SubrangeType	= "[" ConstExpr ".." ConstExpr "]".
Brand	= BRANDED [TextLiteral].
Fields	= [Field { ";" Field } [";"]].
Field	= IDList (":" Type & ":=" ConstExpr).
Methods	= [Method { ";" Method } [";"]].

Method	= Ident Signature [":=" ConstExpr].
Overrides	= [Override { ";" Override } [";"]].
Override	= Ident ":=" ConstExpr.

C.4 Expression Productions

ConstExpr	= Expr.
Expr	= E1 { OR E1 }.
E1	= E2 { AND E2 }.
E2	= { NOT } E3.
E3	= E4 { Relop E4 }.
E4	= E5 { Addop E5 }.
E5	= E6 { Mulop E6 }.
E6	= { "+"	"-" } E7.
E7	= E8 { Selector }.
E8	= Ident	Number	CharLiteral	TextLiteral	Constructor	"(" Expr ")".
Relop	= "="	"#"	"<"	"<="	">"	">="	IN.
Addop	= "+"	"–"	"&".
Mulop	= "*"	"/"	DIV	MOD.
Selector	= "^"	"." Ident	"[" Expr { "," Expr } "]"	"(" [Actual { "," Actual }] ")".
Constructor	= Type "{" [SetCons	RecordCons	ArrayCons] "}".
SetCons	= SetElt { "," SetElt }.
SetElt	= Expr [".." Expr].
RecordCons	= RecordElt { "," RecordElt }.
RecordElt	= [Ident ":="] Expr.
ArrayCons	= Expr { "," Expr } ["," ".."].

C.5 Miscellaneous Productions

TypeName	=QualID	ROOT	UNTRACED ROOT.
QualID	= Ident ["." Ident].
IDList	= Ident { "," Ident }.

C.6 Token Production

To read a token, first skip all blanks, tabs, newlines, carriage returns, vertical tabs, form feeds, comments, and pragmas. Then read the longest sequence of characters that forms an operator or an Ident or Literal, as defined here.

An Ident is a case-significant sequence of letters, digits, and underscores that begins with a letter. An Ident is a keyword or reserved word if it appears in Table C-1 and an ordinary identifier otherwise. The special terminal DQUOTE represents the double-quote character.

Literal	= Number | CharLiteral | TextLiteral.
Ident	= Letter { Letter | Digit | "_" }.
Operator	= "+" | "–" | "*" | "/" | "." | "^" | ":" "=" | "=" | "#" | "<" | "<" "=" | ">" "=" | ">" | "&"
	| "<" ":" | "=" ">" | "," | ";" | "|" | ":" | "." "." | "(" | ")" | "{" | "}" | "[" | "]".
CharLiteral	= "'" (PrintingChar | Escape | DQUOTE) "'".
TextLiteral	= DQUOTE { PrintingChar | Escape | "'" } DQUOTE.
Escape	= "\" "n" | "\" "t" | "\" "r" | "\" "f" | "\" "\" | "\" "'" | "\" DQUOTE
	| "\" OctalDigit OctalDigit OctalDigit.
Number	= Digit { Digit }
	| Digit { Digit } "_" HexDigit{ Hexdigit}
	| Digit { Digit } "." Digit { Digit } [Exponent].
Exponent	= ("E" | "e" | "D" | "d" | "X" | "x") ["+" | "–"] Digit { Dibit }.
PrintingChar	= Letter | Digit | OtherChar.
HexDigit	= Digit | "A" | "B" | "C" | "D" | "E" | "F"
	| "a" | "b" | "c" | "d" | "e" | "f" .
Digit	= "0" | "1" | ...| "9".
OctalDigit	= "0" | "1" | ...| "7".
Letter	= "A" | "B" | ... | "Z" | "a" | "b" | ... | "z".
OtherChar	= " " | "!" | "#" | "$" | "%" | "&" | "(" | ")" | "*" | "+" | "," | "–" | "." | "/" | ":" | ";"
	| "<" | "=" | ">" | "?" | "@" | "[" | "]" | "^" | "_" | "'" | "{" | "|" | "}" | "~"
	| ExtendedChar.
ExtendedChar	= *any character with ISO-Latin-1 code in* [8_240..8_377].

C.7 Reserved Identifiers

Table C–1 lists the keywords and reserved identifiers in the Modula-3 language.

Table C–1 Reserved Identifiers in Modula–3

ABS	CARDINAL	EXIT	INTEGER	NEW	RECORD	TRY
ADDRESS	CASE	EXPORTS	INTERFACE	NIL	REF	TYPE
ADR	CEILING	EXTENDED	ISTYPE	NOT	REFANY	TYPECASE
ADRSIZE	CHAR	FALSE	LAST	NULL	REPEAT	TYPECODE
AND	CONST	FINALLY	LOCK	NUMBER	RETURN	UNSAFE
ANY	DEC	FIRST	LONGREAL	OBJECT	REVEAL	UNTIL
ARRAY	DISPOSE	FLOAT	LOOP	OF	ROOT	UNTRACED
AS	DIV	FLOOR	LOOPHOLE	OR	ROUND	VAL
BEGIN	DO	FOR	MAX	ORD	SET	VALUE
BITS	ELSE	FROM	METHODS	OVERRIDES	SUBARRAY	VAR
BITSIZE	ELSIF	GENERIC	MIN	PROCEDURE	TEXT	WHILE
BOOLEAN	END	IF	MOD	RAISE	THEN	WITH
BRANDED	EVAL	IMPORT	MODULE	RAISES	TO	
BY	EXCEPT	IN	MUTEX	READONLY	TRUE	
BYTESIZE	EXCEPTION	INC	NARROW	REAL	TRUNC	

D

Answers to Selected Exercises

This appendix contains answers to those exercises in the text marked with "[A]."

D.1 Introduction

1. a. semantic; b. syntactic; c. lexical; d. syntactic; e. semantic.

3. The comment ends on the last line. It completely encloses the comment on the second line.

5. a. 20; b. 0; c. 11.

D.2 Declarations

1. Only statements a, c, f, and g are true.

3. a. legal, type REAL; b. legal, type INTEGER; c. illegal; d. legal, type EXTENDED; e. illegal; f. legal, type TEXT; g. illegal.

5. Variable a will have the value 10; variables b and c will have the same value, but that value could be any integer.

D.3 Statements

1. Only statements a, c, e, f, i, and j are true.

3. Assignments a, b, d, and e are legal, although a "helpful" compiler might treat d as illegal. Assignments b, d, and e will require run-time checks, although d's check can actually be made at compile time.

7. A "tasteful" solution in Modula–3 is

```
WITH t = recs[j, k] DO
    t.a := x;
    t.b := y;
END
```

although you could also write it as

```
WITH T = Recs[j, k], a = T.a, b = T.b DO
    a := x;
    b := y;
END
```

D.4 Basic Types

1. Only statements d, e, and g are true.

3. a. INTEGER, 3; b. INTEGER, 3; c. CARDINAL, 10; d. PizzaToppings, PizzaToppings.Mushrooms; e. VeggieToppings, PizzaToppings.GreenPeppers.

5. The values are the same when T is type INTEGER, when T is an enumeration type, and when T is the subrange type [a..b] and a = FIRST(B), where B is the base type of T.

7. The answers are all signed integers (INTEGER): a. 3; b. FIRST(INTEGER); c. 16; d. 1; e. FALSE; f. 1; g. 7; h. −1.

D.5 Structured Types

1. Only statements c, f, i, j, and k are true.

3. a. TRUE; b. 27; c. "omes "; d. ' '.

5. a. Set{1..3}; b. Set{2}; c. Set{1}; d. Set{2, 3}; e. FALSE; f. TRUE; g. TRUE.

8. a. 1..10 should be [1..10]; b. no errors; c. 1..10 should be [1..10]; d. initializer cannot be a user-defined function call; e. record fields cannot be open arrays.

9. We need index variables for each array; without knowing the proper types, we rely on the values of FIRST(a) and FIRST(b) to initialize and type the variables. We choose to control the assignment with a FOR loop that iterates the proper number of times. Each array index is incremented independently, but the increments must be guarded to avoid incrementing an index past the last value of the index type on the last iteration, which is a checked run-time error.

```
VAR
    aIndex := FIRST(a);
    bIndex := FIRST(b);
BEGIN
    FOR i := 1 TO MIN(NUMBER(a), NUMBER(b)) DO
        a[aIndex] := b[bIndex];
        IF aIndex < LAST(a) THEN INC(aIndex) END;
        IF bIndex < LAST(b) THEN INC(bIndex) END;
    END;
END;
```

D.6 Procedures

1. Only statements a, c, d, and f are true.

2. The mode of X is READONLY; the mode of Y is VAR; the mode of Z is READONLY. WITH never introduces VALUE mode.

5. The program prints "0" if the mode is VALUE and "10" if the mode is VAR. If the mode is READ-ONLY, the program will not compile because the assignment to a[i] in the procedure is illegal.

D.7 Exceptions

1. Only statements a, b, f, and g are true.

2. The answer to both questions is No. The Ada language provides a mechanism to accomplish (b), and most Ada compilers provide a library interface for (a) in response to user demand. Time will tell if this is a significant deficiency in Modula–3.

4. The radius parameter, the height parameter, or both may be faulty. To generalize the problem, we'll use a formulation that allows any procedure to use the exception for a set of bad parameters:

```
CONST MaxArgs = 32;
TYPE ErrorSet = SET OF [1..MaxArgs];
EXCEPTION BadParameters(ErrorSet);

PROCEDURE Volume(r, h: REAL) : REAL RAISES {BadParameters} =
VAR errorSet := ErrorSet{};
BEGIN
    IF r <= 0.0 THEN errorSet := errorSet + ErrorSet{1}; END;
    IF h <= 0.0 THEN errorSet := errorSet + ErrorSet{2}; END;
    IF errorSet # ErrorSet{} THEN RAISE BadParameters(errorSet); END;
    RETURN 3.1415926536 * r * r * h;
END Volume;
```

7. Procedure A can have RAISES { }, since the only exception that can be raised within A is handled there and not propagated. Procedure B should have RAISES {Exc_Q} because the TRY-FINALLY statement will not prevent Exc_Q from propagating outward.

D.8 Interfaces and Modules

1. Only statements b and h are true.

3. Only the names T, r, and Z are visible. Although B, C, X, and Y are visible in the interface, they are not visible in the module.

6. Which answer is printed is determined by whether A_1 or A_2 is initialized first, which is not specified by Modula–3. The same situation can arise when interfaces are exported by only one module, if a structure such as shown in Figure 8–3 on page 151 is present.

D.9 Generics

1. Only the statements c and h are true.

2. The statements b, c, f, g, and h are true. Keep in mind that generic units aren't *anything* until they are instantiated.

D.10 Dynamic Programming

1. Type pairs a, c, and e are the same. In b, IntPtr <: REFANY. In d, the types are not related by the subtype relation.

4. Revelations a, c, and d are illegal.

7. Only b and g are legal. a is illegal because the type must be a reference type (add REF before AR-RAY). c is illegal because it includes an extra parameter. d is illegal because it omits the lengths of the open dimensions of the array. e is illegal because you cannot allocate a REFANY reference. f is illegal because you cannot call NEW on a nonobject opaque reference type.

D.11 Objects

2. A is not necessarily a descendent of B, since the subtype relationship can apply to nonobject types whereas "descendant" refers only to object types. On the other hand, derivation does imply a sub-type/supertype relationship among object types, so D is a supertype of C.

3. Both calls will have the same effect because the value of obj has type Obj. If obj contained a value of a subtype of Obj the calls could be different because the subtype could have overridden the method m.

5. There are two possibilities. If x is a field, then class will have type Class. If x is a method, then the type of class will be a subtype of Class given by the object type expression

    Class OBJECT OVERRIDES x := X; END;

7. It must be branded when it appears as the concrete type in a revelation.

9. a. a := b is legal and cannot result in a run-time error, because any value that could be stored in a variable of type B would have the necessary characteristics to satisfy type A. d. d := c is legal, but will cause a run-time error unless the value in c has type D or F.

11. a. Yes; c. No; REFANY includes only traced reference types; e. Yes; this will make the storage un-recoverable, but it is not illegal.

13. The name method can no longer be supplied because the same Entry can now be stored under more than one name. The main idea behind the change is to remove the myName and next fields from the Entry type, so that the declaration in Section 11.5.1 on page 220 is

    TYPE PublicEntry = OBJECT
      METHODS
        print(wr: Wr.T) := NIL;
    END;

and the revelation in Section 11.5.3 on page 222 is

```
REVEAL Entry = PublicEntry BRANDED OBJECT (* no fields *)
OVERRIDES
   print := PrintEntry;
END;
```

Then, define a new data structure to hold the names and links in the Symbol module:

```
TYPE Cell = REF RECORD
   myName: TEXT;
   next: Cell;
   entry: Entry;
END;

REVEAL Table = PublicTable BRANDED OBJECT
      buckets: REF ARRAY OF Cell := NIL;
   (* the rest is the same *)
END;
```

Finally, change the procedures in the Symbol module as needed to search down the chain of Cell types instead of the Entry types.

D.12 Threads

3. No. RETURN is defined as raising the "return exception" (page 140). The LOCK statement intercepts the exception and unlocks the mutex, then reraising the exception.

8. Always lock the account with the smaller account number first.

```
PROCEDURE Pay(from, to: Account; amt: EXTENDED) =
VAR lockFirst, lockSecond: Account;
BEGIN
   IF from.acctNumber = to.acctNumber THEN
       RETURN;    (* or fail... *)
   ELSIF from.acctNumber < to.acctNumber THEN
      lockFirst := from; lockSecond := to;
   ELSE
      lockFirst := to; lockSecond := from;
   END;
   LOCK lockFirst DO
      LOCK lockSecond DO
         from.Amount := from.Amount - amt;
         to.Amount := to.Amount + amt;
      END;
   END;
END Pay;
```

9. Testing for alerts inside p ruins the alertability of Repeat since TestAlert clears the alert flag, causing Repeat to continue calling p. The general principle is that it's better to raise Thread.Alerted when an alert is seen, so that higher-level clients can be advised of the situation. This would apply to Repeat itself.

10. If an exception is raised in S2, mu will be released more than once, (hopefully) a checked run-time error. This is probably the simplest solution:

```
LOCK mu DO
    S1;
    Thread.Release(mu);
    TRY
        S2
    FINALLY
        Thread.Acquire(mu);
    END;
    S3;
END
```

An alternative is to use two LOCK statements:

```
LOCK mu DO S1 END;
S2;
LOCK mu DO S3 END;
```

D.13 Low-Level Programming

1. Types a, c, and f are likely to be illegal.

6. Types a, b, d, f, g, and i are legal in safe or unsafe interfaces or modules. Types c, e, and h are legal only in unsafe interfaces or modules.

8. u+4 has type ADDRESS; t+4 is illegal.

Index

Operators and Punctuation